PRAISE

"UAW members at the University of California are on the cutting edge of the American labor movement. Their 2022 strike was groundbreaking and it taught us all lessons that continue to resonate throughout our union today. This book offers a thrilling look at the daily work that made that strike possible. Anybody interested in joining with their coworkers to take collective action and win big should read this book."

—Shawn Fain, President of the United Auto Workers

"The oral histories collected in this extraordinarily compelling book constitute the most intimate and revealing strike history I've ever encountered. At Homestead in 1892 and Flint in 1937 we can only imagine the day-to-day hopes and fears of rank-and-file workers and on-the-ground organizers. But those emotions and sensibilities are on full display in this detailed history of the 2022 University of California strike: from the resolve and friendships generated during the long weeks of preparation to the euphoria of the early, massive picket lines, and on to the doubts and conflict that came with contract ratification. In this set of nine oral histories, solidarity, militancy, and union democracy cease to be abstractions, but become tactile, tangible, first-person realities."

—Nelson Lichtenstein, coeditor of *Labor's Partisans: Essential Writings on the Union Movement from the 1950s to Today*

"Collective power is built from the ground up. We can create the future we deserve through solidarity, determination, and courage. That's how student and graduate workers built and led and won a historic strike at the University of California. Their journey to victory is a roadmap for workers everywhere—whether you're in a classroom, a lab, or on the frontlines of any labor union. In their own words, nine academic workers show us how they organized, escalated, and won real change—and how we can, too."

—Sara Nelson, International President of the Association of Flight Attendants-CWA

"When I marched on the boss as a teenager to organize my workplace, I experienced firsthand the transformative power of collective action. That same power was unleashed on a massive scale during the 2022 University of California strike, as thousands of young people discovered their ability to shape their future through solidarity and labor organizing. This book brings the strike to life through the voices of those who made it happen, showing us the hard work, solidarity, and persistence required to win material change. Whether you're a college student learning about unions for the first time or a seasoned union member, this is a must-read for anyone who believes in the power of collective action to create a better world."

—Hugo Soto-Martínez, Los Angeles City Council member and lifelong union organizer

"*Out of the Lab, Into the Streets*, provides a rare honest, revealing, and instructive book on the unforgiving but essential work that goes into union organizing told through unguarded first-person accounts of UC academic workers as they fought for their rightful place in labor history. In doing so they affirm that every worker, regardless of their job classification or socioeconomic status, can be an organizer and can win representation of a union that they deserve but only if they are willing to do the hard work. All workers engaged in present-day struggles for representation would benefit from reading this modern account while also remembering to draw on lessons from the many landmark victories that comprise our rich labor history in the United States and beyond."

—Dolores Huerta, American labor leader and civil rights activist who cofounded the United Farm Workers union alongside Cesar Chavez

"*Out of the Lab, Into the Streets* is an invaluable look into the behind-the-scenes work of organizing. The stories told by these workers, of both their backgrounds and their daily experiences planning and leading a strike, make human and familiar the daunting work of organizing for power. Through their stories, readers can feel not only the excitement and fear, but also the excruciating work that comes with taking collective political action, and can imagine themselves having the courage and commitment to take on big fights."

—Astra Taylor, cofounder of the Debt Collective and author of *The Age of Insecurity*

Out of the Lab, Into the Streets

An Oral History of the 2022 UAW Strike at the University of California

Edited by Aleida García Aguirre
with Molly Vine and Patrick Dexter

Dedicated to Dr. Daniel Weinberg, 1996–2025
Tireless organizer, brilliant scientist, steadfast friend

Out of the Lab, Into the Streets: An Oral History of the 2022 UAW Strike at the University of California

ISBN: 979-8-88744-157-3 (paperback)
ISBN: 979-8-88744-158-0 (ebook)
Library of Congress Control Number: XXX

Cover design by John Yates / stealworks.com
Interior design by briandesign

10 9 8 7 6 5 4 3 2 1

PM Press
PO Box 23912
Oakland, CA 94623
www.pmpress.org

Printed in the USA.

Contents

INTRODUCTION PART 1

Oral History Methods and Themes

In November 2022, forty-eight thousand academic workers at the University of California (UC) went on strike for six weeks in what became the largest-ever strike in the history of the US higher education sector. This strike was historic not just for its length and scale, but also because it was part of a new wave of union organization in the US. The labor movement that led to the strike was coordinated by two union locals, which encompassed four bargaining units and eleven campuses. Each campus, unit, and union local has its own political tradition and history. For example, postdocs and academic researchers had never struck before, and the student researchers' unit had just won their battle for union recognition in 2021 and did not yet have a first contract.

Despite their differences, as a result of the strike all forty-eight thousand academic workers won some of the strongest contracts for any group of higher education workers, with many receiving double-digit percentage wage increases. But the strike was historic for reasons beyond the material gains it produced for workers. In the organizing leading up to the strike and the decisions throughout, tens of thousands of workers participated in intense debates over strategy—an uncommon exercise in democracy for large-scale US workplaces.

This book tells the story of how UC academic workers built the 2022 strike and set a new standard of militancy in one of the fastest-growing sectors of the labor movement. In doing so, these academic workers also learned lessons relevant to organizers everywhere about the effectiveness of collective power, cemented through worker-to-worker organizing, militant escalation strategies, and cross-union solidarity. Readers with interests in labor history, political organizing, identity politics, the political economy of higher education, and various other topics will find valuable lessons in studying this collective undertaking.

The 2022 strike was a point of arrival and a process. In the first sense, the strike came about as a result of union organizing, both the organizing of the strike itself and the deeper history of worker empowerment through unionization. But as a process, the strike drew together workers across campuses, disciplines, job classifications, political affiliations, and identities. Drawing on oral history interviews, this book documents the lived experience of the union organizing and power building necessary to establish and sustain the strike.

Nine narrative chapters interweave the first-person stories of nine UC academic workers with whom we held comprehensive and sensitive interviews between February and April 2023. Diverse in their identities, from different campuses, and with dissimilar trajectories in academia and in union organizing, the nine workers narrate a wide range of processes, events, and experiences that converged in the 2022 strike. These accounts include the struggle of UC student researchers to win union recognition, the events that led to cross-unit solidarity, the longtime political debates inside United Auto Workers Locals 5810 and 2865, the stalling strategies of the UC in the bargaining process, the personal toll of organizing, and the exercises in democracy that expanded exponentially in the last third of the strike. The workers also reflect on overcoming the challenges of organizing within a hierarchical and isolating workplace like academia, and discuss how their fight holds potential to transform the industry of higher education.

Through Workers' Eyes: Our Approach and the Challenges of Oral History

The strike and the union organizing that led to it were documented in real time by a variety of news media and online leftist magazines. This existing documentation is fragmented, overgeneralizing, and primarily focuses on factual descriptions and political analysis of the union strategies to confront the UC in bargaining and the tactics of internal organizing. The experiences of workers during the strike and throughout the history of union organizing at the UC are often restricted to glimpses that—although rich—do not fully capture the knowledge and capabilities that lie in everyday organizing.

Our aim in this project is to provide a broad audience with an overarching description of the entire strike, its historical context, the ground-level organizing leading up to it, the everyday experience of the fight, and its implications for organizing among UC academic workers. In addition to building a comprehensive and complex narrative about the strike and the workers who made it possible, we also hope to illuminate the process of *the making of the academic working class* by listening to the workers themselves as they reflect on their experiences.[1]

To fulfill these aims, it was essential to meet with the workers using a methodology that would allow both us and our audience to grasp who they are, understand their trajectories in academia, and recognize their path toward seeing themselves as academic workers who could act to defend their interests. This last understanding was crucial, especially in light of their decision to strike. Oral history and memory studies methodologies helped us select a handful of workers who could articulate the diversity and challenges of both academia and union organizing as academic workers. We then designed in-depth interviews to capture their experiences.

Once the interviews were complete, we transcribed and edited them, then gave them to the workers themselves for review and comment. Through this process, we confronted numerous challenges. First, the thematic richness of each interview made editing complex, as we worked to preserve the speaker's narrative while also telling a clear story across the book. Although we agreed on the importance of this editorial approach, our diverse professional backgrounds led to differing views on what elements were essential or dispensable in each story. In the end, we chose to focus more on detailed experiential descriptions and analytical insights into the UC academic workers' labor movement, particularly the strike, while deemphasizing personal stories about social backgrounds and career trajectories.

Second, the interviewees engaged with us openly and candidly, assuming that we shared a fundamental understanding of the UC 2022 strike's chronology, the organizing efforts that preceded it, and the political and strategic debates that played a role in the academic

1 "The making of the academic working class" is a direct reference to the work of E.P. Thompson, and the concept of "the making of the working class" as a process instead of a fact resulting from historic material structure. E.P. Thompson, *The Making of the English Working Class* (Victor Gollancz, 1963).

workers' mobilization. However, during the editing process, we considered it imperative to incorporate succinct, accessible information to make concepts understandable to a broader audience. We aimed to make this intervention assertive yet minimally intrusive.

A third challenge was the timing of the interviews and the book itself. Alessandro Portelli, a key figure in the theorizing of the oral history tradition, emphasized that the timing of the production of a narrative about the past significantly influences its content. In other words, the timing of when a narrative is crafted is significant, as it leaves an imprint on the story. The individual and social processes that occur between *when* the events happened and *when* they are remembered impact the narrative rhythm, the chronological sequences, the causal relationships, and the global analysis constructed by those who remember. This means that, over time, participants may revisit and critique their own accounts as their perspectives change, which became evident in the final stages of editing, as the interviewed workers not only made factual clarifications, but also fine-tuned some analyses and reorganized some narrative sequences. It is likely that when this book is published, the same workers who spoke with us and those who were close to them during the strike will critically engage with their own statements and those of their comrades. They may see themselves differently, question their past, and look with surprise at some elements they stated as certainties. And, of course, they will continue to agree on certain aspects of their narratives, reinforcing the importance of specific characters and events.

These reflective processes, where one looks back to understand how something came to be, are inherent to human experience. However, in the context of building and strengthening labor organizations, it is crucial to encourage reflection as an ongoing process to ensure the organization does not become politically stagnant.

The interviewees, for example, immerse us in the vivid emotions they experienced as their union became more and more central to their lives on and off campus. This organizational growth was strengthened by a parallel and related process: the formation of a culture unique to academic workers. This culture is characterized by a common understanding of grievances, sufferings, aspirations, demands, morality, humor, ways of working, and labor relations. It also encompasses the importance—though disputed in definition—of certain political concepts for their organization, such as democracy and transparency. This culture among academic workers led to the formation of friendships and solidarity networks, contrasting with the previously dominant isolationist logics of academia.

We hope this book will be a mirror for workers in higher education and other industries who are organizing unions and fighting for better working conditions. But readers should note that the narratives we have woven, and the way they are interwoven, represent just one approach to understanding the events, experiences, and processes around the labor movement of UC academic workers and the 2022 strike. We expect this book to be followed by others that will include perspectives from individuals on other campuses, with different political affiliations, and various social and professional backgrounds.

Who Are the Interviewees?

The UC academic workers who make the university work daily are the protagonists of this book, telling their own stories about organizing toward their first strike, and then striking. Academic workers have historically aligned various local and federal laws with their aspirations to organize and improve their living and working conditions. They strive to shape their union, both locally and nationally, and have been instrumental in growing the labor movement by bringing in younger generations.

The oral history we pursued required in-depth interviews, with more than one session per interviewee, as we aimed to provide exhaustive narratives illustrating how workers can come to realize they want their workplace to change and decide to undertake that change collectively. The depth of the interviews meant we could select only a handful of workers. Our selection process was guided by several criteria. First, we aimed to showcase the varied histories of union organizing across different campuses and bargaining units. Second, it was crucial to provide insight into the day-to-day realities of academic jobs, which meant we needed to interview workers with diverse job titles and career paths within academia. When interviewed, two of the interviewees worked as postdocs, one was working as an academic researcher, and the other six were PhD students who worked as teaching assistants and/or student researchers. Third, we sought to explore the variety of routes workers can take toward union involvement, ranging from long-term organizers to those who became active just weeks before or even during the strike itself. Fourth, we wanted to give space to different political evaluations of strike strategy, the decisions made by the elected bargaining team, and the ratification process. Fulfilling this last criterion proved challenging, as no workers from UC Santa Cruz, a campus known for its vocal opposition to certain bargaining and strike strategies, agreed to participate in the project. Ultimately, the nine workers interviewed here belonged to five different UC campuses: Kenzo and Curtis from UC Berkeley, Aarthi and Emily from UC Davis, Maddy and Kien from UC Irvine (UCI), Dez Manuel and Elsie from UC Los Angeles (UCLA), and Joyce from UC San Diego (UCSD). While we sought to be comprehensive, we also want to underline that our approach does not intend for any voice to speak for other workers.

Exploring the Themes Within This Book

The Path from Personal Hardship to Collective Resistance

The interviews illuminate how workers came to feel that their daily working conditions, resulting from management decisions, were morally unbearable. They also show how workers realized that change could only be achieved through collectively organizing and withholding their labor. Finally, they reveal that workers' grievances—whether impoverished salaries or a lack of protections against abuse—are not, by themselves, enough to cause a strike. Rather, mass action comes about only when a large number of workers understand their grievances to be the result of decisions made by those in power. This understanding can only emerge when worker-organizers create conditions—through organization—that allow their coworkers to witness their bosses' explicit rejection of their deeply felt demands. According to the interviews, the shift from individual dissatisfaction or suffering to collective grievance occurred in union spaces ranging from mass actions to one-on-one conversations. This transition was facilitated by escalating actions in which workers saw how the veneer of a progressive public institution could hide management's truly oppositional interests.

The interviewees shared with us that, typically, academic workers are aware of the less-than-ideal working conditions even before starting their positions at the University of California. This awareness is consistently confirmed once they begin their jobs. In the narratives collected for this project, most workers extensively recount their demanding supervisors, endemic abuse and harassment, low pay, and lackluster benefits. They often accept these conditions due to their passion for and commitment to their research projects, and the belief that higher education will eventually lead to better job opportunities and compensation in the future—a hope they soon recognize as unrealistic, as academia continues to lose its function as an engine for achieving social mobility. However, within organizing spaces, workers find validation and a shared determination that conditions can and should improve. Engaging in worker-to-worker organizing helps them realize that their struggles can be collectively addressed.

The Union as Community

During the interviews, the workers devoted considerable time to reflecting on their social lives before and after becoming actively involved in their union. They usually begin by stating that in addition to being a breeding ground for abuse and harassment, academia's inherent dynamics foster isolation. Postdocs and academic researchers are portrayed as the most affected by the lack of community.

For most interviewees, getting involved in organizing marks a watershed in their experience of isolation and community building. Workers find that their union is not only a means to secure workers' rights but also a long-desired community with whom they share moral values and political beliefs.

This new community breaks down the barriers among workers that are institutionally imposed by academia, as well as those arising from inertia, such as separation by program, laboratory, discipline, job title, campus, generation, and nationality. Rooted in the fact that academic workers across the US higher education industry face similar working conditions, this community unites them with shared interests.

The collective practices involved in union organizing, from one-on-one conversations to large rallies where workers lead as speakers, challenge the boundaries of academic work titles, lab walls, and disciplines. These practices culminate in a collective experience that gives birth to an academic working-class culture. This culture—characterized by a specific worldview, set of values, and ways of doing things—unites workers for future challenges, enabling them to confront subsequent battles in a more coordinated and robust manner.

However, the link between union and community does not seem to be inherent to all union organizing. On the contrary, some interviews highlight that community building was possible thanks to the organizing model promoted locally by their union—an organizing union, as opposed to a service union. This same model, the interviewees explain, enabled UC academic workers to build a strong and extensive base of actively involved union members.

When closing their interviews, most workers return to the theme of the relation between union and community, but with a particular focus on the experience of the strike. They suggest that community is key when confronted with the challenges of striking, both in providing peer support and managing internal disputes and divisions. The definition of community here goes beyond simply sharing a space; it involves a commitment to participate in specific union activities, such as meetings and one-on-one conversations, and ways of resolving conflicts, like talking to each other. This sense of community is not just about togetherness and support, but also about active engagement in union processes.

No Way Like the Union Way

Academic workers, like their peers in other industries, have developed everyday practices to dodge some forms of abuse and make their daily life more bearable, such as voicing complaints with their colleagues and taking on additional institutional tasks to avoid being available at all times to their boss. However, when academic workers engage in organizing, they realize that their union offers a distinctly more impactful way to enact change. The first experiences of union organizing shift their perspective on individual demonstrations against power and reinforce the importance of collective practices to oppose injustice and inequalities.

Many discover that their union is a powerful, yet complex, vehicle for fighting for broader social justice objectives that they value, both inside and outside of the workplace. For instance, workers with experience participating in political actions, such as Black Lives Matter demonstrations, come to see that the fight for racial justice is intertwined with the fight for workplace rights and power.

Related to the discovery of the union as a community, the interviewees also mention that this new community is substantially different from other higher education communities in which they participated with the goal of transforming their working conditions. When postdoc Joyce Chan joined UAW Local 5810, she brought with her experience from institutional higher education groups like diversity, equity, and inclusion (DEI) committees, which were portrayed as the means to address inequalities and abuse in universities. But in Joyce's experience—as in Aarthi Sekar's—those groups led to deep frustration due to their limited effectiveness in securing a better workplace. Despite these discouragements, Joyce continued to seek a community of workers to challenge the status quo. So, when she joined her union, she quickly began organizing her coworkers, orienting them to their rights, and building worker-led spaces so others had the means to empower themselves.

In her narrative, she remembers a pivotal moment in the lead-up to the strike when UC San Diego academic workers took disruptive action to support an international postdoc who had her job and visa status unjustly terminated. Joyce was asked to play a key role in the organization of the grievance process and direct actions that reinstated this postdoc's position. For Joyce, engaging in this successful fight during a time of relative calm prepared her to take on bigger fights, culminating in her ability to navigate situations of open conflict with the university during the 2022 strike: "The mobilization around Dr. Jiang's case was the moment when everything felt real for me. It was empowering. Prior to that, I only heard first person accounts or written records of workers' actions getting results, but seeing it happen gave me so much hope and it opened up a lot of possibilities in my mind."

The Strike as a Political School for Workers

The UC 2022 strike has lessons for the broader labor movement. Strikes of this scale are uncommon, and the new forms of organizing and striking, developed by groups of workers who had never struck before, will be of vital interest to all those involved in labor organizing. The strike was an exercise in union democracy that reminds us of the internal discussions held by workers during the labor upsurge of the 1930s and 40s.[2]

2 For a succinct analysis of some of the disputes within the working class in the Midwest during this time, see Staughton Lynd, "Part 2: Rebuilding the Labor Movement from Below," in *Doing History from the Bottom Up: On E. P. Thompson, Howard Zinn, and Rebuilding the Labor Movement from Below* (Haymarket Books, 2014).

The way in which the interviewees present and illustrate the intense discussions and division they experienced during bargaining and ratification encourages readers to delve into a critical question: How does one determine whether a contract is satisfactory enough for ratification, or if continuing to strike is the more strategic choice?

Participating in the strike taught workers that even with prior knowledge about strikes, there is still much to be learned about how to navigate the struggle both collectively and individually. This gap in knowledge can only be bridged through the direct experience of striking. This is not to say that prior experience organizing and academic knowledge of strikes is meaningless. What workers suggest in their narratives is that preparation for a strike should focus on more than just tactics and strategies, it must put in place structures and practices for mass decision-making. Workers also acknowledge that it is not necessarily possible to practice decision-making at the same scale and at the same pace as it occurs during a strike, and confronting complex challenges requires workers to adapt to constantly changing situations.

Simultaneously, workers emphasize that the strike is not only a strategy to achieve some demands, but acts as a political school for them and their peers. During the strike, workers must rapidly familiarize themselves with one-on-one organizing and all that it entails—such as direct, personal interactions aimed to agitate and educate coworkers and move them to action—as well as the historical context, the role of their union, how to engage in bargaining, and how to participate in internal political debates. Joyce Chan points out this disconnect between theory and practice: "No one can teach you the effort it takes to get a strike off the ground! You can only experience it yourself when you're actually prepping for it.... In the online class I took with APALA [Asian Pacific American Labor Alliance] about organizing, the most we learned about the day-to-day of any strike was something like, 'They talked to their coworkers and, within a month or whatever suddenly they were on strike.' It was like, 'Magic! Everyone agreed and it happened!' No [*laughs*]. That's not how a strike happens."

Mass Mobilization Builds Class Identity

According to the narratives, the loud and broadly coordinated strategy implemented in the months before the strike successfully drew many UC academic workers to union organizing. Maddy Duong, an academic researcher at UC Irvine, got hooked into union activities during the mass membership meeting that every campus held in October 2022 to grow support for a strike authorization vote. Postdoc organizer Elsie echoes Maddy's experience when she recalls that the UCLA mass membership meeting encouraged many people to participate in the actions that led to the strike authorization vote, such as meetings, walk-throughs, and one-on-one conversations. Being on the ground and listening to workers discuss their experiences at UC helped them recognize they belong to the same class. According to Elsie, this realization sparked feelings of solidarity and a sense of urgency to join and contribute to the movement. "At the end of the Big October Monthly Membership Meeting (BOMMM) everyone was so excited and hyped up about it. People who I'd never met before signed up and came to their first strike planning meeting shortly afterwards. During the BOMMM we had cards for people to write down the name of five persons to talk to about what was going on. And people filled those cards and talked to those people! That was probably the first organizing task for a lot of people."

The Strike Is Felt in the Body

Almost every worker interviewed for this book mentioned an unexpected aspect of the strike: the physical toll that the strike took on them. They anticipated the need to put experiments on pause and prepare the undergraduate students for the potential impacts of their absence, all of which they accomplished. However, they describe the act of going on strike as stepping into a realm filled with unfamiliar situations and dynamics.

Emily describes the Sunday before the strike as a time of preparation for facing the unknown, yet with the understanding that self-care would be sidelined by the union's needs. This involved stocking up on easy to prepare food, preparing multiple thermoses ready for the cold weather of Northern California in November, and doing the last big laundry loads for weeks, among other things. Aarthi also provides a particularly detailed and vivid account of personal exhaustion experienced during the strike.

Dez Manuel emphasizes that participating in a strike is not an activity undertaken to feel good. By its very nature, he asserts, a strike is a conflict—an inherently uncomfortable situation that workers must endure to improve their lives. Despite his intense discipline and satisfaction with the strike, he acknowledged that he was "glad it's over! It was really intense, and with intensity comes positives, comes negatives.... I wasn't sleeping. I was barely eating. I was running myself into the ground."

Addressing Division

Solidarity sentiments grew stronger in the lead-up to the strike and during the strike. However, workers disagreed whether solidarity alone could achieve their demands or if a more strategic vision was necessary to overcome the immense power of the employer. Emily points out multiple instances where workers diverged on the political strategy to follow, especially when the path to achieving a righteous demand in the bargaining process seemed questionable. These divergences occurred despite the fact that most workers shared the same goals.

Some workers, like Kien and Dez Manuel, talk about the importance of the organizing experience in tuning their political expectations, sentiments of solidarity, and sense of urgency. This implies that while class identity and solidarity are crucial for improving working conditions and the social status quo, the experience of organizing and the resulting empowerment are equally essential.

The necessity of expanding union participation presented new challenges. Interviewees reflect on the difficulties of building consensus when workers have so many different political trajectories, educational backgrounds, and expectations. Together, the narratives of all interviewees demonstrate that collective action and one-on-one organizing offer a way to unite these ideological and emotional differences. When workers are all together, those who might otherwise have been afraid of interrupting traffic in a march find that this tactic can be joyful and empowering. In such collective experiences, ideologically radicalized workers can come to embrace the importance of fighting together instead of alone. As Emily Weintraut, a UC Davis worker interviewed for this project, stated: "Ever since we've been organizing one-on-one and we're actually talking to our coworkers, we have super huge union membership. I want to highlight this: just because your coworkers don't agree with you, that doesn't mean they're inherently wrong. What will revolutionize the labor movement is empowering all workers, and the way that you do that is one-on-one. With the one-on-one conversations there is give and take. I was mobilized by it and empowered by it! And I was empowering other people and mobilizing other people."

As Emily also points out, disagreements are an inevitable part of a mass organization. The complexity of navigating disagreement needs to be directly addressed in labor organizing literature. Yet we find that popular books about organizing give little space to conflict and dissent among workers themselves while fighting the boss.[3] This book highlights how workers deal with different kinds of disagreement, and the ways that these debates emerge and evolve. This topic is of relevance for organizers and workers, and it also contributes to broad debates about democracy in mass organizations.

UCLA worker Elsie Jacobson saw a tension between workers who had been actively organizing in their union for months or years before the strike and those who became active during the strike itself. For workers who were engaged in organizing throughout the process of unionization and contract negotiations, the strike felt like the culmination of a long story of building power. They saw their capacity to win and leverage the power of the strike as a result of this longer trajectory of inspiring people to engage in collective action. Meanwhile, some workers who became active around the time of the strike felt that this was their one opportunity to take agency and apply their theories of social change. Elsie put it this way:

> There's always the sense that we could have done more—I don't mean just during the strike. However, I don't really have any regrets around what happened during the strike because I kind of see the strike as like the end result of everything we did over the last couple of years, so there was not a huge amount that I could have done to change any of those outcomes. Of course, prestrike there's always more organizing that can be done.
>
> And what I wonder is . . . many people didn't know what was going on before and now they just got involved and the strike was happening and now all of a sudden it's over and maybe they didn't get to make, you know, those hard decisions and maybe

3 See, e.g., Jane McAlevey, *A Collective Bargain: Unions, Organizing, and the Fight for Democracy* (Ecco, 2020); Jane McAlevey, *Raising Expectations (and Raising Hell): My Decade Fighting for the Labor Movement* (Verso, 2012); Kim Kelly, *Fight Like Hell: The Untold History of American Labor* (Atria/One Signal Publishers, 2022).

> they felt like a bit left out of it. And I understand those feelings and I understand that might be frustrating. But then from our perspective it's, "Well, you know, you can't just jump in at the last minute and take the ship in a different direction."

For Elsie, as for other interviewees, disagreements had different outcomes depending on how they were addressed and how dissent linked to individual trajectories inside the union. Here lies the question of how workers gain authority to lead the decision-making process. For some, this authority is gained by long-term organizing within the union; for others, it is gained by the perceived sharpness of their theoretical approach. For others, all workers have the same authority, regardless of their involvement and political education. These three stances all rely on an underlying political theory and can intertwine and change over time.

An Old Debate: Theory Versus Practice

Speaking directly to organizers and workers in the higher education sector, this book addresses an old debate about the dialectics between political theory and practice in the labor movement and the formation of working-class consciousness.[4] It is no secret that academic workers, particularly those from the humanities and social sciences, study and theorize social movements, institutions, and power relations. Academic workers have historically carved out space in universities for expressing gender nonconforming identities, for questioning policing and penal institutions, for building noncapitalist housing experiences, and for addressing racial inequality in the US. All this informs the theory and practice of workers in their union and the fight for a better life. Nonetheless, inside the workers' collective there are important debates about how much their efforts should be guided by theory as opposed to previous experience. How do theory and practice feed each other in the higher education labor movement? Dez Manuel Fonseca, a UCLA worker, shares the following:

> One of the challenges I think academic workers face is that we think about a lot of stuff in theory. Our job is theorizing—often

4 See E.P. Thompson, *The Poverty of Theory and Other Essays* (Monthly Review Press, 1978).

> abstract theorizing, not from practice. It's important not to let academic theorizing substitute for the actual hard work of organizing. Theory can only come out of struggle. And it can only serve to inform practice.
>
> Am I the same person as I was before the strike? Oh, no! Politically, not at all [*laughs*]. I don't know how anybody can be the same after.... It was the craziest thing I've done in my life. Probably, the most intense experience of my life. I keep talking about regrets and like wishful thinking and there's things I would have done differently, things I wish we did differently. I'll take with me for a long time the experiences and the lessons I learned.

Workers reckon with the difficulties of defining victory, particularly within an organization of thousands of first-time strikers with widely ranging expectations of what a strike is meant to accomplish. For some, the transformative nature of the contracts was an unmitigated success; others lament shortcomings or the flaws in the process. For yet others, the contracts were never the only goal. Visible social formations within the union emerged from the strike based on distinct visions of its purpose.

Navigating a path through new challenges that emerged during the strike has by no means been simple. Sometimes, a political identity compels workers to not accept any success other than absolute change. Other workers find their political identity compels them to situate their gains within the never-ending working-class struggle. Many interviewees reflect on the ways in which their understanding of how to push for militancy in their union transformed throughout their time on strike. Kien Le, an international graduate student worker at UC Irvine, reflected:

> From the beginning, I always planned to vote no on the contract, just to maintain a kind of radicalism. And then later on, once I saw the whole vote no campaign, I could not even cast my no vote anymore. That was when I decided, "You know what? I cannot respect the people who don't participate and then vote no." I know that wasn't everyone, but from my perspective it was many people. If you show up and keep fighting and you still want to vote no, I respect you. But if you never show up and vote against the

> agreement we won, just to make us fight for you more, I cannot agree with that. That's when I realized a lot of other people have different ideas about what the union is. Many people think it's a service, and it's not. No matter what you want, you need to show up to the picket, you need to participate, because that's the only way that we can win.

Organizing and fighting, as practice, transforms workers' subjectivity, making them more willing to change what they find unjust (including dynamics within their own organization). For organizers in higher education and academic workers fighting to be unionized, this book will discuss how UC academic workers not only increased their union membership but strengthened the involvement of workers from different departments and political backgrounds in the debates and decision-making in the union. While the rate of union membership as a percentage of the national workforce in 2024 is at one of its lowest points since the early years of unionization, workers at UC have increased union membership by tens of thousands. They achieved this first by growing membership within their existing union and then by organizing new units of previously unrepresented workers.

Ripple Effects

By and large, the academic workers interviewed for this project are part of the new, younger workforce in the US. They belong to a generation of workers who are economically precarious despite their high level of formal education. Although academic workers have grievances unique to their jobs, they share the experience of exploitation with other working-class people from different generations and industries.

The organizational and political skills that academic workers have developed are transferable to other environments and struggles because they, as individuals, have been transformed by their experiences. It's quite possible that those who came to be defined as leaders during the UC strike will continue to encourage other sectors to get involved in social transformation. Similarly, those who began their journey as organizers may thrive in these roles in whatever industries they find themselves in the future.

Understanding that people have the power to effect change is not neutral; it profoundly impacts individuals and intersects with their cultural beliefs. During their fight for fair contracts, many of them transformed into worker-organizers and some stepped into new identities as movement leaders. The ripple effects could be profound, as Aarthi describes:

> We now know that we have the power to make fundamental changes to how we work and the future of how academia is going to be moving forward. The UC strike has inspired other academic workers across the country to unionize. It has pressured other institutions to acknowledge that they are not paying living wages to academic workers. The UC strike has generated thousands of new leaders across the state—hundreds of incredibly motivated workers with the understanding that now we have the power to change our workplace and we're going to only keep growing. The UC strike has generated the knowledge that as we move into new sectors, we can unionize all of the engineering, all of the teaching professions, all of the biotech industries.... Just so many different sectors need unions.

Overview

From the early stages of the project, we extensively debated how to structure the narratives. We mainly discussed two options: present each worker's narrative in a seamless, unbroken form, or segment the workers' narratives into thematic chapters. We finally chose the latter. Our decision was based on the belief that this structure would more effectively achieve two key goals: to facilitate a clearer dialogue among the workers' narratives, and to illustrate the nuances of the dialogic transformation process between the workers and their organization. This process refers to how both the workers and the organization influence and reshape each other through dialogue, reflecting the evolving relationship and mutual adaptation over time.

The narratives show that union organizing is a complex process, influenced by both the time period and the specific generation of engaged workers. Furthermore, this process is shaped by the institutional knowledge of the union and the type of organizing model workers and their union choose. As workers organize in their union, their preexisting notions of institutional knowledge, the role of unions, and the nature of strikes undergo a transformation. Simultaneously, the act of organizing reshapes workers themselves (for instance, they start identifying as *workers* and students or academics at the same time), affects their relationships with each other and their supervisors, and more. By presenting their stories in an interwoven manner, it becomes easier to discern the complex process in which workers and their union mutually nourish each other.

The layout of the chapters, both thematic and chronological, not only showcases the diversity of the voices of UC academic workers and their union but also allows us to observe how the organization evolves over time. More specifically, it reveals how the dynamics of the strike and the picket lines varied within a single campus, between campuses, and throughout the duration of the strike. We see, for instance, how the initial seven to ten days of the strike were full of energy, followed by nearly two weeks of intense internal tension and little progress at the bargaining table. However, this tension either diminished or shifted focus as workers used direct actions to continue making progress.

In chapter 1, "From Academic Worker to Worker-Organizer," we delve into the diverse backgrounds of the workers—who they are, their social origins, their journey to the University of California, their daily academic life, and the challenges they faced at work. Additionally, workers narrate how they came to see themselves as workers and the significant role that participating in union organizing played in this self-realization.

Chapter 2, "Setting the Stage," focuses on the organizational efforts that preceded the 2022 strike. Seen from the present, it may seem that such organizational efforts were a way of preparing for the strike, which is why we chose this chapter's title. However, while these events were unfolding, not all workers foresaw that their activities in the summer of 2022 would lead to their first-ever strike. This chapter shows not only the strategies and actions leading up to the strike but also the emergence of emotions surrounding collective organization and the University of California's stalling in the bargaining processes. These emotions, in turn, become part of the driving force behind increased involvement in the union and future actions, including the strike itself.

Chapter 3, "Thrills and Chills," takes us through the emotions and experiences of the workers in the first ten days of the strike. The first day holds a special significance in this narrative. It wasn't just the start of a novel form of struggle for many UC academic workers, but also a day filled with such energy that it inspired many workers, who initially intended to participate only briefly, to become fully committed to the strike's organization.

Chapter 4, "Past Becomes Present," is devoted to the following ten days, a period marked by escalating tensions within the union due to internal political differences that originated years earlier. These differences surfaced at various times, notably during the prior contract negotiations in 2018 and during the wildcat strike of 2019–20, and again in the 2022 strike. While some interviewees felt these differences were evident since the summer of 2022 (or even earlier), the decisions made by the bargaining team toward the end of the second week and during the third week of the strike sparked discussions that laid bare these conflicts. As a result, more workers realized that the internal differences within the union were deeper than they had initially thought.

In chapter 5, "What's Appalling? UC Stalling!," workers discuss the shifting energy and expectations on the picket lines. With minimal movement at the bargaining table for graduate workers, tensions rose and strategic disagreements, both new and old, surfaced.

In chapter 6, "The Second Wind," workers recount the later stages of the strike, in which they responded to a lack of progress at the bargaining table with a series of militant direct actions during which many workers faced arrest. These actions also became a source of controversy in the broad debate over strike strategy.

Chapter 7, "Contract Contention," chronicles the end of the strike. After the escalatory actions described in chapter 7, the UAW 2865 bargaining team entered into mediation with UC in order to try to make more rapid progress. Mediation soon produced a tentative agreement that contained substantial gains over previous offers. There was fierce debate over whether or not to ratify the contract, but workers ultimately voted to ratify by a margin greater than 25 percent. Workers remember the week of the ratification vote as one of the most emotional of the strike.

Chapter 8, "Outcomes and Autopsies," looks at the implications of the strike for each worker interviewee as well as the academic working class more broadly. Workers share reflections on strategy, conflict, and community that suggest future challenges and powerful potential in organizing at the UC.

—Aleida, Molly, and Patrick

INTRODUCTION PART 2

The Long History of the University of California–United Auto Workers

UC Berkeley Sproul Plaza on the first day of the 2022 academic workers strike

For many, the buildup to the 2022 UC-UAW strike began the prior year, as organizers laid the groundwork for what would ultimately become the largest strike in the US that year. In reality, the strike was closer to forty years in the making. We argue that the strike represented a direct continuation of the efforts initiated by University of California graduate students when they started to organize a union in the 1980s.

This history is important to understanding that the power behind the 2022 UC-UAW strike had been building up for decades, not just years. In terms of sheer numbers, the 2022 strike was the largest and boldest action undertaken by the fast-growing higher education wing of the labor movement. This sector has grown in power over the past few decades, but until recently the public paid little attention to it. Part of the significance of the UC-UAW strike is that it catapulted higher education workers and their issues to the front pages of newspapers nationwide. By shutting down the nation's largest university system, the strike made clear the value academic workers provide to society; hundreds of thousands of undergraduates had their classes and finals disrupted and canceled and world-class laboratories with multimillion-dollar annual budgets were forced to cease all research activities.

The strike's significance also lies in what it won. By bringing the collective power of four bargaining units totaling forty-eight thousand workers to bear on one employer, workers made gains that had previously not been possible. Through the strike, workers won raises as high as 80 percent and made a host of other meaningful changes to their working conditions as well. But these victories were complex, and the strike also led to an intense debate among workers over whether or not the achievements could be conceptualized as a victory. A significant portion of the workforce voted to continue the strike rather than accept the terms of the settlement. In this regard, the strike was also significant as a large and public display of union democracy.

Striking Against the Nation's Largest and Most Prestigious University System

The historic nature of the 2022 UC-UAW strike stems partially from the unique situation of the University of California itself. The University of California is alone among American higher education systems in both its scale and its conception. A massive, ten-campus system, it enrolls over 230,000 undergraduates and 60,000 graduate students per year and employs over 230,000 staff. Managing an enterprise of this scale involves quite a lot of money, so it should come as no surprise that UC's most recent annual budget exceeds $47 billion. Any labor action undertaken in this context was destined to be talked about in the superlative.

But the UC is unique not just in its scale but also in its dual mission to do world-class research and to educate California's diverse working class. UC spends over $5 billion each year on its research activities[1] and UC researchers consistently develop more US patents than researchers at any other university system in the world.[2] This elite research takes place alongside its mission to make higher education accessible to working Californians. In UC's 2020 undergraduate cohort, 44 percent were first-generation students, being the first in their families to attend a four-year university, and 33 percent of UC undergraduates received Pell Grants, meaning they come from families with annual incomes below $30,000.[3] According to UC statistics, approximately 80 percent of UC undergraduates are nonwhite,[4] with half of UC campuses federally designated as Hispanic-serving institutions and the other half seeking that status.[5]

This context elucidates some of what was at stake during the strike. To many workers, the UC seemed to be prioritizing too heavily the parts of its mission related to elite research at the expense of its ability to make research and education accessible to workers from diverse backgrounds. There was a stark tension between UC's goal to educate California's diverse working class and its inability to support a workforce from that same class. Not only this, but UC's importance to the broader population of the state meant that workers could harness popular discontent and use it as a tool to build support for their strike. By disrupting the education of 230,000 undergraduates whose families come from all backgrounds and all parts of the state, workers made the impact of their strike felt far beyond the confines of the ten campuses.

---

1 University of California, *Budget for Current Operations: Context for the Budget Request* 2023–24 (University of California, Office of the President, Budget Analysis and Planning, n.d.), p. 11, https://www.ucop.edu/operating-budget/_files/rbudget/2023-24-budget-detail.pdf.

2 "The University of California Leads in US Patents," UC Newsroom, June 12, 2018, https://www.universityofcalifornia.edu/news/university-california-leads-us-patents.

3 "Undergraduate Students: Admissions and Enrollment," University of California, Accountability Report 2024, accessed May 4, 2024, https://accountability.universityofcalifornia.edu/2021/chapters/chapter-1.html.

4 "Fall Enrollment at a Glance," University of California Information Center, accessed May 4, 2024, https://www.universityofcalifornia.edu/about-us/information-center/fall-enrollment-glance.

5 "UC Hispanic-Serving Institutions Initiative," University of California, Equity, Diversity and Inclusion, accessed May 4, 2024, https://diversity.universityofcalifornia.edu/actions/minority-serving-institutions/hispanic-serving-institutions-initiative.html.

History of UC-UAW

The early days of what would later become UAW 2865 and UAW 5810 were full of false starts and setbacks. While today academic workers are undeniably in the midst of an organizing surge, in the 1980s there were only four graduate workers' unions in the nation. Teaching assistants won union recognition at the University of California in 1999, following a decade-long organizing drive and decades of previous attempts to unionize UC graduate workers. As early as 1938, a group of UC Berkeley workers under the banner of University Assistants and Readers (UAR) agitated for a higher minimum wage for academic employees.[6]

UC graduate workers sought union recognition at several moments in the 1960s and 1970s, and chartered variously with the American Federation of Teachers (AFT) and the American Federation of State County and Municipal Employees (AFSCME). These early efforts all fizzled out eventually, but the 1979 passage of the Higher Education Employer-Employee Relations Act (HEERA), which extended the same collective bargaining rights previously granted to California state employees to employees of the California State University and University of California systems, created a clearly defined pathway to unionization for UC employees.[7] HEERA, however, was silent on a key issue: whether or not teaching and research assistants were employees (and thus had collective bargaining rights) or merely students.

Despite HEERA's lack of clarity, graduate workers at UC Berkeley organized the Association of Graduate Student Employees (AGSE) with the intention of becoming a formally recognized labor union and settling this issue once and for all. AGSE voted in 1986 to affiliate with an international union and joined the United Auto Workers, which was the only organization willing to put up the financial resources to grow AGSE into a statewide organization.

The next eight years saw various statewide organizing campaigns take root as well as various legal fights, and by 1994, workers had shown California's Public Employment Relations Board (PERB) that there was majority support for unionization at all eight University of California

---

6 Ricardo Ochoa, "Barbarians at the Gate," *California Public Employee Relations,* no. 143 (2000). Ochoa's essay offers a more complete history of graduate workers' early attempts at unionization.

7 Ochoa, "Barbarians at the Gate."

campuses (two of the present ten campuses did not exist at the time). After a two-year fight, PERB ruled in 1996 that teaching assistants, tutors, and readers were employees and thus eligible to unionize but that research assistants were not. As a result of this ruling, eligible workers soon began organizing to win recognition at all eight campuses. By 2000, they succeeded, winning separate but identical contracts at each campus. In the next round of bargaining, which took place in 2003, these eight contracts were merged into one statewide contract and UAW Local 2865 was born.

The Higher Education Labor Movement

Though it immediately became the largest graduate worker union, UAW 2865 did not arise in a vacuum. Exploring the early years of graduate student unionization around the nation helps demonstrate the longer arc of efforts preceding the 2022 UC-UAW strike. The first academic student employees union to win recognition was the Teaching Assistants' Association at the University of Wisconsin-Madison, which achieved this milestone in 1969 and joined the American Federation of Teachers as AFT Local 3224 by 1974.[8] Following in their footsteps, the Graduate Employee Organization at the University of Michigan secured recognition in 1974 and was also affiliated to the American Federation of Teachers.[9] Before the 1990s, only two other graduate worker unions had gained recognition: the Graduate Teaching Fellows Federation at the University of Oregon, recognized in 1977,[10] and Graduate Assistants United at the University of Florida, which finalized its first contract in 1983.[11]

Following the successful unionization efforts at UC in 2000, waves of graduate unionization continued to break primarily at public universities in historically liberal states where public sector employees either had or could win collective bargaining rights. In the University of Massachusetts system, graduate workers at UMass Lowell and UMass

---

8 "History," TAA, accessed May 4, 2024, https://taa-madison.org/history.

9 "GEO History," Graduate Employee Organization, accessed May 4, 2024, https://www.geo3550.org/about/history.

10 "Our History," Graduate Teaching Fellows Federation, accessed May 4, 2024, https://gtff3544.net/about/history.

11 "GAU's History: With Love Since 1972," Graduate Assistants United, accessed May 4, 2024, https://www.ufgau.org/history.html.

Boston won recognition as UAW 1596 in 2001. On the West Coast, teaching assistants in the massive California State University system won recognition as UAW 4123 in 2004. That same year, teaching assistants and research assistants at the University of Washington, chartered as UAW 4121, ratified their first contract. Notably, UAW 4121 would go on to follow a similar trajectory as UC-UAW, expanding to eventually include postdocs and academic researchers.

Today, the higher education sector is in the midst of an organizing surge that has seen graduate workers continue to unionize and has expanded to new types of workers as well. As of 2024, over 150,000 graduate workers had won union representation alongside over 15,000 postdoctoral scholars.[12] The surge is ongoing and higher education workers ranging from adjunct faculty to administrative professionals continue to announce new campaigns on a regular basis.

Postdocs Enter the Stage

The success of graduate worker unions inspired other groups of academic workers to unionize. One such group is postdoctoral scholars, workers who have completed their PhDs and continue working in a university research setting in a temporary position for one to five years. Postdocs have time-bound appointments; individual appointments can vary significantly, but there is a five-year cap on the amount of time workers can spend as postdocs before moving on to other parts of the academic workforce. Postdocs work primarily, but not exclusively, in science, technology, engineering, and math (STEM) disciplines. Usually, there is a direct path from graduate worker to a postdoc position, which also means there is a constant flow of workers with union experience into nonunion postdoc job titles.

UC postdocs formed the first standalone postdoc union in the nation when they organized UAW 5810 in 2009. At that time, postdocs only had union representation as part of larger faculty bargaining units at the universities of Alaska and Oregon and Rutgers University. The formation of a postdoc union at UC is notable because the University of

---

12 William Herbert, Jacob Apkarian, and Joseph van der Naald, *2024 Directory of Bargaining Agents and Contracts in Institutions of Higher Education* (National Center for the Study of Collective Bargaining in Higher Education and the Professions, 2024), https://research-data.hunter.cuny.edu/ncscbhep/2024DirectoryofBargainingAgentsandContractsinInstitutionsofHigherEducation.pdf.

California is the single largest employer of postdocs, employing about 10 percent of all postdocs in the nation.[13]

The formation of UAW 5810 catalyzed a wave of postdoc organizing that is still ongoing. Since 2010, postdocs have formed unions at the University of Washington, Harvard University, Columbia University, Mt. Sinai Hospital (in New York City), California Institute of Technology (CalTech), the National Institutes of Health, and more. These successful unionization drives have led to more organizing, and new classes of workers, such as career researchers (known at UC as academic researchers) and contingent faculty continue to form unions at UC and beyond.

UC-UAW 2018–22

As we have described, the 2022 strike was the product of decades of organizing. But the four years immediately preceding it proved to be especially important. During this time, several events took place that were essential for the strike to occur and succeed. Notably, these events included the 2018 election of new leadership in UAW 2865 that was supportive of grassroots organizing, the recognition of the academic researcher unit of UAW 5810, the UC Santa Cruz wildcat strike, and the formation of Student Researchers United-UAW. These developments brought thousands of additional members into the labor movement, and made it possible for a union of forty-eight thousand workers to go on a multiunit, statewide strike in November 2022.

Changes in UAW 2865

The UAW 2865 that ratified the 2022 contract was much more powerful and participatory than the one that ratified the 2018 contract. The surge in engagement stemmed from a meticulous and successful organizing program that sought to boost membership and encourage democratic involvement within the union. There is no perfect metric of participation, but one simple proxy metric is participation in the ratification votes themselves. In 2018, 4,374 voters participated in the UAW 2865 ratification vote, whereas in 2022 this number rose by 323 percent to

13 Katie Langin, "Fewer U.S. Scientists Are Pursuing Postdoc Positions, New Data Show," *Science*, March 25, 2024, https://www.science.org/content/article/fewer-u-s-scientists-are-pursuing-postdoc-positions-new-data-show.

18,483.[14] Furthermore, in 2022, four years after the new administration was elected, 63 percent of workers were union members, which significantly contrasted with the 36 percent rate to which membership had fallen in 2016 and the 45 percent membership rate during 2018 bargaining.[15]

At the same time that union leadership changed, the institution faced a threat that underscored the need to enlarge its membership base: the 2018 Supreme Court ruling in the *Janus v. AFSCME* case. This decision, the result of decades of antiunion legal activism, changed a long-standing practice among public sector labor unions by ending the collection of "fair share fees." Previously, all workers represented by public sector unions were required to pay fees to cover representation costs, and those members who wanted could become formal full members by paying additional dues. The *Janus* ruling eliminated fair share fees, which meant that if a worker represented by a public sector union did not choose to fully opt into membership, they would contribute nothing, while still receiving all the benefits of union representation. The changed political landscape for unions brought on by the *Janus* decision made it even more important for the new leadership of UAW 2865 and UAW 5810 to succeed in expanding membership and organizing new groups of workers into the union.

In addition to building membership numbers to encourage internal democracy and strengthen the institution, the new leadership also wanted to expand membership beyond humanities and social sciences workers, who had been predominant in the union. From 2018 on, the UC-UAW sought to build an organizing structure in science, technology, engineering, and math (STEM) departments. This strategy would be necessary to build a strong UAW 2865 because STEM workers constitute a sizable proportion of all UC academic workers. Without the participation of STEM workers, union leaders could not truly contest the power of their employer. Additionally, organizing STEM workers laid the groundwork to eventually form Student Researchers United-UAW, a STEM-heavy union.

---

14 "SRU Contract Ratification Results," UAW 2865 Mailchimp, December 23, 2022, https://mailchi.mp/6f8d2bd383ea/2865-sru-contract-ratification-results.

15 UAW 2865, "UAW 2865 Membership #s, 2008-22," unpublished internal document.

Academic Researchers Join UAW 5810

While changes were taking place in UAW 2865, another group of UC academic workers simultaneously pursued unionization. Academic researchers, an umbrella term that refers to approximately 5,000 career research employees who work in UC labs and research centers, filed for union recognition in October 2018 and won recognition of their own bargaining unit in April 2019. They ratified their first contract in November of that same year, after a contentious bargaining campaign and a majority-participation strike authorization vote.[16]

The formation of the academic researcher unit brought an additional 5,000 workers into UAW 5810, which already represented about 6,500 UC postdocs. This was an important step for the higher education labor movement because it was one of the biggest advances yet made into the STEM workspace. By organizing unions, academic researchers and postdocs gradually increased the proportion of workers represented by unions in UC labs, leaving student researchers as the obvious next candidates for unionization.

The 2020 UC Santa Cruz Wildcat

In late 2019 and early 2020, graduate workers at UC Santa Cruz held a wildcat strike (i.e., a strike that has not gone through the union's official strike sanction process) in protest of the high cost of living in Santa Cruz and their low wages. A total of 233 graduate student instructors and teaching assistants refused to submit grades for the fall 2019 academic term. Under pressure from the university, and struggling to rally additional support from their coworkers at UC Santa Cruz or from graduate workers on other campuses, most of the strikers submitted grades in January. Still, a smaller group of workers persisted in withholding grades and refused to teach their scheduled classes in the winter of 2020. When the UC Santa Cruz administration formally fired the last fifty-four striking workers in February 2020, there was renewed outcry, but efforts to widen or intensify the strike largely did not succeed. The significance of the wildcat strike waned, and in July 2020, leadership of UAW 2865 secured an agreement from

---

16 Michael Price, "Nontenure-Track Researchers Ratify First Contract with the University of California," *Science*, November 14, 2019, https://www.science.org/content/article/nontenure-track-researchers-ratify-first-contract-university-california.

the university to rescind all disciplinary actions against the strikers and to rehire them for the fall 2021 term.

Though limited in scale, the wildcat strike was a national news phenomenon whose impact was felt through the 2022 strike. Many participants and observers felt the 2022 strike was a continuation of the fight in 2019. The wildcat shed light on divisions within the union which informed the ideological tensions in the 2022 strike. Several participants in this project reflect on the ways in which the wildcat impacted their understanding of the union.

Student Researchers United-UAW

The recognition of Student Researchers United-UAW in 2021 was a milestone in the long march of the higher education labor movement through the STEM workplace, previously thought of by some as an impenetrable bastion of antiunion conservatism. Student researchers at the University of California participated in the 1980s and 90s organizing drives that led to the formation of UAW 2865, but a 1996 ruling from California's Public Employment Relations Board (PERB) excluded them from union representation. In an effort to change this, graduate workers sought to pass a law in the California legislature in 2010 to formally recognize student researchers as workers with full labor rights. Workers successfully passed this law through the legislature twice but were defeated by two successive vetoes from then-governor Jerry Brown. It was not until their third attempt in 2017 that the combined pressure from the broader labor movement in California ultimately succeeded in passing the law and securing the governor's signature.

In August 2020, UC student researchers began circulating union authorization cards, beginning what became a two-year fight for union recognition. In May 2021, workers submitted to PERB approximately ten thousand authorization cards, meeting the necessary standard to win recognition. PERB verified majority support for unionization in August 2021, but UC refused to certify the union because of a spurious argument over the legal status of a subset of the workers whose funding came primarily from state and federal grants. For several months, workers engaged in a combination of direct actions and political lobbying that brought UC into a PERB-administered mediation process. When mediation did not quickly produce recognition, workers held a strike authorization vote in November 2021 in which 10,890 student researchers voted to strike if necessary. The results of this vote brought renewed urgency to mediation, and on December 8, 2021, UC agreed to drop all of its disputes and recognize the new union unit in its entirety.

The significance of this campaign to the 2022 UC-UAW strike cannot be overstated. First and foremost, the formation of Student Researchers United-UAW exponentially increased the power of UC academic workers by bringing an additional seventeen thousand union members into play. Second, the 2021 recognition campaign provided a trial run for many of the tactics used during the strike, including organizing a successful strike authorization vote and persevering in the face of stiff opposition from UC. In doing so, it helped tens of thousands of workers previously unfamiliar with unions and union strategy quickly gain meaningful experience. Third, it changed the relationship of power between workers and the UC because workers could now credibly threaten to shut down UC's research operations in addition to its instruction. Many oral history participants reflect on the importance of student researchers to the 2022 strike.

CHAPTER 1

From Academic Worker to Worker-Organizer

UC Davis workers picketing campus at the beginning of the strike in November 2022

Where I Come From

Emily Weintraut

I'm Emily Weintraut; my pronouns are she/her. I'm a proud girl from South Jersey. I'm a student researcher and a teaching assistant in the Food Science Department at UC Davis since 2021.

I was the first of my family to go to grad school, so this was a very new thing for me. My parents went to college, but they left before finishing. Later, my mom went back to school to finish her teaching degree. My dad is in IT, one of my brothers is a software engineer, and the other is a chemical engineer.

All of my life I wanted to be a gynecologist; sexuality and sexual health are subjects I'm very interested in and passionate about up to this day. In undergrad I was in premed, and I shadowed a gynecologist who provided medical consultations that went for over an hour, which is super rare. But he didn't make much money and had to have a separate job. I thought that that was the kind of doctor I'd like to be, but I also realized that path was not feasible for me. And then I panicked because I had made decisions around med school. But one day, I watched a video about the founder of one of the first kombucha drink companies in the US, GT's Kombucha, and that piqued my interest, and I thought that there was a lot of research to be done in the field of food science and health. So I decided to go to grad school instead of med school, and I'm happy with where I am. Never would I have expected to be here! I know tons about my research field, but I feel like I'm out of my depth on everything else. But funnily enough, I don't study kombucha, I study beer because my boss has funding there.

Dez Manuel Fonseca

My name is Dez Manuel Fonseca. I'm a third-year PhD student in history at UCLA—hopefully I'll be a PhD candidate by the time this book comes out [*laughs*]. I'm from southeastern Massachusetts. I've worked as a teaching assistant and currently I have research funding via the Graduate Research Mentorship Fellowship.

I come from a working-class background. My parents are immigrants from Angola and Cape Verde. My dad is a repairman; he works in everything related to electronics and hardware. He got fired after the 2008 recession and was self-employed for a while, but he just got his first union job this year! My mom is a medical interpreter at a hospital in Massachusetts. I'm the only person in my family to pursue grad school. I went straight to grad school from undergrad. You know, immigrant family background, it's like a stereotype. My parents made *everything* about school and I had to always get good grades. School is what I've been good at, but I also enjoy it. And although school was what I've always done, I didn't know anything about doing a doctorate.

I went to UCLA because I wanted to work with my advisor. Also, I wanted to have a union because I did some organizing in my undergrad.

Plus, the funding package I was offered from UCLA was better for me than what other schools offered. I guess that's how I got to UCLA, a couple of different factors.

I started my program in September 2020, and because it was during the pandemic, I was working from Massachusetts over Zoom. When I moved to LA in 2021, I didn't know anybody. Moving to LA was pretty isolating at first because I didn't have a community beyond my program; but at the same time, being isolated was okay to stay focused on my work. My second year was when I started teaching. I just committed to working to be the best teacher that I could be, and I really liked it! Then, in April 2022, I got involved with our union for the April 26 action, and then I attended more and more membership meetings. Our union was my first substantive community beyond academia in LA. Overall, each year of my program has been completely different: first was coursework, second year was teaching, third year was basically organizing [*laughs*].

Elsie Jacobson

I'm Elsie Jacobson. I'm a postdoc at UCLA in the Department of Biological Chemistry. My pronouns are she/her. I am from New Zealand; I grew up in a small town called Pāuatahanui. I've been living in the US and doing this postdoc for three years. My dad's an engineer and my mum works at the city council and parks department.

I grew up on a small farm. I was always really into biology and trying to understand how things worked—particularly all the animals I was surrounded by. As a kid I dreamed up photosynthetic Martians with ice-melt-based reproductive cycles and got my first anatomy lessons dissecting fish with my dad.

I didn't know about academia as a career path or what being a scientist was. I thought being a scientist was sitting in a corner in a white lab coat doing something uninteresting. But in university I got into science, and I enjoyed doing genetics. Later, I got a lot of research experience at a biotechnology company where I worked for a couple of years.

To be honest, I did a PhD because my job was getting boring, and because I realized I needed a PhD for my professional development. I did my PhD at Auckland University researching how cells respond to mechanical changes by taking cells and making them squeeze through very small holes and looking at their DNA. It sounds from another world, I know [*laughs*]. The more research I did, the more I realized that this was something I wanted to do as my career, so I decided to do a postdoc because that's the continuation of the research journey.

Being from New Zealand, it's quite a common thing to do your PhD locally then go to the US or the United Kingdom to do a postdoc. If you go to the US, there's an expectation that it is a lot of hard work, but also there is the expectation that you'll gain more research freedom and funds.

Probably the biggest disruption to my expectations was the pandemic. I started my postdoc in November 2019 and I got sick when the pandemic started, in mid-March 2020. These are difficult times for me to remember because all of a sudden, my nascent postdoc was stopped by both the pandemic and by me getting really, really sick. It changed my life. It has been a very challenging three years in a way that I definitely didn't expect when I came into this postdoc. But I also didn't expect so much good stuff to happen, like the strike!

Just so you can get an idea of how sick I got, I'll tell you this: Before I got sick, I was always active, I was never home. My husband—who was doing his PhD—and I would get up at 5:30 and go to the gym. I was really into powerlifting, and I was lifting twice my body weight and going running and stuff. In February, before getting sick, I did the Firecracker Run in under an hour, which is a 10K race that goes up around Dodger Stadium. And I was obviously working in the lab full-time.

Suddenly, I got sick and it cut my energy levels by an enormous amount. Long COVID shares a lot of symptoms with chronic fatigue, and something that happens is that you can become exercise intolerant. For most people, if they do exercise, they can just keep building up and get fitter and fitter and healthier and healthier, but for me, if I tried to do that, I would get really, really sick. It has been a whole restructuring of my life learning to take care of myself in a way that I never had to before.

Kenzo Esquivel

My name is Kenzo. I am a fourth-year PhD candidate in the Department of Environmental Science Policy Management at UC Berkeley. I study sustainable agriculture and soil science. I'm focused on California farmers and farmworkers in my dissertation research.

I am from Pilsen, a predominantly Mexican working-class neighborhood in Chicago. I identify strongly as being from the Midwest. My dad is Mexican American. My mom is Japanese. I am the first in my family to go on to a graduate degree, and to navigate elite institutions of higher education, which shapes my involvement and perception of these spaces.

Pursuing grad school has in some ways been the path of least resistance, which is incredibly ironic to think about. I ended up studying science in undergrad because I went to a public science and math magnet school in Illinois for high school. That set me on a trajectory of identifying as a strong student, and shaped my feeling that I could best contribute to society through STEM. I went into college planning to pursue environmental science. Through my undergraduate studies I began to develop my identity as a scientist, and by the end of it I was thinking a lot about the intersections of ecology, climate change, and environmental justice. And because of these interests, I thought that the best way in which I could contribute was by doing research.

In my late undergraduate I got a research position which led me to apply to one master's program, which I ended up getting into and attending. After that, I thought about a PhD as a next step in opening up more doors because I could focus on research, but also pivot to more community-engaged or policy-engaged work around the environment. I didn't come into Berkeley thinking about being a part of the academic institution. I had little understanding of what it was "to be in academia." And I specifically came to Berkeley because it was an environmental science, policy, and management program, and I thought it would give me the flexibility to explore interdisciplinarity. I came in identifying quite strongly as a scientist, which now makes me laugh a little, and now I think of myself much more as an interdisciplinary scholar.

Maddy Duong

My name is Maddy Duong; my pronouns are she/her. I've been working as an academic researcher in the Fruman Lab at the University of California Irvine [UCI] for over two years. I started after graduating with my BS at UCI.

My dad immigrated here from Vietnam when he was young, and my mother has been in the States for many generations, but her family is from Ireland. My mom—who raised me for the most part—worked for a juvenile detention center.

How did I decide to be in academia? I think a lot of immigrant families feel education is a way to secure success and financial stability. That was something that was ingrained in me from the beginning with my aunts and uncles. They all went to college, whether they used their degree or not, that's another story. It was never a question that I was going to go to college. And so, I did, and I fell in love with research. I stayed in academia for that reason.

Everybody in my family went to college. That's what first-generation children do. They think that's the key to economic stability and success in their career. I think that's still true if you get your education and use your degree somewhere else; if you stay in academia, you are not going to make a lot of money. For me, studying biology was either to do research or to go to med school, and I knew I didn't want to go to med school. Also, there's something compelling about what the university does, "Oh, they study cancer and they're trying to fix all of these world problems." So, you are kind of blinded by the goodness of the work. But then when you actually go to do it, you realize that there are many people doing the work who aren't treated well or well enough, really. Principal investigators can be very abusive toward people in their labs and expect that people work more than forty hours a week. But we stay for the work. I know that people feel motivated and personally connected to the work. I know so many people that work in cancer because somebody in their family was affected by cancer. And that's the reason that keeps them there; it's definitely not the money or the work conditions.

As for community or relationships as a worker, I'd say that I didn't even know any other academic researchers *until I went on strike*. It wasn't until the strike that I found a community of academic researchers.

Joyce Chan

My name is Joyce Chan; my pronouns are she/they. I'm a second-year postdoc currently, in neuroscience. I've been in the University of California San Diego, UCSD, for about a year. I was born in New York City, and I lived there my entire life prior to coming to UCSD. I identify as Asian American. My mother is Taiwanese and my father is from Hong Kong and southern China. My family would be considered middle class because my father worked as a computer programmer for the New York City government and my mom stayed at home and raised me and my sister. I also identify as disabled; I recently came to terms with this identity.

Our union is the biggest community-building space I have in UCSD. I'm constantly repeating this: It's really hard for postdocs to make connections because we don't have a cohort; we are employed by a principal investigator instead of a PhD program, which leads to a very growing and large sense of isolation. This is a really big issue especially for international folks, because they get here with a mentality of coming in, publishing as much as possible, taking up as many skills as they can, and getting out. But then everything falls to the wayside because they're so focused on productivity that they don't consider how this quality of life hampers that productivity.

Curtis Rumrill

My name is Curtis Rumrill. I'm a fifth-year doctoral composer at UC Berkeley. I grew up outside of Syracuse, New York. My dad started working as a greenskeeper in a country club of Syracuse University and eventually became the manager. My mom worked in student support services at a college in Cobleskill.

While I'm a composer primarily, I also have a history in community organizing and labor organizing. I came to UC Berkeley after ten years working in labor organizing; I was a staff rep for a nurses union. After I had my first kid, I needed to shift away from the exceptionally demanding job I had. I applied to doctoral programs and was accepted into UC Berkeley. I moved to Berkeley in January 2018. From the union perspective, I've been in UC Berkeley for the ratification of the 2018 contract, and I also worked under the 2014 contract when I first arrived here.

Kien Le

My name is Kien, last name is Le. I'm a third-year PhD student in visual studies at UC Irvine and a teacher's assistant for the film and media program. I grew up in Vietnam. When I grew up, I had some difficulty navigating my life and figuring out what I wanted to do. I knew for sure I want to study abroad because growing up as a gay man in a conservative country like Vietnam wasn't easy. I felt like my voice never mattered. For example, I could never participate in any election. So, I think that's one reason why I pursued higher education; and I also participated in the labor movement because I feel this way I can be heard.

When I was in high school and even in middle school, when I was in Vietnam, I wasn't the brightest student in my class. In fact, I always was in the bottom. And it wasn't because I'm dumb or anything because when I took the standardized test, I scored better than other people. It wasn't that bad! But I just felt I never wanted to learn anything because I felt like it was all just indoctrination. So that was one of the reasons why I wanted to study abroad where I can explore what I'm interested in, you know. For example, as a gay man I want to know how to navigate my life. So, a major part of my background research is about the history of AIDS activism. I did a kind of independent study with my advisor who taught me a lot about how gay men and the queer communities organized in the 1980s and 90s! That was not something that you can learn in Vietnam. Also, I want to pursue higher education because I feel I need so much to learn!

Aarthi Sekar

My name is Aarthi Sekar; my pronouns are she/her. I'm a graduate worker at UC Davis in the Integrative Genetics and Genomics Program, and have been for *seven years*. Also, I have been helping organize with our union for about three years now. I started off organizing for the student researchers campaign and was the Local UAW 2865 unit chair bargaining team member for Davis during and leading up to the strike.

My family's a family of immigrants; we arrived in the United States when I was seven. We are a classic Indian family leaving India to come and get in on the Silicon Valley expansion in the mid-nineties. Education has always been a big priority in my family. My parents had an expectation for me to pursue my studies, but also pursue getting settled, and having a family. I think [*laughs*] I've done one better than I have the other.

Although my family is middle-class Indian, well educated, there wasn't an expectation for the women of the family to pursue education after undergrad or college. So, although there was support for me in going into my PhD program, my family and I have diverged in the expectations of how to live life.

I pursued a PhD because I came out from an all-women's college where there was an expectation to go into higher education, but also because after working six years in both a private industry and a nonprofit research institute, I realized I was never going to be able to have agency over my own work, nor any real respect for it, without holding a PhD. And so, that pushed me to go back to school and be a graduate worker.

Academic Work

Aarthi Sekar

Entering academia, my expectations clashed with reality. I anticipated a collaborative PhD environment with substantial support, but faced feelings of isolation and loneliness. And, based on my working experience, I was surprised with the lack of worker support, including no recourse for discrimination or hostile behavior, no vacation time, and no rights.

My research focused on human genomics and genetics, involving both laboratory experiments and creating libraries of sequenced human genomes to explore differences in cortex size between humans and chimpanzees. I study what makes us uniquely human. Before I was involved in any attempt to change my workplace, my routine involved long hours in the lab, often extended into late evenings, and if I had more data to analyze, I would eat dinner and get back on my computer. I remember answering messages to my principal investigator and other lab mates at 10 or 11 p.m.

My day-to-day in terms of experiments would vary widely because the aims of my dissertation were pretty unique and disparate from each other, and because of the constant and never-ending cycle of grants. Acquiring grants is something that consumes a lot of the work of grad workers. My principal investigator would have grants that she was constantly applying for, and there was a very urgent expectation for me to generate data to get these grants for the lab.

I also wasn't expecting to have to be almost in a marriage-type relationship with my professor. I didn't realize that was sort of an inherent expectation in academia. I don't know if "marriage" is the right word. It felt like I was tied to one person for years to get my degree, for better or worse [*laughs*]. That's what made it feel like a marriage.

The relationship I had with my principal investigator was probably very similar to many people's, but also very different. What's constant for everyone is that she was my sole most important connection to success in my PhD, and if anything corrupted that relationship, it was guaranteed that I wouldn't be able to succeed. And that felt like an unhealthy and unfair dependence.

When I entered my PhD, I didn't take the opportunity to do rotations in different labs. Back then, I wasn't capable of taking a bird's-eye view, and I got caught up in my current lab because it is known as a good lab, because it is cutting edge. But I wasn't able to set down boundaries in the one relationship where you are beholden to one person for the success of your PhD. For example, if I was struggling with my anxiety, my principal investigator would suggest that we would go on runs together. And I sensed that if I said no, I was losing the opportunity to be a better graduate student. And it was unhelpful because during those runs, we would have conversations about my mental health—which was a breach of privacy. I ended without a healthy personal boundary. There was an expectation for all of us in the lab to post our availability on the shared calendar. And we have to post everything, including doctor's appointments. So, I started feeling awkward, thinking, "What about me going to therapy? Do I say, 'Aarthi at therapy'" [*laughs*]? It got to a point where that was really unhealthy. And this is related to the expectation in academia that research is your life and any type of energy that you are putting toward other things is not okay, like you are not a good scientist. But nothing was ever going to be enough. Then you have imposter syndrome with the feeling that no matter what you do, it's never going to be enough. And it just becomes crushing and debilitating. And then you have no privacy. You don't have any room to be yourself. It took me to a very dark place where I started losing a sense of what made me *me* over the course of being in this lab.

Feeling not enough, and being constantly harassed were two things I shared with all my labmates. And we talked about it, but in a particular way. We would complain, cry together, and share anxieties, but that didn't help us to stop being terrified and say, "This is unacceptable."

After my qualifying exam, at the start of my third year back in 2018, I was struggling with strong depression and anxiety. But I found a place that made me feel like I belonged, and where I was able to organize events for our community. And so, in spite of my principal investigator's disapproval, I became student chair of the recruitment program, which opened other doors to keep on organizing and gave me a way out of the never-ending work in my lab because I had institutionalized activities to attend.[1] It was around that time when we formed the diversity, equity, and inclusion [DEI] committee. Forming the DEI committee was huge for me because I had spent three years feeling as though everything I did was worthless, but now people were thanking me after every event. So many of my fellow graduate students in our program had experienced overwork, lack of boundaries, or lack of support; some were getting yelled at in their qualifying exam with racist remarks.

When we started our committee, the faculty loved the idea since they could showcase it on their websites and brochures. But—for the most part—they didn't address the underlying issues. They made excuses while people continued to face yelling and bullying in exams and labs, often due to their accents or assumptions about their intelligence based on their origin. We proposed ideas like a fund for "Broke-tober" to get institutional support, but nothing really changed.[2]

Dez Manuel Fonseca

As a teaching assistant, I'd teach two classes starting at 8 a.m., and since I live pretty far away from campus because the Westside of LA is so expensive, my day began around five. I'd catch the bus by 6:30 to get to campus by 7:30. On the busy days without a packed lunch, I'd buy the cheapest option on campus—a five-dollar chicken nugget meal—which was not the healthiest, but it kept me alive. To avoid traffic, I'd leave campus before 3 p.m. or after 7 p.m.

My research centers on the decolonization of Portuguese Africa during the 1960s and 70s, particularly focusing on Cape Verde's anticolonial history and its ties with Guinea-Bissau and Angola. My advisor is an expert in Black Marxism, racial capitalism, and anticolonialism in the third world.

---

1 Across the UC system, institutional programs support the promotion and recruitment of PhD students and postdoctoral researchers. At the departmental level, a group of current graduate students participate in recruitment activities that organize visits, events, and outreach to prospective students.

2 The term *Broke-tober* comes from the fact that upon entering graduate school, pay is not typically provided for two months, meaning one's first deposit arrives in November. October is thus a very financially difficult month for most graduate workers; and this difficulty limits who can aspire to graduate school. Aspiring students need to have saved thousands of dollars to survive those months and the relocation expenses for nonresident workers.

I've never romanticized academia. I never thought of it as a dream job or a super impactful job in the world at large, even though I'm very passionate about my research. One of my professors used to say that his job is no more or less morally superior than working at any service job. That resonated with me.

Academia is seen differently by different people. Some see it as a dream job, others as morally superior [*laughs*]. And although it's true that being an educator is important, I think that it is more important and impactful being a K–12 teacher than a professor. There's a lot of, for lack of a better word, "bullshit" in academia [*laughs*], and it no longer offers the job security it once did, turning what was supposed to be a structured apprenticeship into a precarious position, unless you already come from money. I feel everybody, particularly in the department of history, understands that.

I knew the pay wasn't great coming in [*laughs*], but I managed to find a decent living situation because I'm single. Still, I'd end the month with barely fifty to a hundred dollars left. So my expectations and reality have been similar. What has been different is that I got involved in labor organizing as an academic worker—which I delayed starting due to adjusting to a new city and new responsibilities.

Explaining my job to my family has been a challenge; they think I'm paid to be a student, but really, I'm paid for the work I do in addition to my program. This is part of why PhD programs can stretch up to eight years—you have to work to live.

What I always say is that if somebody offers me a job, I'll take it. But statistically it is highly, highly unlikely I will get a job as a tenure track professor. All the positions that are available are adjunct positions. And I know that's because of austerity measures in university, the neoliberalization of the university, and offsetting costs.

Kien Le

When I began my PhD, I knew that faculty members are not my friends. I think there needs to be a clear boundary between supervisors and employees, which is different from the widely spread, naive idea about higher education: You work for your advisor and you guys become friends to create this fantasy about a perfect workplace. That is not true anymore—if it ever was! Having a union is helpful because it helps to set a boundary between your research as a student and your employment. It helps you when you are being overworked, protects you from getting your job rescinded.

You go into graduate school and you only work with your advisor, you only talk to grads, you become so committed to your academic job and then you don't know what is going on out there. The pitfall of graduate school is that it isolates people. Before we built up our organizing and this strike, people would just care so much about their own research that they have no idea what their colleagues or coworkers are going through. The strike really changed that, like, "Hey, you have to go to the picket, you have to do walk-throughs, you have to know how it is really fucked up out there, and that not everyone is on the same level as you are."

Kenzo Esquivel

I knew how it felt to be a part of an academic community because I did a master's. Coming into Berkeley, I was expecting the graduate experience to be one of finding academic peers with whom to nerd out and develop research interests, specifically around agriculture and ecology and its intersections. I was expecting to be trained to be an independently minded scholar who is able to think critically about our food system and be a part of the research that could advance sustainability and justice in the food system. And at least within my core lab community, I feel like these expectations have been achieved.

I chose UC Berkeley partly because of my principal investigator, who seemed like someone I could grow with intellectually and who understood his advisory role holistically. Another reason was Berkeley's reputation for valuing students beyond just their research outputs. And finally, for its active involvement in food, social, and labor justice movements.

Three and a half years in, my relationship with my principal investigator and lab community remains strong, but the broader department hasn't fostered a strong cohort dynamic. We've had some shared classes, but they haven't really facilitated bonding. Early on, I connected with nonwhite students through the Graduate Diversity Council. In June 2021, we demanded the department take more significant actions toward racial justice, such as improving teaching, mentorship, and recruitment efforts to enhance diversity and equity. This action galvanized us and guided our activities for the following years. Despite these efforts, I've still felt somewhat isolated and haven't found the broader academic community—beyond my lab—I was hoping for at Berkeley.

Curtis Rumrill

I think that the music department isn't committed to our growth as composers. It feels like our role in the department is to teach the undergrads so that the faculty focus on their artistic careers. My professional career was on a faster upward ascent before coming here. Right now, the Bay Area isn't the music scene it used to be. So, it's been isolating. We are living off of the connections we had before we came here; we're watching our careers hit a plateau. And you sign up for this expecting it'll set you up for a job in academia later, but those opportunities no longer exist unless you are an already reasonably famous composer. You get a job in academia by being famous in the field. Being in a program that isolates you and slows your professional growth is tough. Facing the reality that you're not really advancing in your career, you are simply just taking a low-paying job, and you're moving your family across the country for that, it's hard. Moreover, the broader issue is that academia's viability is waning, not just for music but for the humanities in general. We're all in the same sinking boat.

Emily Weintraut

I didn't have that many expectations coming to UC. In undergrad people would make jokes about how poorly people are treated and paid in grad school. That's how I knew I would do a lot of work and be underpaid. And that was how it was, except it wasn't as bad for me because I did rotations, and I found a boss I'm happy with, and who does not overwork me. I spent years in retail and minimum-wage jobs; I refuse to be mistreated as an employee. I had heard horror stories from my friends in grad schools who were working twelve to fourteen hours a day, six days a week. And I was very grateful that was not me. But still, the financial struggle, it's been an issue.

On Black Friday 2021 I got a retail job here in Davis to get a bit more of that community, but also to make some money because I had only gotten *one paycheck* at that point because the university pays us in arrears that first quarter—you start working at the end of September and your first paycheck is November 1; that's what we call Broke-tober. On top of not being paid, I was spending a lot of money because I was moving, and although I had some savings from my jobs in undergrad, I really needed the money.

I like working in retail; I've worked in retail since 2017. People underestimate the social game you need in academic work, and I think my retail experience has actually prepared me for that. I have gotten a lot of great opportunities because of my extroverted tendencies or because I realize how important it is to reach out. When I started retail, I would go straight into an anxiety attack when I would get yelled at. Eventually, you build up an immunity to that, and there's a lot of skills you develop dealing with the stress of a customer service or minimum-wage job.

Elsie Jacobson

I do basic research, which is trying to find out new things about biology. For instance, I have been studying X chromosome inactivation, a process where an entire X chromosome becomes silenced if there is more than one in the cell. It's a fascinating model of gene silencing, which is where this project started, but it has led to me studying the X chromosome in placental development, evolution, and disease. Something I love about basic research is the freedom to follow a project in unexpected directions, just picking up the most interesting thread and following it.

My day-to-day changes continuously. I mostly control my own time, which is both freedom and responsibility, as I have to make progress on my project—find something no one has found before, and generate enough evidence to support it—mentor my students, manage collaborations, write grants to fund the lab, and present my work at seminars and conferences, as well as service tasks like organizing seminars and lab maintenance. Most days I work until I can't work anymore and then I just try to rest as much as I can for the next day. And some days that's a full day and some days it's not a full day, but my principal investigator has been really good the whole time. We are both learning how to accommodate my disability. We've learned that if I don't rest when I need to rest, then it gets worse and worse and worse.

When I was in New Zealand, I had heard horrible things about working conditions in the US. Actually, a lot of the things that are in our union contract that we had to fight for are *mandated by law in New Zealand*, like parental leave, sick leave, and paid time off. Consequently, coming to the US was somehow scary. I got excited when I found out that UC postdocs have a union and therefore that we have rights and benefits. I remember the exact moment I received, signed, and returned the membership election form. It was my first time being a union member.

Early Union Involvement

Kien Le

My first two years at UCI, it was during the pandemic, and I didn't get involved in my union. I signed up as a member because ... only crazy people would not sign up! It is just the first step, you sign a union card, it's an easy step to do! And so, I signed up. But for the first two years, I never participated in anything. I kept getting updates from the union. So that's how I learned about things.

I remember when we got the email from our union asking us to fill out the questionnaire to ratify our demands. It was a year ago, I think. And before that, we elected a representative for our bargaining team and an alternate—not all the people I voted for won, but that's okay. For me, whenever I have a chance to cast my vote, I will cast it; and regardless of the outcome, I'm going to respect the majority. But we are going to fight for the minority group too.

It wasn't until the summer of 2022 that I found my summer job offer was rescinded. That's when I reached out to people from the union and told them what happened and that I didn't think it was legal. So, the union stewards helped me with a grievance. Twenty-four hours after we went into the step two meeting arguing that it is unlawful for the university to do this, I got my job back! And I got more involved with the union after that, not because I felt like I owed the stewards something, but because I realized having the union, having this kind of network of support really helps each of us going through graduate school. I don't want to sound sentimental, but ... for international students it's like having another family to be there and to help us get through this.

Joyce Chan

I helped out in the case of a postdoctoral scholar from China, Dr. Li Jiang, who was working at UCSD and was pressured by her principal investigator to fabricate—and therefore, to falsify—data, but she refused to do it. And as this disagreement was happening, she found out she was pregnant, and of course she informed her principal investigator, as you would with your employer. And her principal investigator essentially dangled in front of her the idea of renewing her contract and her visa if she continued to do good work and of course, not contest her principal investigator's methods. Then seven months into Dr. Jiang's pregnancy her principal investigator didn't renew her contract, and she was in a dire situation because she would have to fly back home to China, which was in lockdown because of COVID, and quarantine for a couple of weeks during the end of her pregnancy. So, Dr. Jiang was facing losing her job, health care, and visa status, and because of how sudden things happened, she probably wouldn't have been able to find another job in a different lab in time to not be affected. And it was shocking but not surprising to see how the university sided with her principal investigator.

Our union mobilized around her case, and finally the dean of the department of health sciences caved to our pressure and got Dr. Jiang a new position in a different lab at UCSD, allowing her to keep her employment, health insurance, and visa status. This was my very first rally, so it was a big deal for me, personally.

The mobilization around Dr. Jiang's case was the moment when everything felt real for me. It was empowering. Prior to that, I only heard first-person accounts or written records of workers' actions getting results, but seeing it happen gave me so much hope and it opened up a lot of possibilities in my mind. And as much as I try not to dwell on the past, I think about all the people I tried to help during my PhD and how a union would have made a huge difference. Having a union means we will be able to help so many more people in the future.

Emily Weintraut

I started my program in 2021, before Student Researchers United was recognized by UC. But as teaching assistants, I learned we could be members of Local 2865 during recruitment, around February or March 2021. I remember I had seen a headline about UC workers filing their cards to form what came to be Student Researchers United, and I asked about it during recruitment, and a coworker—Sierra Durham—talked to me about it. Back then, Sierra was a grad student in food science, during the strike she was a bargaining team member for postdocs; she left UC recently. That was my first exposure to our union.

I also knew about unions because my mom and other people in my family are teachers. Although I didn't have much experience in unions, I've seen how effective unions could be in getting rights for workers and improving working conditions. I've seen the Amazon and Starbucks campaigns. But I've also seen the degradation of working conditions across certain areas and how unions can change that. And growing up, I watched my teachers never going on strike, but constantly being on the edge of doing it. They were the kind of teachers that won't go on strike because they care too much about the education of their students. This political position is problematic because those teachers—my teachers—were desperate to fight to improve their job conditions, but they loved their students so much, and then it became a moral dilemma.

I'm going to say something that I know sounds weird, but I became active in our union, just by being active. I kind of just did. I know when I signed the card, I thought "Well, obviously I'm going to be a union member." I didn't question it. After that, when we had the first strike authorization vote for Student Researchers United, Sierra invited me to a meeting and I went. She got a couple of people from our department to go. And I remember I thought that the people in that meeting were kind of intense, meaning that they knew so much. And I, in contrast, had experienced grad school for just three months.

Later, in the spring of 2022, after the recognition of Student Researchers United, I was asked to go to some meetings in Central Park in Davis to talk about our contract. Sierra invited me directly, and—as you can imagine—I cannot say no easily, so I went. At first, I felt again like people were intense, but I kept going and the more I learned, the more I was like, "Yeah, we need to do this!" First, I tried to keep a distance because I was so overbooked in my undergrad—I was in charge of multiple organizations, I was working retail twenty hours a week, I was doing research in a lab, I was a full-time student, I was a resident advisor, I had no personal time! So, I had planned to not do anything outside of work in grad school. But the more I learned in those meetings, the more I naturally got involved in it. I never wanted to be involved, but thought that if I didn't help as much as I could, I would feel bad about myself.

Personally, the first meetings were tough because they were on Zoom, and people were already organizing. There was no intro to the union, and I had no idea what was happening. But I never felt judged for just being there. Eventually, in our biweekly organizing meetings, there's always this moment where someone asks, "Who wants to facilitate the next meeting?" And then ... silence. I always felt this internal pressure to volunteer, even though no one was pushing me. I'd sit there thinking, "How is no one else volunteering?" So, I'd end up saying, "I guess I'll do it." That's how I got roped into everything.

As I got more involved, I felt empowered, but also realized how hard it was to break free from the mindset that being underpaid and overworked in grad school was normal. It took time to ask myself, "Why am I being mistreated like this?"

A lot of people joined our union the same way. My first meetings were casual, in Central Park, where people hung out with drinks. That's probably why I kept coming back, to meet others. Different people from my lab, like Sierra, got really involved as we neared the strike. Everyone engages with the union at their own pace, and that's okay.

At first, I was just attending meetings, staying quiet because everyone seemed so smart. I was nervous—it was my first union, my first strike. But after I facilitated a meeting, I thought, "Wait, these people aren't smarter than me. We're all just figuring it out together." By September 2022, I surprised myself: "I can organize!"

As I was getting to know all these people, I was building trust with them for numerous reasons. And trusting them was one of the reasons I got more and more involved. These people were spending their weekends, spending their summer, months ahead, organizing—I wasn't as involved over summer because I was teaching a UC Extension course and working two other jobs, one in retail and one at a brewery. But when I got to work with them, I was thinking, "These people are putting their time in, they're putting in extra time to do this, they care about it." So I didn't even question if I trusted them, I just did.

Around September 2022 we switched from almost exclusively Zoom meetings to regular in-person meetings. I think our regular in-person meetings were inaugurated by an event like a happy hour specially organized to get to know people. And from that point on, meetings got a lot easier.

One clear memory I have from when I started going to union meetings is that there was so much going on that we needed to meet constantly. I think in general people have so many meetings that are so unnecessary and could have just been an email [*laughs*]. But in the buildup to the strike, and during the strike, not a single meeting could have been an email and it was very specifically timed out: "We'll spend five minutes on this subject; you have to make a motion to extend the time if you want, et cetera." It was this very rigid structure. But then, interestingly, once we had regular meetings in person, we were becoming friends and keeping that rigid structure was a challenge sometimes because someone would make a joke, and we'd all laugh. It was definitely more fun to be in person. And once you know people in person, the Zoom dynamic also changes, you can send direct messages or just chat about what's going on in the meeting. But if you don't know anyone, you're just sitting there and keeping your thoughts to yourself.

Aarthi Sekar

I knew about the existence of UAW 2865 a year into graduate school. I knew Local 2865 was around and that teaching assistants had a union. But since I was on a research fellowship being paid for my research work, at that time I was barred from being a teaching assistant. So, it was not something I paid attention to for a good part of my graduate experience early on.

I remember when the campaign to unionize academic researchers took off in late 2018, Neal Sweeney—the president of Local 5810—did a walk-through in my lab. I remember I was sitting at my desk when I saw him and asked him what he was looking for, and he said, "I'm with our union." And I almost jumped out of excitement, "Is it happening now?!? Are we going to have a union?!" But as soon as I told him I was a graduate student, he said, "No, not you. Do you have a lab manager around?" So I—with absolute disappointment—brought over our lab manager and Neal talked to him to sign the union card. After that, I wondered why we didn't have a union, and that became more and more frustrating because there is no way for us to resolve anything in our workplace; if we are fucked, we are fucked, and that's the end of the conversation. The only solution available to most of us was leaving the program. And I wasn't thinking I was going to do anything about it, but it was very much in my mind that something needed to happen.

It's funny. I didn't know much about unions at all. No one in my family had experiences in any union. When I started talking about unions all the time, they thought I was going to be arrested; that's the context they had. But I was so hopeless and I was feeling so despondent about my experience in graduate school so far that I was ready for any kind of rope to be thrown. I didn't know if having a union was the answer. I just knew that—in a very general way from what I learned in elementary, middle, and high school—collective bargaining is good, and that unions have been important for workers to have rights. And I couldn't have even said it that way. Aarthi in 2018 would have said, "I feel unions would be good." But I was so *desperate* for some kind of ability to have a say in the conditions of my workplace.

On January 2020, maybe late 2019, I had a really informal conversation with Don Gibson, who organized with UAW 2865 at Davis; we talked about how horrific it is for grad students or anybody who is an academic worker to find housing that's affordable in Davis. And a couple weeks later, I got an email from Don cc'ing Garrett who back then was a lead organizer during the Student Researchers United campaign in Berkeley, and an essential part of that union. So, this email suggested Garrett and I should meet. And I thought, "Sure, no idea who this person is, but why not?" Because I was ready for *any* rope.

And so, Garrett and I met for coffee right near my lab, we sat down, and he handed me the climate survey about experiencing harassment and discrimination in the lab. And I filled the survey, I was like, "Yes to all of these!" And then he asked if I had heard of what a union is, and asked, "What do you think about graduate student researchers having a union so we can actually make sure that we have better protections in our workplace?" And I said, "Yeah, that sounds completely necessary." Later that week we went on a walk-through. That was wild, I had never done a walk-through before. I liked the fact that I was just going up to people asking them, "How do you feel about your workplace?" and people being, "It's kind of shit," almost like whispering.

In this walk-through, Garrett had the first conversation, and I had the conversation right after that, and I remember my second conversation was with Ellen Gregory and Jamie Ho, who were crucial parts of the Student Researchers United campaign and the strike that just happened, and are amazing leaders in the College of Biological Sciences. It was definitely ingrained in my head, that conversation. Both of them were like, "What are we going to do about it?" There was agreement and a growing understanding that we needed a union, but it felt nebulous. It felt like we were having a conversation that some people probably didn't want us to be having and we were doing it anyway; it felt like we were finally taking ownership of our space. And it was really, really exciting. I still think of that first walk-through very fondly.

Building trust one-on-one. I started trusting Garrett a month into our interactions. I immediately—from our first conversation—trusted Garrett more than any faculty member I had a conversation with, because everything he said and the way he explained it made sense to me. But I really trusted Garrett and leaned on him—in terms of trying to become an organizer myself—because Garrett was so good about follow-ups. Every single conversation that I had with Garrett, we had an extensive debrief that really helped me. I would ask all these questions and he would take the time to answer every single one. And every month he would just call me—like randomly—and he'd be like, "What do you think of this?" And I'd be like, "Why is Garrett asking me what I think of this?" But then it started happening over and over again, and I was like, "Okay, maybe I have something to contribute." And that was when I realized, "Oh, it's not just that I trust this person to help me, he trusts me to help lead this campaign and build something together."

Because of the DEI committees and my personal experience, I wanted for us the ability to not be bullied in our workplace. That was the main thing. Yes, I thought we deserve higher pay, we deserve child-care support, better rights for international researchers, but the fact that we can't even have any acknowledgement that we are bullied in our workplace! I didn't understand. We could barely talk to each other about it without feeling like our principal investigators would find out and we would get fired. That's wild! I wanted the ability for us to come together and—without fear—have protections to not only address the bullying but have the bully reprimanded. And it became very clear in the short amount of time after Garrett brought up the idea of unionizing graduate student researchers that the DEI committees were not going to do anything about bullying and that forming a union and coming together as a collective was the only way we were going to win those protections.

I could go on talking about the fight for Student Researchers United for hours, from getting the cards to delivering them and fighting for recognition of our union. The card delivery action in Oakland was amazing. I love thinking about that day. First of all, it was just a beautiful day! But second, after organizing on Zoom during a pandemic, we were finally getting to see each other face-to-face for a historic day of submitting our petition to become a union. I felt really incredible being part of something so, so powerful with my coworkers from eleven different campuses and research sites.

We turned in the cards in May 2021 and won recognition in November 2021. In between, we had incredible rallies. I've never seen that many of my coworkers come together in one place at Davis ever before. We also met with legislative folks. It was all-hands-on-deck, and around that time I softly transitioned to lead organizer.[3] It meant a lot of walk-throughs with our coworkers before the strike authorization vote for recognition.[4] I remember the strike authorization vote being incredible and one of the most challenging things I'd done up until that point in time.

At this point in my life, I'm so much more excited to call myself an organizer, and I still have so much hesitation to call myself a scientist, and it's not because I feel like an amazing organizer, no, but because I have a huge amount of pride about being one. I feel empowered and I feel a confidence and ownership that I've never felt about being a scientist or an academic researcher at all, ever.

I'm in this battle because *I know I deserve better*. But most importantly, I know *all of us deserve better*. I'm not in this fight because of any kind of literature or ideology. To be honest, I've read like two sentences of Marx. I don't know if that's something I should claim, but I have no interest in reading Marx—I'm exaggerating, I'd like to read him sometime. I know we deserve better because of my experience and because of all of the experiences of my friends and my coworkers. I'd rather listen to my coworkers than read Marx; and I believe in the power of my coworkers to change how we live and work.

I mean, there comes a point when you hear day in and day out of the harassment or the panic attacks people are having in the middle of the night because they are unable to pay their bills, or buy food to get by, or because they're sleeping in their cars, or because they're terrified of stepping into the lab because they don't know how their principal

3 A lead organizer is responsible for coordinating organizing efforts in a particular workplace or area, in this case on a particular UC campus, as well as meeting with other lead organizers to plan and implement the union's statewide strategy.

4 Some workers, like Aarthi, discuss two different strike authorization votes. The first happened in November 2020, to gain recognition for student researchers, and the second in October 2022 was to approve the strike that began in November 2022. The 2020 campaign achieved its goal of winning recognition of the student researcher union without escalating to a strike.

investigator is going to treat them. And their dignity is lost and they are living in constant fear. You hear countless stories. You just hit a point where you're like, "Why are we all doing this?"

The only reason that I was able to acknowledge in a bold way and stand up for my rights was because I had those conversations with my coworkers and we all acknowledged together that this isn't okay. If I had just done it on my own, it wouldn't have happened.

What's an academic workers' union? It's when we come together to fix things that aren't working for us—whether it's pay, protections, or research conditions. Instead of a few people talking to their principal investigator or department chair separately, a union unites hundreds or thousands of us to negotiate with the people who control our working conditions. And it works because we act together. How does it feel to be a union member? I love it! Just saying it makes me feel proud.

Kenzo Esquivel

I have been involved in our union since I got to Berkeley. I came in knowing that I wanted to be involved because I served as a department steward during my master's program. I remember asking members of my lab via email about their perception of our union before coming to Berkeley. In my first year I got plugged in and then, in April 2020, I was elected as a head steward.

Part of why I became involved is because I grew up in a union household. My dad is a union carpenter in Chicago. From a pretty early age, I made the connection between that and my family having financial stability. During the 2008 crisis, for example, my mom was laid off, and there wasn't that much construction work, but we had health insurance and regular pay. And I knew that I had good vision insurance because every time I got a new pair of glasses, the seller would comment on how good our insurance was. So yeah, growing up I was conscious of what unions were and I had the sense that it was the union that allowed for us to live comfortably.

Also, I was pretty involved in campus fossil fuel divestment and anticop stuff in my undergrad, and I was plugged into a movement to get the university to open a level-one trauma center. All of these campus groups worked together and there was a strong student organizing community. When I came into grad school, I already had an understanding of what it was to organize, and what it meant to think about power as organized people. The University of Michigan, where I did my master's, had a strong grad union, the Graduate Employees' Organization, and I got plugged in there early. I volunteered to be a department steward, and for two years I attended union meetings and helped get department colleagues plugged into our union.

When I arrived at Berkeley, a couple of friends who were in their second year connected me with our union orientation quite quickly. First, I went to a contract enforcement or know-your-rights training my first semester and a campus organizing committee meeting. By the end of my first semester, or the very start of the second, I got more plugged into organizing activities. I remember that during my first walk-through with Garrett we found some graduate student instructors right after their sections and talked to them about getting signed up as members of the union. During the campaign to create Student Researchers United, I attended a few initial meetings and helped with small tasks like distributing sanitizer kits and collecting signed cards in my department, even putting up a statement on our website. While I participated in one-on-one conversations and enjoyed reconnecting with colleagues during the pandemic, I didn't take much ownership of the process. Although I was excited when we delivered the authorization cards in May 2021, I still felt somewhat removed from the collective effort.

The strike was on my mind and in my general consciousness since the spring of 2022. I was thinking about spending the summer building the capacity of the organizing committee of my department, and building a sense of awareness of our union—which after the 2019–20 UC Santa Cruz wildcat was not super active. Being the only head steward in the College of Natural Resources at the time, and informed by conversations with leadership and knowing the contract campaign was coming up, it felt crucial to have conversations with people in my department to have a strong showing if we were to call for a strike authorization vote, even if it didn't happen for a while.

Before the spring, I tried to be involved in the shaping of the bargaining survey. The bargaining survey was so important. My primary involvement, along with a group of folks, was figuring out what bargaining frameworks we could apply around environmental issues within the confines of the labor contract. Also, we did some research around what other unions have done about environmental issues in the past. Ultimately, we ended up including things like transit benefits and biking as the main framing around the environment and infrastructure development.

When we articulate our priorities as a union, core economic things always rise to the top. I think sometimes there is a struggle to balance the inclusion of issues that may not be as important for a larger swath of campus, but are crucially important for, say, student parents or disabled workers. But I do think that most of those issues ended up being in the bargaining survey.

At the beginning of the fall semester, I wasn't sure if a strike would happen. But it felt like a real possibility, and I was extremely motivated and energized around it. The conversations back then were focused on encouraging people to attend the bargaining sessions and talking about their impressions. Because, at that point, we had been bargaining with the university already and had not made progress on any of our big issues because a lot of the big-ticket issues—like wages—got left for last.

Those early conversations were also about people understanding that bargaining wasn't against their advisors—with whom they might have a good relationship, or not. Then, the most challenging ones were with graduate student researchers and fellowship folks, who had questions regarding what it'd look like to stop dissertation research, who qualifies under the new student researcher contract, how funding would be impacted when their pay was coming from external funds, et cetera—there was more clarity and easier movement among graduate students instructors. When we eventually started talking about the strike, folks were more concerned with logistics and less with the concept of going on strike, thanks to the fact that we agitated folks in a slow and steady way. Certainly, there were a few harder conversations and some people didn't want to talk about the strike. But I would say the majority sentiment in our department was not necessarily too difficult to move toward the possibility of a strike.

Elsie Jacobson

I became a member of our union as soon as I arrived, and I got more involved around six months into the pandemic. Part of the reason was being really sick and realizing how many protections I had just because of our union. I always knew unions were important, but this was a new level of awareness. Because my first-year contract could only be one year, I was so nervous about getting sick five months into it. Really, I was anxious about not getting my contract renewed. But I can't imagine how much more anxious I'd have been if I knew they could fire me at any time, like before we had a union.

I really appreciate the fights and wins of the postdocs that came before me. The security and peace of mind that my contract gave me meant that I was able to rest and recover and improve over the course of 2020. Without it, I'd have been overworking myself and getting myself sick. The amazing health insurance that we have obviously made a huge difference. As do the twelve days of sick leave and the twenty-four days of paid time off. I can't imagine being a UC grad student researcher with no union and getting sick as badly as I did. What would I have done? That's why as soon as my brain was working again, I reached out to Local 5810 and I joined the organizing committee meetings.

I was aware of the Student Researchers United campaign because James, my partner, was a grad student. We talked endlessly about the campaign as it unfolded. Union organizing has been a huge part of our lives for the last three years. After most grads signed union cards with Student Researchers United, I became more involved in postdoc bargaining. Bargaining began in June 2021, and by November we held a successful strike authorization vote on Zoom, pushing UC to negotiate seriously and recognize the student researchers' union.

In preparation for and during the 2021 strike authorization vote, we had a pretty good organizing committee and a pretty active Slack [a messaging platform]. We had a meeting or a phone bank every week. We had orientations on lock. All of our orientations were one-on-one because they're much more effective than group orientations. We'd get lists of postdocs every week and we'd assign them to a peer. It was a really good system. Orientations were really important for building membership, building awareness of the union, finding new leaders, and talking about the strike authorization vote and other stuff that was going on.

To be honest, the 2021 strike authorization vote was the first time that I experienced a super active union. Before that, we weren't organizing with a goal in mind beyond expanding membership and making sure that everyone knew their rights.

Postdocs were the first unit to bargain with the university—as I said, we began in mid-2021. But since the university wasn't offering us anything decent, we were able to align our bargaining with the other units. The other thing that helped us to get the negotiations aligned is that our last contract tied postdoc wages, and raises, to the National Institute of Health postdoc scale. So, even though we were out of contract for like a year and a half, we still had raises, which is the major concern of being out of contract.

Compared to 2021, we did a lot more organizing in person leading up to the strike and that helped us all to really believe that we were going on strike. The 2021 strike authorization vote was a softer threat, but in 2022, we thought the strike was inevitable, so we were preparing people for it. Organizing in person made a genuine difference because it helped to build trust in each other and have hard conversations about the challenges of going on strike. This time, we were focused on local organizing. Instead of campus-wide meetings, buildings or groups of buildings met separately—for me, this was the Biomedical Sciences Research Building, Boyer, and Molecular Sciences Building—and we planned walk-throughs the whole time. Given that UCLA is large and diverse, organizing based on the physical location and field of research helped us connect with other workers. The walk-throughs were absolutely essential because we went to every lab and tried to talk to every person and hear their concerns and their thoughts about everything. And personally, I didn't have any negative reaction from anyone. There definitely wasn't any animosity. Although there was one grad student who I talked to that was worried that we were asking for too much in negotiations and that the UC wouldn't be able to afford to do research anymore. This concern was a common thing that a lot of people heard.

Leading up to the strike, all the units coordinated and worked more closely than ever before. In 2021, there were two strike authorization votes happening in parallel: one to get recognition for Student Researchers United, and the other one for postdocs. It wasn't until the summer of 2022 that the collaborative organizing with the grad students was running smoother than ever. That's when we started having these building-specific goals and the building-specific meetings where we all, postdocs, grads, and academic researchers, worked together on a regular basis, and we merged organizing committees. I remember all these details because that summer, James and I went to New Zealand and got married.

To be honest, even though we were talking about the potential of a strike, I didn't know how it would be possible for postdocs to strike in the numbers that were necessary. And that was definitely a scary, scary thought. It was clear that we needed to have a really big show of force. It was clear that we all needed to be 100 percent prepared to strike. When we had the strike authorization vote and the university didn't budge at all, I realized we were going to have to strike. But part of me didn't believe it was going to happen until the Sunday night before it started!

During a lab trip to the beach, I spent the entire car ride intensely telling a nonmember about how messed up UC's behavior was—and it worked, he signed up! We all have PhDs and do highly skilled research, yet they treat us like "trainees" and pay us fifty-five thousand a year starting. On top of that, UC's response to the pandemic was awful, with no real acknowledgment of what we went through. My principal investigator's attitude was, "No one will care, just keep moving," which reflects how academia works.

A postdoc can be such an awful job that you only do it if you're so passionate or obsessed about it that you're willing to live in an apartment that has sewage floods going unfixed, like me! My UC apartment recently had a sewage flood. For us this was the first time, but these floods happen all the time, and so do the leaks from the ceiling and the black mold. Many of us postdocs are in our thirties and maybe we're looking to have families, maybe we want to move on with our lives and not be stuck in this place forever. And we shouldn't have to choose to either stay in academia or have a life, because when you force people to choose, you end up losing a lot of good people to corporate jobs; you end up losing a lot of diversity as well because, who can afford to put their life on hold? Who can afford to not have enough money to send home to their families? Who can afford to have kids when their parents live out of state or in another country?

Dez Manuel Fonseca

What was my knowledge of union movements before getting involved in my own union? I studied US history in undergrad and in grad school, so I know there's been a concerted effort to destroy the labor movement in this country, which was really strong—and socialist—in the twenties and thirties and forties. I know the Communist Party was strong in building the militancy of UAW, until the communists and socialists were kicked out. The Red Scare, the McCarthy era, the Cold War were kind of the first assault, then labor leadership made an alliance with the Democratic Party and with the government to not oppose capitalist governance in the US. The Reagan era was a neoliberal assault on labor. That's kind of the theoretical understanding I had of the labor movement.

My first experience with the difficulties of organizing in labor was in undergrad, in Tufts University, Boston. I helped the undergrad campaign of the dining workers to form their union with UNITE HERE Local 27. It was similar to what we do here: one-on-one conversations, forming relationships, in-person meetings, having a clear strategy. I was responsible for secretly expanding the group of undergrads that helped the workers deliver a letter to the president's office. We had a rally of hundreds of students in a small campus to support workers and fight against retaliation. It was incredibly emotional seeing the joy that the workers experienced when they won their union. Sitting here now, I can see the parallels not only to our campaign but other workers at USC [University of Southern California] or Caltech [California Institute of Technology] or even shit like Starbucks, Amazon.

I can't think of family experiences in unions as I was growing up. But we do have a couple of stories that involve organizing. A couple of uncles in Guinea-Bissau were involved in the anticolonial struggle; one of them was a member of the Communist Party and a sympathizer of the dockworkers that were massacred in Pidjiguiti in 1959 for going on strike to demand independence from Portugal.

One of the reasons I decided to come to UCLA was because I knew teacher assistants had a union, UAW Local 2865. I knew about the contract negotiations that were on course back in 2020; I knew that the contract was going to expire during my third year. It seemed so far away when I got here, but three years later I was able to be part of the negotiations! I actually had a talk with the history department's steward, Michael Dean, during my visit day. After that, I signed a union card at my orientation. I actually don't remember my orientation [*laughs*], but I know I signed up to become a member!

My real involvement happened thanks to a one-on-one conversation with, again, Michael Dean. As a result of that conversation, Michael and other coworkers asked me to participate in planning a mass action that was going to happen on all UC campuses on April 26, 2022, to demand fair contracts for all four bargaining units. April 26 was a catalyst because after that I started going to bargaining sessions and membership meetings.

Oh! And I almost forgot this probably big thing [*laughs*]: I was also asked to be the new history department steward. And I did. As a steward, I was getting people to the bargaining sessions, organizing the history department organizing committee meetings, and following up the grievances that were filed before me.

That spring we had union leadership elections, where I ran to become steward—although the election was uncontested. Before I even agreed on running for the steward position, I did my research on the background of the two slates. At first, the slate that piqued my interest was the one that had messaging around antipolicing and BDS [Boycott, Divestment and Sanctions], which are issues I'm also committed to. But the problem was that I hadn't seen them on the ground. One person I asked about the slates was Michael Dean. We talked about different strategies for strengthening the union and what it takes to have a militant membership because what was important to me was forming connections with people who were actually committed to the union.

I ended up voting for the slate that Michael supported, and I did that based on the trust I had in him as an organizer. Michael and I were not close friends, but he was just an actual presence in my department and *I saw him organizing*. I also saw the people from the slate he supported doing walk-throughs, sending emails, being involved in different campaigns. In a union, that's the number one thing: are the people that you're working with and voting for committed to building up the union, and making the union as strong as possible so that you can accomplish wider social gains?

One last reason why I got involved in our union was the People's Summit in Los Angeles, in June of 2022. I'm familiar with some organizations that held the summit, so when they called for endorsements, I spoke at an organizing committee monthly membership meeting and proposed that we, as Local 2865, endorse it. And we not only endorsed it, we sent workers to attend, myself included.

I wanted to be not just an observer, but a participant in helping our union in the best way that I could. So, me and a few other people started a social sciences organizing committee that congregated departments in fields like history, geography, sociology, et cetera, because we all have similar working conditions and share a location. It made sense to organize together. We started out in June with four or five people over Zoom, and by August or September, we had ten to twenty people regularly, but sometimes forty people looped in. It became a really good place to make sure that different departments were well organized, and we could take responsibility to find leaders in the departments with low participation.

In the months between spring 2022 and the strike, I joined other union organizing spaces where I could tell people had been organizing for months if not years before me. There, I focused on understanding the dynamics, strategies, and tactics that were being discussed. That's what I was competent to do because I didn't know shit about what an unfair labor practice charge was, what an economic strike was, what "table talk" meant, and all the interpretations about the bargaining table. I didn't know who the bargaining reps were, I didn't remember voting for them! I knew nothing about bargaining. Absolutely nothing [*laughs*]!

I've learned a lot in less than a year. I'd say a union is a group of workers organizing together to better their working conditions and their livelihoods. It sound cliché, but really, "We *are* the union." The best way I can describe it is that our union is just us; it's just workers who make all this shit happen, who develop and implement organizing plans. You understand that the union is the workers just when you are organizing, that's how you realize that the workers' goals happen only when there is a sizable amount of workers organized and organizing. And, what's organizing? It's meeting regularly, designing plans, doing walk-throughs, getting new members signed up, having one-on-one conversations to get people involved in campaigns and in fighting against retaliation, filing grievances; all that shit only happens when workers are doing it. And during the high peaks of our movement, like a strike, we need thousands of workers *actively involved and actively participating* to make shit happen. And how does it feel to be a union member? It feels very empowering!

Within the academic space, I would say that when you organize in a union, the academic work makes more sense. Fighting to make your workplace better makes your academic work more fulfilling and less alienating. Academic work is very alienating. When you think of your work as a passion project, you are alienated from your work. From my experience, organizing in a union helps my work make more sense, like I'm providing a service to the university. I'm being exploited as a worker [*laughs*] but providing a service as a union organizer.

Finally, related to what a union is for me, a strong union is built through in-person one-on-one conversations. You need to see your coworkers as real people going through the same struggles, which you only truly understand by talking to them directly, not through speeches or online posts. It was those one-on-one talks with Michael, the history department steward, that got me involved. He listened to my concerns and treated me with respect. Since then, I've consistently done organizing work every week. Before those conversations, I was just dipping in and out.

CHAPTER 2

Setting the Stage

Dez Manuel Fonseca speaking at the Big October Monthly Membership Meeting at UCLA

"You Can Only Get Slapped in the Face So Many Times"

Aarthi Sekar

Academic workers, union members, decided to go on strike because it had been months and months of our side making all the attempts to negotiate in good faith with UC. The bargaining team drafted up a proposal, doing a massive undertaking of surveying all in-unit members for their input on what demands we really need. We analyzed that data to see what the issues and sub-issues are. For example, with dependents, is the issue dependent health care? Is the issue childcare support? For international researchers, is it support of visa renewals? Is it job contract timelines or length of employment? It took months. There was so much work done; there were good faith bargaining efforts that were made at the table, so many efforts to demonstrate collective action and to show UC that these are rights that are so important and pertinent to us and that we deserve them. It's not something we should have ever had to demonstrate, but we did in massive numbers. And with all of that, UC was refusing to actually negotiate in good faith with us. I lost count of the number of unfair labor practice charges. Every single bargaining session you would go to prestrike, they would always be late, they were incredibly dismissive, they always came unprepared. If we had proposals ready, they had barely anything to say, they would come back weeks later without any kind of input on the proposals. And we all witnessed it.

UC did not deem the livelihoods of workers to be that important, because if they did, they would have made a real effort to actually negotiate in good faith with us. And you can only get slapped in the face so many times. I think that level of disrespect was felt widely because we had hundreds of people go to those bargaining sessions. And after them, people would talk about how awful UC's labor relations team acted—showing up an hour late, et cetera. People witnessed not just that, but the rude tone that they would take, and some of the things they said demonstrated how little they think of us. It was the straw that broke the camel's back because on top of the pile of things you deal with on a daily basis, they are then dismissive of us. That pushed us. We organized people to come to these bargaining sessions to witness management's disrespect because it's necessary for workers to collectively witness how they treated us and dismissed us.

Kien Le

To get my department ready to escalate toward a strike, we wrote a letter to the faculty and the dean of the school of humanities. It sounds easy, right? But it required a lot of labor for the letter to be written because many people participated and we wrote it in a collaborative way. So we felt like, "We need to be in this together, as many signatures as we can have." And it was a shocking moment for me because some people just refused to have their names listed on the letter! Some people just never respond. And that was when I recognized there's a big difference in the levels of participation. Some people are like, "I'm going to sign this right now, let's go!" And some people just say, "I'm worried if I sign this letter, it's going to impair my relationship with my advisor." Things like that. So basically, I had to talk to people in advance and answer all of their questions and help them understand.

That's when I realized the amount of labor that it takes to make something like the 2022 strike possible! Just one-on-one conversations and talking people through their doubts. And you have to resolve them, right? So, one-on-one conversations ... I don't remember how many conversations I had [*laughs*], but they were a lot! And then we got the majority of workers to sign the letter, we gave it to the faculty asking them to sign on and send to their higher ups. Many faculty members signed the letter, many didn't. So that was when we realized like, "Oh, this is going to be a big fight." And the dean of the School of Humanities even refused to meet with us when we tried to deliver the letter to him.

Big October Monthly Membership Meeting and Strike Authorization Vote

Maddy Duong

I got involved with our union after one of the organizers in UCI came into my lab bay during a walk-through and casually asked, "Hey, how do you feel about all these issues?" They were talking about pay, nonresident supplemental tuition, things like that.[1] Then they invited me to a rally to talk about the possibility of going on strike. When I say they "invited me," it sounds like the event was exclusive, but it was open to anyone. That walk-through was a game changer for me; it led me to the Big October Monthly Membership Meeting (BOMMM), and that's where I really got hooked. The stories I heard there compelled me to go on strike. That action got me motivated to help improve the lives of my coworkers. And also—because I'm planning on being a graduate student—I had a personal investment for the future.

---

1 Nonresident supplemental tuition is an additional fee charged to graduate students who are not residents of the state where their university is located, such as out-of-state or international students. It's a significant extra cost on top of regular tuition, often impacting those who may already be financially strained.

I knew about unions before and I knew that it was important to be a member. My uncle is a high school teacher and he does stuff with his union. During the pandemic we talked about unions and he urged me to join the union at Ralph's, the grocery store where I was working at the time.

Emily Weintraut

The first big action prestrike was the BOMMM. We organized the BOMMM one-on-one. We would be in pairs to do walk-throughs. So, I'd go up to my coworker, sometimes my friend, I'd go up to other people in my department, in my building, and I'd ask if they had heard about bargaining or the BOMMM, giving them information, inviting them to the BOMMM. And people's responses were usually positive. One challenge of organizing is that a lot of communication is done by email, and a lot of people ignore a lot of emails if they don't have to read them. It's not a dire thing, but it's a challenge. However, when you talk to your coworkers on a walk-through, they get on board.

I don't think that you connect with people if you don't have a one-on-one exchange. Talking with people was empowering and mobilizing for me, yes, but it was also mobilizing for others to have someone to validate their experiences. And then I could tell them, I can vouch for the fact that people aren't treated as badly in other departments and by other principal investigators. And they would also realize that. Empowering people and spewing at them are divided by a fine line. Sometimes people are good with where they're at, and if that's the case, you don't want to tell them, "Your life sucks!" Empowering people is more subtle, "Okay, you are fine right now, but you deserve more. What can we do to get you more?" That's why those one-on-one conversations are really important, because if you're just speaking *at* people, like spewing at people what they need or should do, it's not going to connect as if you were having these one-on-one conversations. A big strategy that we used was asking questions like, "How would this change your life?" And having people think about that. We're talking about UC committing unfair labor practices, but on top of that, we were talking about what people care about, "How would having childcare change your life? How would having nonresident supplemental tuition remission change your life? How would having higher wages change your life?" And we would workshop that and build off of each other.

One-on-one conversations were mobilizing to me because I learned that, for example, some people in certain departments are only given 25 percent employment, so they're making half of what they need to stay afloat, which is just disgusting.[2] It was mobilizing talking to international students who are forced to pay nonresident supplemental tuition because their departments will not cover it. I talked to one international student who is married and doesn't make enough money for his wife to come to the US, and he is living in a shared room because he cannot afford his own room. A lot of that stuff is really mobilizing. That's the thing, I never went into organizing thinking I have horrible working conditions. No. My boss is good. I don't have a family to support. But also, I have a lot of financial difficulties, and I've worked three jobs at once to scrape together. I went into organizing thinking of *us*.

I had tons of one-on-ones! I'm amazed just by thinking about it, but still, not as many as I would have wanted. I mainly did walk-throughs in the departments of food science, viticulture and enology, and microbiology. I also did walk-throughs in biological and agricultural engineering, and I did some stuff in nutrition and helped in animal science. A lot of the organizing is more so done on a building basis just because people in different grad groups and departments will work in a variety of areas. I did have a lot of conversations and a lot of group conversations, and a lot of them were difficult.

Conversations blur in my memory between the BOMMM and the strike authorization vote. In general, there were different kinds of difficult conversations. For example, there were negative comments from people saying that our union sends too many emails; we do, we send a lot of emails, and they have a lot of important things, and people get sick of it. There were some other people that I talked to who were incredulously asking, "But why would UC do illegal things?" Those were hard conversations because I didn't have the experience to explain it in a different way than just, "They're greedy." A lot of the people not wanting to vote for the strike were scared that their boss would find out that they even voted in the strike authorization vote. There were a lot of international workers who feared it was illegal for them to vote.

---

2 Student researchers are often offered a 50 percent assignment, which implies twenty hours of research work, but they often spend forty-plus hours in the lab. Here Emily is saying that some student researchers are offered only 25 percent of employment and salary, but work forty-plus hours.

People would also say, "If I go on strike, I might not be able to graduate, and I'm here just to get my degree and get a job." However, in spite of the fear of going on strike, people morally agreed.

And then, in STEM there was a nonzero number of people who believe we make too much money as it is. That was surprising! And that obviously comes from a place of privilege or a weird kinship with their boss where they think that striking is an action against their boss. But going on strike was not an action against faculty, it was an action against poor wages and workplace abuse. It was against the UC's illegal actions and the UC's abuse of its academic employees. The one-on-one conversations were about reframing that. And that was very difficult for some people.

There's so much indirect retaliation in academia because you're trying to get a degree, a thing that can act as a sort of prestige for opening up more job opportunities. And because you want to get prestige, you accept being overworked and abused. At least in STEM, there is that culture of abuse and overwork. Once I told a faculty member about how I know people who, on top of being underpaid, work twelve hours a day for six days a week, and they didn't even blink because faculty don't think that's unreasonable. There were people who were afraid to talk during our walk-throughs because their boss works directly adjacent to them and they were afraid of retaliation.

Principal investigators can fail us or deny us funding if we derail from our schedule, and the way they do it is because we have to register as students and get credits for fulfilling research. But we also have to find a teaching assistant job, and do a full forty hours of research. We see this very manipulative abuse often in academia. Principal investigators will threaten visas for international workers, which is just horrifying! They'd say, "If you do this or that, I'm not going to renew your visa." Your boss has a lot of control over you, they are the only one who can vouch for you, or decide if you are going to graduate in four, five, or ten years. And people take the abuse because they're trying to get a degree.

Our union is not against faculty, our union is against abuse. But if you're an abusive faculty, then yeah, we're going to fight against that. We always say, "Our union is by, for, and of our members." Our union is for the members. We are just trying to make life better for us. And it does have this effect where it benefits other people. You increase grad workers' wages, other wages are going to have to increase too for lecturers and adjuncts and other things like that because they want to keep the hierarchy of wages. But also, teaching assistants are happier if they have less work burden—they're better educators for their students.

At UC Davis, we held the BOMMM on October 13 at 5 p.m. I remember being scared because getting four hundred people at 5 p.m. on a Thursday was going to be difficult because people are tired toward the end of the week. What I know from my coworkers is that they go home as soon as they finish their lab work.

It was a bit nerve-wracking for me because Sierra wasn't going to be with me, and it was going to be my first time organizing by myself. I had to lead my department to the BOMMM, and although food science people are late to every event, I made sure we were on time. I was scared at first because other departments were trickling in, and I didn't see that many people. Then more came in, and more, and more, and I didn't realize the magnitude of it until I stood up to do my speech. I started shaking when I saw how many of us were there. I didn't think I had public speaking anxiety, but my hand was shaking, *my leg was shaking* because there were so many people there!

Basically, this is what I said in my speech, "I moved across the entire country to come to one of the top programs—because UC Davis and Cornell are seen as the top programs in my field in the US. I changed my license from New Jersey to California so I could gain residency, even though being from New Jersey is a big part of my identity. And guess what I did this summer? I worked a manual labor job and a retail job that both paid me minimum wage because I didn't get funding from the university. And I'm now currently working those two jobs and my normal research job and assistant teaching. I'm working three jobs at once just to stay afloat and to not go too far into debt. I did a clinical trial where I made six hundred extra dollars, thank God! And I was still in the red. So, I'm at this world-renowned program. I am doing groundbreaking research in the food industry. I'm working as much as I can and I'm barely able to pay my rent and stay afloat." And people connected to my speech; they were supportive.

After me, Sarah and Porter gave a speech about childcare. They schooled us on childcare. It was mind blowing to me how expensive it was. I knew some of it from other people, but they went in-depth about the exact amount that their childcare was going to cost. And that was big to me. I think everyone there agreed that we make too little fucking money, and that it is insane that you're in a world-renowned program working two other part-time minimum-wage jobs.

The BOMMM at Davis had over seven hundred people. I had never grasped that concept before! It feels insane because most union meetings I had gone to had maybe twenty people. I had never been to a massive event at Davis yet, so seeing all those people was mind blowing to me. I was thinking, "Holy shit, people really do care!"

Seeing that was more empowering and it made me feel more of a kinship, like, "We're all these different campuses, some of us have academic rivalries or whatever, but we're all here fighting for the same things."

The strike authorization vote was next. I remember I was so worried because the initial point of contact for the strike authorization vote was getting the ballot sent to your email, but people don't read their email. So, when we found out that we had not only hit our goal for day one, but exceeded it, I was surprised and excited. We got more votes on day one than we did in the entirety of the Student Researchers United strike authorization vote even though we had less time to prepare for it.[3]

During the strike authorization vote, we began every day with a morning huddle to inaugurate the walk-throughs, and we ended with a debrief. I was there every single day, I spent the whole week of the strike authorization vote going around talking to people, and for so many people it was such an easy talk because we had done walk-throughs before. We would ask if they were able to vote and, immediately, they would vote. The hardest conversations were with people who were scared of retaliation from the university or from their principal investigator, but other than that, it was very easy. And people were saying, "Yeah! Fuck the UC."

We were anticipating an exponential decrease every single day following day one of the strike authorization vote, but that's not how it went! We still got so many more votes every single day. The initial votes,

3 The Student Researchers United strike authorization vote was held in October 2021 to demand recognition. For more on the Student Researchers United campaign and their strike authorization vote see workers Elsie and Aarthi.

day one, were from people who were more connected or who were at the BOMMM. But afterwards, we continued walk-throughs, and we continued to get more votes every single day.

Besides one-on-one conversations, I talked to some classes. I gave a guest lecture in a class where I'm a teaching assistant around the strike authorization vote. There were a couple of hundred undergrads in my lecture hall. Before talking about kombucha, I gave a speech, "These are the current conditions we're dealing with. This is what the UC is doing to us." I got resounding applause after that, and I didn't expect it. I was so scared of their reaction. And then people came up to me and told me they didn't know what was happening.

Dez Manuel Fonseca

When the fall term began in 2022, I was on the ground every day doing whatever preparations for our Big October Monthly Membership Meeting, and for the strike authorization vote. But I was also working to get more people involved. My main goals were having one-on-one conversations and building trust, asking people about their workplace conditions, their financial conditions, and whatever people thought was an issue in their lives. One of my genuine goals was listening. And while I was doing all that, I was realizing that organizing toward the strike was the next big action we could take. I was realizing that, based on the strength of our union, we were—collectively—in a unique opportunity to organize a strike threat. That opportunity wouldn't always be there because you can be at the end of a contract negotiation and not have a strong active union; that's more common than not. Our union was trying to reverse that trend.

A lot of people in the humanities and social sciences struggle to conceptualize what is their work as a student, and what is their work as a worker. And the way I see it, that differentiation doesn't even exist because we are producing something for the university when we're doing our individual research as "students." My dissertation will be property of the University of California, and I can get a Ford Fellowship or any other fellowship and I don't even know where that money goes. A lot of it doesn't actually go to me [*laughs*]. And because your advisor oversees your research and there is a blurred boundary between your work and the academic relationship, people think that if they were to go on strike, their advisor would get mad at them, and that relationship is important for their professional future. People need the recommendation letters, they need to get into conferences, they need their papers to be accepted in journals; they need connections. People don't get a professional position standing alone.

I always knew that a strike was the only way to win even a slice of the demands that we had. Our strike was legally an unfair labor practice strike. There were a lot of other unfair labor practices that stalled bargaining for a long time. I remember, for example, that UC's labor relations team didn't hand over the most basic information that our bargaining team asked for. I don't know if it was negligence or malicious shit, but UC dropped the ball.

But for most of us, the underlying reason we went on strike is that we have a super low-paying job. There are people in my department and all over the campuses who pay like 60, 70, 80 percent of their paychecks in rent. And oftentimes it goes right back to the university for their expensive campus apartments.

We planned the Big October Monthly Membership Meeting in the regular statewide organizing meetings, which were on Zoom. I helped to organize the BOMMM in UCLA. I did a lot of turnout. I did walk-throughs every day in different buildings. I had one-on-one conversations with people who had no idea of the campaign and we talked about our demands. I handed out the QR code to RSVP for the BOMMM and access more information. I also helped to schedule the rally and the speakers. I helped to make sure we had all the supplies we needed, like the bullhorns, the vests, and other stuff.

We organized a walk party from Bunche Hall for all social sciences. I helped with getting social sciences people hyped and walking together. We organized a walk party from Bunche Hall, which was one of the most fun parts—we had the bullhorn with the sirens on and went walking through the building halls announcing that we were having a rally, getting people together, and we eventually met up with other walk parties and coagulated into a giant body of hundreds of workers. Me and another organizer, Rachel, were picking up workers, doing impromptu speeches in the courtyard, agitating, mobilizing, walking all together to the rally. It was mad cool! Hundreds of people descending from the steps, chanting. We had chant leaders; people were in vests. I also helped with crowd control and held on to the mic. I also ended up being delegated as one of the speakers. I learned I was going to have a solo speaking role the day before the BOMMM; I gave a speech about wages, one of the most widely felt issues.

We learned a lot about organizing rallies by doing the BOMMM. We learned we should marshal people in closer because it easily gets spread apart; we learned we should get people to chant in low periods, making sure it's always busy. We learned we have to be ready to respond to questions and interruptions or people on the open mic saying unrelated things. For example, there was a person who started talking about Jesus on the mic, so I was like, "Cool, but not here. Unless it's related to labor, you could make it related to labor." He didn't though [*laughs*]. People were confused, and I just started a chant. That was funny.

Personally, I learned that all rallies need organization. We wanted to bring a sentiment out of workers—workers realize we don't make enough money, we realize we are exploited, we realize the immense value that we produce at the university. We wanted to take out the latent knowledge that people have about their conditions, and transform it into a positive and progressive force. Contrary to popular belief, rallies don't just happen spontaneously. We carefully organized the BOMMM to ensure it had a purpose.

The overall energy was incredible. It was a roaring success: a real moment of unity. There was a connection between the organizers of the rally, the speakers, and the emcees, and the people were calling for a strike authorization vote. The BOMMM spread consciousness and awareness of our strike threat and of bargaining in a way that we didn't have before. It was a real marker. After the BOMMM the conversations about a potential strike were more open, they were happening in more spaces, more people were participating in it. And across campuses all the BOMMMs looked pretty successful.

The week before the strike authorization vote, it was all-hands-on-deck doing walk-throughs on schedule and having conversations. We did nitty-gritty organizing work with the people who were signing up as strike captains. For me, that week was a lot of walk-throughs in engineering and biosciences because the infrastructure was weaker for student researchers than it was for academic student employees because we've had a union for two decades and they just formed theirs.

When the strike authorization vote results came out, I felt really good. 75 percent of workers voted and 97 percent of those voted yes. It was a huge success! And from my perspective, it was a success because we had a strong, visible social media campaign, we had a really good website that was an important tool in our tool kit. And man, we had an army of people doing walk-throughs, dozens of people signing up for several hours a week! And that's how we were able to do it. There's no shortcut. There's no magic trick. You go, you talk to workers, you build a relationship with your coworkers. That's what the slogan is about, "educate, agitate, organize."

Curtis Rumrill

For me, the fundamental purpose of the large strike vote was as a demonstration of power to the boss. We had internal metrics that we were trying to hit because that's how you get some idea of how you're doing in organizing. But the purpose of a gigantic strike vote and a supermajority yes vote is to make a strong statement to the boss, "We have this much power, you need to come to the table in a serious manner."

In 2022, some folks from the Academic Workers for a Democratic Union caucus were worried that the threat of the strike would be used to get a contract without actually going on strike. I think that there was a sincere concern that every time there was a metric attached to some sort of organizing goal, that that metric wasn't meant as a goal to be reached, but a barrier to prevent us from being able to go on strike.

But going on strike was a foregone conclusion because the purpose of this strike was to change the balance of power in the long term. The mere threat of a strike would not be enough to do that. When your goal is to change the nature of your relationship with your employer, you actually need to pull the trigger on the strike.

Kenzo Esquivel

At UC Berkeley, the Big October Monthly Membership Meeting was held on Memorial Glade, which is a big grassy area on campus. We filled that space up like I had never seen before for a union-related event. We had postdocs, academic researchers, grad researchers, and graduate student instructors all speak. We also had individuals who were not part of the planned speeches come on to offer the feelings from specific departments about why they felt ready to strike. Having the opportunity to hear people who were not part of the planned speakers was incredibly mobilizing.

Departments from across campus each came to the BOMMM with big signs bearing their department names, and collectively we formed a huge crowd. I think this element of seeing so many departments was incredibly energizing. And for a lot of people it had been a long time since the last time they'd been surrounded by that many people. That also added to the novelty of it. People were really energized and excited about being part of a large community that was ready to strike. And people were excited to get their first union shirts.

We had small-group breakouts, which gave us a great opportunity to give new leaders a role in facilitating the meeting and getting a sense of what it is to be in a leadership position. That was the first time that we got some of our departments' new first years taking a role and marching over and facilitating the breakout group. Folks in attendance also had the chance to talk to one another across their department.

There was a sense of unity at the BOMMM, at least for me, and how I perceived that space was that those historical divisions really didn't feel at play in that moment. The departments that were more aligned with the wildcat were also out there. If I remember correctly, pê feijó—from the Department of Rhetoric—was one of the speakers responsible for riling up the crowd, and certainly her department was more wildcat aligned and ended up being more vote no aligned during ratification.

By the time the BOMMM happened, we had built a strong base, and the excitement was palpable. There was an electric energy of empowerment and solidarity as people from across campuses gathered, realizing the fight was everywhere. It helped everyone see that we had the numbers and power to strike.

Before the strike authorization vote, I was offered a temporary staff role to help with the preparations, but I declined because I had already committed to a conference in Puerto Rico. Though I wasn't present for the strike authorization vote, it was a key test of the infrastructure we built. While I checked in remotely, our strike captains exceeded expectations, achieving a higher-than-average turnout. It was clear our department's organizing was strong, and though I was nervous about the strike authorization vote, it became a collective victory.

I was asked to be on staff around mid-October. Jess gave me a call and said, "Hey, you're doing a lot of important and good organizing work in your turf, but would you be interested in taking on a little bit more responsibility and structure as a part of paid staff?" I guess I was asked because as a not-paid-staff organizer in my head steward role I had organized my college and the College of Natural Resources, but I hadn't been doing a ton of active organizing outside of my department community. So, the invitation to be on staff was about expanding the scope of my work as an organizer and obviously being compensated to some extent to take on that extra work. I was both honored to be asked, and also thought that realistically it probably didn't make sense because I was going to an academic conference and I wasn't going to be around for the week of strike authorization vote.

It felt almost like a promotion, an opportunity to have a little bit more of an impact or a little bit more ownership over the potential success of our strike. And I struggled because, to me, the conference was a professional development opportunity, a commitment I'd made to my colleagues, and the opportunity to be on staff felt a little bit ... I'm looking for the right word ... the offering of being on staff was challenging my own values and what was more important to me. Obviously, I had been working toward the strike for literally years in little pieces, but I also wanted to go to the conference in Puerto Rico and I wanted to meet the colleagues that I'd been talking to for months. Also, I was supposed to moderate a panel and be on a panel, so it felt shitty to pull out a month before the conference. Anyways, I feel I ultimately did have the space to make my own decision and I did end up attending the conference. At the same time, there were definitely moments that were difficult because of what I decided.

A different staff organizer made me feel uncomfortable about my decision. They repeatedly brought up the fact that I was going to "Costa Rica." And they were guilt-tripping me to do stuff before I went to my conference. That felt not good because it was like an erasure of the work that I'd put in, and it felt weird that they considered guilt-tripping me to ask me to do things instead of doing it in a way that felt relational. So that felt shitty. And I still think about that. And that should not be how a staff organizer is functioning in our union.

Joyce Chan

Workers in UCSD, we held our BOMMM in front of the Geisel Library. It was a big gathering that showed us our numbers on the ground—this is who we are, this is how many of us there are. It showed us the importance of being together, and recognizing where we are aligned because, as long as we are all focused on being actionable in terms of pushing forward our agenda as an aligned group, we can be very powerful. The conversations about our differences can happen at a later time because the strike is not the end of our fight.

After the BOMMM, we had a week to organize the strike authorization vote, and then the strike authorization vote itself. I remember it was a lot of walk-throughs, it was a lot of phone banking and texting. I remember doing less science than usual leading up to that because I was so excited to get the first strike off the ground. And during those walk-throughs, all the time we encountered people who were afraid to go on strike. But I think those fears were nothing that a follow-up conversation or having a heart-to-heart conversation can't fix. And even if people disagree with the strike, having conversations with them helps because at least they get to hear the perspective of someone who is seeing the action as very important.

As an organizer, I was really pushing my boundaries and pushing my comfort levels, doing tasks that I would consider myself too shy or too uncomfortable to do. I did it because I knew that it was going to change the lives of many people. For me it was difficult to do walk-through conversations and phone banking, which made me anxious. But phone calls, I think I was doing forty or sixty a day, almost to the point of losing my voice. For me, an anxiety-inducing aspect of doing a walk-through was bumping into hostile principal investigators.

And then, the strike authorization vote results came. In my mind, I knew the strike was going to be approved by 90 percent or more of voters. But just seeing the sheer number of people that voted and just seeing the overwhelming majority—98 percent or something like that—it was really high!!! I was absolutely beaming because the strike was becoming more real. And again, I didn't have any doubt in my mind that it was going to be a majority, but seeing that high participation number—like a high test grade—sends you over.

Elsie Jacobson

The Big October Monthly Membership Meeting felt really different from any of the other rallies and meetings we did before. For my building, for example, we had a team waiting outside to take everyone to the BOMMM, while me and two other postdocs went to every person in the building and invited them to go. For some people, that was the first time doing a walk-through, which was kind of cool.

The meeting ended up having fifteen hundred people. It was crazy! It felt really, really amazing! And I knew a lot of postdocs were there. It was really exciting because, for me, it was the first big thing that we were really doing together. I think a lot of people shared that excitement.

I remember the speakers were sitting up on the grassy slope, looking at the people. We had speeches; Dez Manuel Fonseca went last and his speech was incredible! It was just next level. And there were some people who got up to the podium for the open comment section. I gave my first speech too. I remember it was pretty nerve wracking because I was going to talk about my disability to fifteen hundred people. But everyone in the crowd was so supportive and excited to hear from everyone.

And then, Michael Dean asked the question, "Do we want to do a strike authorization vote? Hands for aye." And everyone's hand went up and everyone yelled and not a single person said no. It was just completely unanimous. He even asked for abstains, but that was it. It was *completely unanimous*, completely positive. Actually, to be fair, it was kind of funny because a couple of people were confused, they were asking, "Are we voting to strike?" And I told them, "No, we're voting to vote," and we laughed.

The vote to have a strike authorization vote was important because it made it felt like escalating to the strike authorization vote was a collective decision. The people in the BOMMM could have said no, and that would have told us something. And if it had been 50/50, we would have had to take stock and rethink our approach. But the fact that it was so overwhelmingly and loudly positive made it feel like it was a collective decision to move forward and do the strike authorization vote with the strike in mind.

At the end of the BOMMM, everyone was so excited and hyped up about it. People who I'd never met before signed up and came to their first strike planning meeting shortly afterwards. During the BOMMM, we had cards for people to write down the names of five persons to talk to about what was going on. And people filled out those cards and talked to those people! That was probably the first organizing task for a lot of people.

The goal for the strike authorization vote was basically to reach the same participation numbers that we had reached the year before, but in half the time. In 2021 we did it in two weeks, and for me, it's a little bit of a blur in my mind. But this time, in 2022, I remember we walked through the buildings over and over again and talked to as many people as we possibly could. We tried to pair a grad student with a postdoc to personalize the conversations and make sure that we were talking about demands that were specific to the specific contracts. And on the weekends, I did phone banking. I certainly got everyone I knew to vote.

I didn't have any conversations with people that were antistrike. I talked to a lot of people who were too busy and didn't want to stop working, and we did our best in those cases. I used all of my organizing skills, "educate and agitate." Sometimes I'd come across a person who'd tell me, "I'm completely happy. I don't need anything to change." But if they were willing to have that conversation, they'd end up admitting that not everything's perfect.

We were monitoring the strike authorization vote results like it was the score of a game. All through the week, we knew how many people had voted, but not the way that they had voted. I wasn't too worried about us getting a majority voting yes. But we were definitely trying to make sure that as many people as possible did vote. Because having those large numbers would mean that all of those people knew about the strike and were in some way prepared for it.

Strike Eve

Kenzo Esquivel

In between the strike authorization vote and the strike, we were working closely with our strike captain network. We had recruited a good group of people who had gone to some trainings and we delegated five to ten people per person for them to reach out to and have concrete conversations about what it meant for each one of them to go on strike. And because of my position as head steward, I took the responsibility of reaching out to a lot of people we didn't know—researchers, academic researchers, and postdocs. I gave myself the hardest turf, which was also the easiest because I would call and do everything I could to find them, but ended up not having that many conversations. My work ended up being a lot more supporting and checking in on the strike captains to make sure that those conversations were happening. That was both within my department and within the energy and resources group, for which I took some degree of responsibility because it is adjacent to my department. I was also helping graduate student instructors think through what the strike could look like. It was at that moment when the strike was obviously getting very real for people.

Aside from the different conversations we were having on campus, we were working at the UAW office. There we were having meetings, and preparing signs, and whatnot. All of that is kind of a blur. I was also getting my own things in order: I needed to power down some of my own analyses, and talk to my undergrad lab tech so that he could work hours if he wanted to. I was also working with my principal investigator to help him plan and navigate what his class would look like.

After the strike authorization vote, a lot of the one-on-one conversations we had with researchers were about assuaging people's fears and answering people's questions. There were a lot of anxieties around how not doing their research labor would set back their dissertations and harm their own progress. We encouraged people to think about how their own dissertation research is related to the mission and revenue of the university, and how withholding that labor affects important research output for the university. Some questions were more logistical, for example, "I have a lab tech who's leaving in December and I really want him to get through these samples. How do I navigate that if I'm striking?" I think it was for the folks who were in research positions where we—organizers—had to work through the different feelings around, "This is my work, this is my own advancement." But also, the folks doing research were the ones who had lab equipment or specimens, and for them, the logistical concerns were many.

For the folks who were teaching, things were relatively cut and dry. Most people felt relatively clear that we were asking them not to do teaching labor: not holding classes, not attending office hours, not grading. That felt rather tangible and specific.

Of all the conversations, the conversations that got people thinking holistically about what it is to be on strike were the most memorable. People needed help thinking through this, a lot of graduate students had never thought about their labor in this way, or being part of a movement in this way, or what it means to try to make an institutional change at this level. Those one-on-one conversations helped people see themselves as being an important part of a broader movement to democratize the university and create equal opportunities for diverse scholars. There were conversations where there was a real sense that this movement wasn't rabble rousing; it wasn't even about just getting a raise. So, getting the opportunity to bring people and tying people's experiences into a broader vision felt really ... that stuck with me.

I witnessed fear of retaliation leading up to the strike, particularly with international workers who were worried about the implications of striking, and people who were worried for them. There was another group of people who were nervous about what the university would do once they found out that they were not doing research. Both types of conversations were pretty straightforward. They just needed to be walked through the various protections that they had, and the fact that there is power in numbers, and that we would fight tooth and nail to protect them from any retaliation.

Dez Manuel Fonseca

After the strike authorization vote and before the strike, I was doing the last of my academic work, because I knew I wasn't going to do it *for a long time* [*laughs*]. I was also focused on doing strike captain trainings on Zoom and in person. A strike captain was a role designated for people who wanted to be more involved, so we were recruiting people to be strike captains by department, and then we trained them in the basics of the strike, like the foundations of the strike: "broad, visible, and complete." "Broad" means as many workers as possible; "visible" means that those workers should be visible; "complete" means that they withhold all their labor. We educated strike captains on different ways of organizing and mobilizing their department—we had a thing called "turf," which meant that every strike captain was responsible for bringing ten to fifteen people out to the picket line. We mostly focused the training on the logistics of the strike, and now I think we should have done more political education on labor and bargaining.

At this particular moment, having social events was an effective way for people to start their engagement. Social events work because people would talk about the hot thing on the block, which was the strike, and they would get excited and that built a trust and a commitment to actually do the thing and walk out. We did a lot of phone banking too! Oh man! The phone banking was crazy, but also very important. I don't like phone banking, I much prefer walk-throughs, but you do what you have to do and I was on the phone all day [*laughs*].

It was a bunch of preparation, just trying to get as many people to go on strike as possible, and doing it on a one-on-one level. We didn't expect to send out a tweet or an email or post in a group chat. From what I've heard from the history of our union, moving toward one-on-one organizing, instead of posting a statement to call for action, has been one of the big strategic reorientations we did as a union. People see a lot of statements all the time; you can go online and see hundreds of competing statements, but when that *one person* reaches out to you and you trust them, it makes a big difference.

When I talked to people, I would get a range of responses. I wouldn't even say there was a predominating spirit or feeling, other than *positive*. For example, I was doing walk-throughs in south campus, in STEM departments, which didn't have a union culture. There I faced a lot of hesitancy... more than hesitancy, I encountered people who had heard about the strike, but didn't know what a strike was. One conversation that really comes to mind was with a group of guys in civil engineering. They all were pretty positive about the strike, they were thanking us for the service of the union, and I asked them, "Can you commit to go on strike and bring your coworkers on strike?" And they said, "I can go if you have a rally at 8 a.m. or 9 a.m. I can leave my office and then go to the rally and come back to keep working." I came across a lot of people who thought that the strike was like a demonstration. People not realizing that a strike means you don't do any of your work.

The feeling about the strike was also related to how actively people had been organizing. Among workers who were not too active, there was personal unease or hesitation, but there was a feeling of internal division going into the strike. And among workers who were thoroughly involved in organizing, there were internal divisions about the strategy of the strike.

In my mind, it was almost impossible that the UC would concede to all of our demands and we would call off the strike. Not a chance. But, to be honest, I would address this issue depending on the relationship I had with the people I was talking to. If people were hesitant toward the strike, I would insist on the importance of every action—the BOMMM and the strike authorization vote—to define if we were going to go on strike. But with the people I had a close relationship with because we were organizing together, I talked more freely about how we had no alternative.

The university did almost nothing in response to the strike threat. What we got was bad messages from the vice chancellor and provost, Darnell Hunt, saying, "Don't worry about the strike, we're negotiating. Operations will resume as normal. Don't expect major disruptions." That was kind of it.

My biggest self-criticism in the lead-up to the strike is the expectations we set, and how we did it. I would tell myself and other people a particular line. I would say, "We're definitely going to get over $40,000." I don't even know what I meant. Did I mean $40,000 minimum base pay implemented immediately? That would have been almost a 100 percent raise, which I imagine has never happened in the history of labor negotiations [*laughs*]. Maybe I'm wrong. I'd love to be proven wrong. I also wasn't thinking about steps, like the experience-based raises we get in our contract. I wasn't thinking about any of that. So, it was this really simplistic round figure number, "If it's less than $40,000 it's a failure." I don't know how I got there, and that was setting expectations.

For me, nonresident supplemental tuition was really important, and I didn't realize that it wasn't a mandatory subject of bargaining until we were in the struggle.[4] So, it was hard not to get our goal because nonresident supplemental tuition is crazy to me. International students have to pay as much as $15,000 or $20,000 a year just to work. It's a xenophobic law in California. But nonresident supplemental tuition isn't a mandatory subject of bargaining.

Generally speaking, I thought that the University of California, the largest employer in the largest state in the United States, would easily give in to our demands. Just like that, as if it's not a giant capitalist, for-profit institution. Eventually I realized that was really naive, and really ignorant of the history of labor and neoliberalism in this country. We are not the first union to ever try to make shit better and I think it was really naive to think that a lot of newly agitated, newly organized people would just hop in and fix UC and fix California after three months organizing.

---

4 In collective bargaining, some topics are mandatory if either the employer or the union introduces a proposal. Other topics are permissive, meaning they can be bargained if both parties agree. Other topics are prohibited. Mandatory subjects of bargaining include wages, hours, and other terms and conditions of employment.

Aarthi Sekar

Going into the strike, I was so excited and I was so nervous. I was so excited that we were organized, that we were ready to show our power on the picket line, thousands of workers to show that we are not backing down and that we are here to fight. I was nervous because I'd never been on strike before! And certainly, because we would be navigating a strike against the largest employer in California.

The previous weeks, I was just trying to think how we were going to organize our coworkers so that on day one and week one of the strike, there would be thousands on the picket line and terrify the UC.

Up to that point, I had imagined that once we were on strike, we would march through campuses and that the media attention would be astounding because it was academic workers on strike at one of the largest universities in the country, and that UC would start bargaining with us because they would realize how discontented their workers were. Looking back that sounds naive!

Maddy Duong

Once the strike was approved by the strike authorization vote, I had a lot of things to do. I was wrapping up all of my experiments. I had a conversation with both of my principal investigators, and they were confused by the fact that academic researchers could participate. Maybe they thought it was only for graduate students. But they didn't say anything more than that. We had a pretty light conversation—maybe because nobody expected it to be so long—to plan out work during my absence.

I was also organizing, having a lot of town halls and things like that. It was hectic! And I was new, but the people who had more experience than me were helping me. I was doing things like getting people to sign for picketing shifts, which was extremely difficult because it really made people think about the consequences of actually going on strike. For example, I knew so many international postdocs who were pretty resistant about going on strike, which was strange to me because they would be positively affected if we made the changes we were pursuing with the strike.

People from my lab were not as optimistic about the strike as I was. In my lab, all the postdocs were also parents—and the grad student who had recently joined is also a parent—and for them, the idea of not having income was really scary. I understand they weren't as optimistic as me, given their conditions. But even if they didn't feel like they could take that risk, I think they agreed and supported the strike in a different way.

As the strike approached and we were getting ready for it, some principal investigators were cool with it and some weren't. And that also had a large part to play in whether people were going on strike or not. I know that people who had principal investigators that were very supportive, they felt comfortable going out to strike; whereas for the workers without that support, withholding their labor was a harder decision for them to make.

Elsie Jacobson

The two weeks leading up to the strike were like a continuation of the strike authorization vote. Crazy weeks. More conversations. Honestly, that's when the more memorable conversations happened because there was a real concern for how long the strike would last. There were quite a few people that were saying, "I cannot strike for a week," or "I can't strike for two weeks. It's not possible. So maybe it's better if I don't strike at all." And I was like, "Well, if we all go out on day one, then the university is much more likely to cave soon and resolve it quickly. Just take it one day at a time." And other people were willing to go out for two or three days. And that was what we started with and we just had to hope that they really would go out for that one day, or two, or three days, and that maybe, like with the BOMMM, being around all this amazing energy and this purpose would motivate them to come out for the following days and weeks. And for a lot of people, that did happen.

Withholding our labor is a serious and hard decision, because it could mean that big experiments you have been building for months start to fail. For example, I was working with another postdoc who was deriving some cell lines for months, and they survived just the first half week of the strike. You have to understand that when you strike, you lose not just the amount of time that you're on strike, it's losing some or all of the progress you've made. I know someone that works with organoids that take months to grow, and there's just no one that can look after our stuff while we're gone. And so, talking about those impacts of the strike was challenging because timing is so critical, especially for people who want to stay in academia long-term and become professors. All these arbitrary deadlines, there's a bunch of fellowships that you can only apply for in specific periods of your PhD or postdoc, and is that one experiment more important than forty-eight thousand people getting better rights? I had some of the hardest conversations ever in the two weeks leading up to the strike.

Personally, going on strike was really tough. I'm still catching up on getting back the data I lost. It's hard to lose research and to lose time, but ultimately, that's fine. We, postdocs, talked a lot about this in the lead-up to and during the strike. We wouldn't have any of the things that we have now if it wasn't for the postdocs who sacrificed before us. I put in perspective what four weeks of strike are compared to changing people's lives for the better, and changing academia for the better as well! What we were doing was not just about us and the University of California, it was about changing academia in the United States. The University of California has 10 percent of the postdocs *in the whole country*, so the National Institute of Health will have to respond. And we were right, we're seeing that after the strike the universities are increasing salaries for postdocs and grad students.

But overall, I was surprised at how ready people were to go. I mean, I certainly had hard conversations, but there were also labs I would go to and say, "Are you ready to go on strike?" and they would unanimously respond, "Yeah!"

What did we expect to win? I guess we were expecting to win improvements on all fronts. We had all the demands, but I think everyone understood that it's a negotiation. My perspective is that we propose the ceiling and right now we're on the floor. And, basically, how much power we have is how close to the ceiling we're going to get.

Joyce Chan

Looking back, to be honest, I knew little about the logistics of a strike. That was not something that was taught to me. The strategy of how to have a conversation about a strike was discussed in one lesson in APALA [Asian Pacific American Labor Alliance], and we also learned a bit about some key figures in Asian American organizing, but I don't think any class would have been able to do justice to explaining what it takes in terms of timeline, putting everything out there—I don't know how to phrase it. The thing is, no one can teach you the effort that it takes to get a strike off the ground! You can only experience it yourself when you're actually prepping for it and having these conversations. In the online class I took with APALA about organizing, the most we learned about the day-to-day of any strike was something like, "They talked to their coworkers and within a month or whatever, suddenly they were on strike." It was like, "Magic! Everyone agreed and it happened!" No [*laughs*]. That's not how a strike happens.

Emily Weintraut

Once the strike was authorized, we had two weeks to figure out how to strike! Personally, I really hoped that we wouldn't have to plan a strike. I asked myself, "Now, what does a strike look like?" A strike is withholding your labor, yes. But what does a picket look like in academia? Especially on a huge campus like Davis! It was rough trying to figure out the logistics. Thank God some people had estimates of that because I could never provide that! It was panic planning a strike and it wasn't like we weren't planning before, but it was so much more real. I remember that before the BOMMM I did a lot of walk-throughs and a lot of organizing, and then once the meeting happened, I thought I could take a break, but the weekend after the BOMMM, we had to plan the strike authorization vote and that's how I started working on union stuff *every single day* and not taking a day off! We needed to plan for small and big stuff, always running, as if we were going late to everything, "Shit! Who has the banners? We got to buy this thing, can someone go to Home Depot and buy this and all of that?"

Around October we rented a union office in Davis, and a lot of organizing happened from there—phone banking, texting people, making sure people were signing up for picket shifts which was a pain because people were not signing up. To be honest, if I was not as involved with our union, I would not have signed up for a picket shift; I would've just showed up and gone off the vibe of where I wanted to be. Getting enough picket shift leaders was a stressful thing. But the picket line, day one, shit tons of people showed up to do the work!

I start remembering and I get dizzy by how much we did in those weeks! I was helping sign people for strike pay. That was a horror. It was so much work! You have to give everyone a fifteen-minute spiel, but people came in at different times, so you would end up with ten people having different conversations at once; and there were all these things you needed to hit because you don't want to have it just in a pamphlet, you want people to be aware: "These are your legal rights.

This is the procedure for *x* or *z*." A strike is very serious and the idea of getting your pay docked is very serious. And I say it was a mess just because it was so much simultaneous work, not because we weren't organized.

I was helping with remote strike pay sign up too, and that was a mess because it was so much simultaneous work we had to do because we had limited time to do it, and the reason we didn't do it weeks in advance was because we didn't want to make people anxious. Just dealing with that, and sending the forms to UAW International every night, it was a lot. We have so many people in our union—which is great—but getting all those people signed up within a short amount of time was difficult and stressful.

I don't think all of our union members knew all the work we were doing in preparation for the strike. There's this idea—and I was of that mind—that "there's the people who do union stuff." But that's not true, and that's why in orientations we push the message that "our union is of, by, and for our members." It's *by* our members, which means the people doing strike pay sign-ups are your *coworkers!* A lot of people seem to think there's more structure in place and don't realize that's not true until they get more involved. Our union is member-run, even though there's staff, and it relies on members getting involved. That's why whenever we reach out to people, we ask if they are willing to get more involved or take some concrete next steps. We try to make people make it *their* union and *our* union rather than *the* union because it's not an effective union; it's not an effective representation if it's just some third party somewhere. And because our union is member-led, we got such an amazing strike authorization vote turnout. That's why we got a great strike turnout at first. That's why we have people so passionate because it is by us and because it represents us.

At first, we were just talking about voting to authorize a strike, not actually striking. I was focused on uniting everyone at the BOMMM to show UC our strength. But when nothing changed in negotiations, I pinned my hopes on the strike authorization vote, thinking, "They might back down like when Researchers United formed." After the strike authorization vote, I thought, "It'll just be a short strike." Eventually, I realized we should prepare for an indefinite strike.

The legal reason why we went on strike was UC's unfair labor practices. But also, we were out of contract and the pay raises that they wanted to give us were shit. I remember saying that what we were initially bargaining for was like over $1,000 extra a month. In contrast, what the UC wanted to give us was maybe $100, which with inflation and rent increases and all of that, it would not have been a substantive raise. We were asking for a pay increase that would make it affordable to be a grad student.

November 13, Sunday before the strike, I was probably stressing out, looking at the weather. Oh! I was also grocery shopping because there wasn't an official thing planned for food and I was doing so much organizing and stuff that I was thinking, "I guarantee I'm not going to have time away from the picket line. I'm also going to feel guilty if I'm not on the picket line, so, how much food do I need?" I was very stressed over what to bring to the picket line, so I overpacked. "Do I need my laptop? I'm not going to have wi-fi, but what if I need to sign someone up for a remote strike pay? And I did occasionally have to do that. I was also feeling a pit on my stomach, thinking, "Oh shit! I'm going on strike. I never saw this for myself!" I actually had never thought I would ever be part of a union [*laughs*]. And I kept thinking, "We're not going to have to go on strike. The UC is going to negotiate a fair deal." And also, we had ordered big strike hoop earrings for us to wear during the strike, and I was also thinking, "Damn, the earrings haven't come in! We can't go on strike without the earrings." That was obviously funny in retrospect; I was just worrying about absolutely everything.

Curtis Rumrill

Even when a strike is legally protected, it's still scary. Thus, we had to do a lot of hand-holding and charting and making sure that our department was going to be 100 percent out on the picket line. Going into the strike, I was nervous that it just was not going to be as powerful and that it was going to falter because the kind of deep organizing that needed to happen had not happened in the way that I think it should happen. I think we made up for a lot of that just by the size. I don't know what the numbers were exactly, I'm guessing 75 percent out, something like that. Not a number that you would normally want to go into strike with. But when you're dealing with forty-eight thousand workers, 75 percent of that is pretty strong. And I've never organized a strike this big. So, at a certain point, maybe it's not possible to do the level of deep organizing necessary to get 90 to 100 percent.

Before the strike, someone from the Rank and File caucus invited some of us strike captains, including me, to a meeting under the guise of, "Let's have a humanities meeting to plan for the strike." During the meeting, they claimed that the union leadership had made a late-night decision—requiring strikers to do shifts on the picket lines to get strike pay—which, according to them, was completely antidemocratic and should be overturned. I became frustrated when I realized that they saw picket lines as unimportant. It became clear to me that the Rank and File caucus saw the strike as an opportunity to overturn the union leadership and reinstate themselves in power.

CHAPTER 3

Thrills and Chills

Workers at UC San Diego assemble on the opening day of the strike

Day One

Joyce Chan

Day one of the strike I remember seeing the sheer number of people and feeling like I could go on all day! I remember being very, very happy. The day was very sunny; it was very warm. I saw so many of my friends at the picket line! I felt like I wanted to dance. I had my ukulele every day for the first week. I was strumming along, and really feeling it. So, by the end of the first day I was like, "Well, I can't wait for day two" [*laughs*].

We even had people who were passing by and joined us! I was always impressed by the number of people that came to our picket line. We had people from community organizations come visit us and march with us or chat with us. We even had a retired firefighter! And I think it just made it feel like the movement was so much wider than we could have ever envisioned.

I have never felt a bigger sense of togetherness like the one I felt during week one. The vibes were fantastic and positive. I was a speaker during our first rally, but since my name was added to the schedule last minute, I didn't know what to say. I was extremely anxious, but I was put at ease when I saw the number of people who were waiting to hear what I had to say. I thought, "Yeah, these are my people."

Elsie Jacobson

On Sunday night we were asking ourselves, "Is anyone going to show up tomorrow?" We were so nervous and so excited. But on Monday morning, when we showed up, people showed up! And we went like, "This is actually happening! Quite a lot of people are actually coming! It's not just us." It was really exciting. However, once we got everyone on the picket line, we were mostly prepared for traditional striking activities, like marching and chanting, and we immediately realized we needed more activities and things for people to do.

That first day people marched for eight hours. We didn't know we couldn't keep the picket alive just with marches [*laughs*]! We were so tired at the end of that first day. The next day we decided to include other things, like a field trip to make some noise and disruption outside of different buildings.

Every day things got a bit more active and we got more stuff on the picket. And the energy was so high and positive that it felt like we were sitting in a festival [*laughs*]. It really felt as if we were building something, even though we'd have to set up and pull down every single thing every day, and every day there were more things to set up and we had more activities, more food was definitely out, and we had more coffee for sure [*laughs*]! We had live music most days. The picket line became a beautiful thing that we built and grew with the creative and social energy from all of us. It was amazing how so many people brought their talents, skills, and ideas.

That first week there was so much marching that we eroded the path of grass that we were marching on and it got incredibly dusty! Then someone went out and bought astroturf—the fake grass—and from that day on, every morning we had to set up the astroturf, and every evening we had to pull it out so the university wouldn't haul it away. Imagine that [*laughs*]! Every day we were doing things to try and make it better. And every day we had more people helping with that as well.

Aarthi Sekar

November 14, I got up and it was the first day of setting up our picket line. We had two big picket locations at Davis: Hutchinson Field and Russell Field. I had the U-Haul full of "UAW, Unfair Labor Practice" picket signs, our loudspeakers, and all the supplies for the pickets, so I dropped them off at 7:30 in the morning. There was so much excitement that people came in unexpectedly much earlier than the 9:00 picket shift start time.

When 9 a.m. rolled around and we had the picket shift sign in, the lines were already just way long for people to sign in to their picket shifts, and people are getting their cards stamped with the historic, "I'm on strike, this is my picket shift." People are holding banners on the corner of the intersections. There are cars that are honking. That day there were two different groups that marched all through campus and then we converged into one huge picket line and there was no seeing the end of that line. As a matter of fact, it was so long that the line just kept marching for minutes and minutes and minutes. We also had a march that went through the biological buildings group and then the chemistry buildings and the engineering section, then through the quad, and then through the humanities area, and with every single area you could feel the chants reverberating off of the buildings, because there were so many of us. We ended up having a rally at noon at the administrative building, Mrak Hall, where we had incredible speakers from different local unions show up and voice their support.

Honestly, people recognizing we were all in it together made the energy amazing. People did not want to stop marching all through that day. We had rallies before where workers from across the departments came together, but we never had a picket line that stretched or crossed campus. This was thousands of people. At Davis it was well over fifteen hundred people, almost two thousand people that were out every day on the picket line that first week.

That first day the conversations were electric. The chants were electric. People were so fired up; they were *angry* that UC was not bargaining in good faith. They were also *excited* that they were doing this together, almost in disbelief, pinching themselves. What we were living through was history, and everyone was aware of that. Later that day, the debrief was incredible because people who hadn't participated up to that point were strategizing to keep the picket line strong. The day exceeded my expectations. I was just *so proud* to be part of what we were doing together. I can't believe that I was part of that day.

And the chants! The one that always comes to my mind is, "My neck, my back, we deserve a fair contract. My neck, my back. We deserve fair contracts!" That was my favorite one. And the signs. I liked all the dogs with their signs! So sweet! There was one dog that had a sign, "UC, throw me a bone." It really resonated with me [*laughs*] because I did feel like, "Gosh, UC just throw us a bone. Come on! You have so much money, just pay a living wage."

Maddy Duong

The very first day of the strike I was nervous. I showed up a little bit early, and there were some people picking up signs. And I got stressed, thinking, "Oh, my gosh, is this all it is going to be?" But people kept coming and coming, and I felt more at ease. And then we had a big rally at the end of that first day, and I spoke at it. I was more than anxious about speaking at the rally; I was terrified! It was awful because I didn't really know anybody at that point. But it was good; people supported the things I was saying. I was supposed to talk about being an academic researcher, but I ended up talking about my future life as a graduate student and changing the culture at the UCs in general. And there were so many people that they also contributed to making me feel okay with striking.

I became a picket leader during the first week of the strike. All it took for me to become a strike leader was showing up and signing up to do work because literally every email sent by our union asked "Do you want to be a picket shift leader?" [*laughs*]. And I, genuinely out of curiosity, stuck around to hear what was going on at the debrief meetings. And there were action items that I felt were something that I could do, so I volunteered to do them. I'm being straight up serious, that's how I was able to be a part of this group of leaders that was making the decisions throughout the strike. It was very easy. And I saw that it was that easy for other people that were not involved either before. We even, at some point later in the strike, were begging people, "Please, if you want to come to the debrief meetings, we can use more hands."

Curtis Rumrill

Both my kids came to the picket line and they both hated the experience while they were doing it. It was an overwhelming experience for them. And then they consistently said they wanted to go back [*laughs*]. Going into the strike, day one, I think things were really good. For a while, the wind was at our back. The divisions were there, but they were mostly like you had to be looking for them.

Kien Le

Day one of the strike, I show up at 8 a.m. and from then on, I was at the picket ten hours a day, every day. It was quite dramatic; we asked people if they had slept and many of us hadn't because we were thinking about the next day. It was insane. I think some people were excited because they got an opportunity to be a part of something. I think the picket lines really brought people in. And for me, personally, as someone who was organizing for the first time, seeing the people chanting and picketing the first time was very meaningful.

Kenzo Esquivel

Day one of the strike, I remember the big rally. We had speakers, and the whole front part of campus was completely full. The turnout was huge. And the energy was electric. We had media there, and since I was a media-trained person, I was getting calls from reporters and talking to a lot of folks.

And I remember there were people who I had never met before asking how to help. I also remember that day one was one of the few times I got behind the mic at our picket line because, for the most part, I don't like being in the limelight, and I preferred to defer the public activity to others. And when I got called up to say a few things in public, I remember being energized and excited by how much energy and how much joy was present there.

That first day, I was running a little late because I have a side gig as a baker, and I was picking up two big bags of pastries that I'd gotten that morning. So, I got to campus right around when people were starting to mobilize for the rally. I got to campus and I was trying to find my people, but it was hard because the crowd was too big. I was at the rally for a moment, and then I went to talk to an ABC 7 reporter; it was my first time talking to media. Being a spokesperson for our union also was very nerve-racking but exciting.

Dez Manuel Fonseca

Day one of the strike felt great. It felt euphoric. We had been organizing for months, many people for years, and seeing it finally coming together was ecstatic. We had all the signs in a U-Haul—the workers made all the signs, we made the order and stapled them all the week before. The picket line started at eight in the morning, but I got there at six. By seven or seven thirty, there were fifteen to twenty picket shift leaders by Bunche Hall to get everything ready. But then a news team came, and it got weird. They wanted us to start picketing, but we weren't ready. So, it was a rush to get all set, the supplies, the food, and the music. I had never done that before, and the people that had, they had never done it on this scale. In a way, we were figuring things out on the fly.

On day one, we marched down Westwood Boulevard, one of the busiest streets in LA. I couldn't believe the amount of people walking down that street! I thought that with an army of people like that, we could take UCLA. I don't know if I'd ever seen that many people before. It felt great, especially for the people who have been organizing this, whether it be for weeks, for months, for years. It was what looked like infinite workers marching down Westwood Boulevard demanding fair contracts, demanding fair treatment.

The first day was not far away from what I thought it would be in terms of what I had to do. I expected to be figuring stuff out on the fly and that's what it was like. You can imagine how many people have signed up and where you're going to put people, but you don't know how many people actually that is, or what it means to be walking in a circle. At least, I didn't. It was just constant managing: take a chunk of people and move them over there; take a chunk from these other people, move them over there; put on this vest, be a marshal, make sure people stand here or there, read these chants; keep people active to keep them engaged. And, on top, all of that had to be done fast and efficiently. I'm going to get tired just thinking about it again [*laughs*]!

That first day I was on autopilot the whole time. For me, there were no feelings. It was just organizing. I wasn't worried about how I felt, not in the morning, not in the afternoon. We needed to do a lot of stuff at the end of the day: the supplies and signs had to be stored, the space had to be cleaned up, we needed to do a debrief with all workers. I was concerned with meeting up afterwards in the union office with some of the organizers that wanted to debrief. For me, the strike wasn't about feelings. It was about what needed to be done next: How are we going to organize the rally tomorrow? How are we going to organize the rally Wednesday? Who will be our speaker? What will be our route? Who will be signing people up for strike pay? Who will bring food? Who will bring the signs? Who will drive the U-Haul? Are we going to switch picket locations? Do we have a police liaison? We had thousands of workers on campus that we had to be responsible for. We had to deal with a lot of stuff that we didn't know we were going to have to deal with until we were in the situation.

Emily Weintraut

Day one of the strike I got there late [*laughs*]. I got there around 8 a.m., other organizers got there at 7, and the picket line was scheduled to begin at 9 a.m. When I arrived, I was kind of lost because I was stressed, but then I started my role as a chant leader. I ended up doing chants for so long that I lost my voice on day one.

I signed up to be chant leader because it seemed easy before I ended up losing my voice! I'm a person who is not picky about the tasks I do. I'm there to help. That's it. If someone tells me to do something, I will do it. But when I was asked to be a chant leader, I was excited, "Sure, I'll do that! That's my vibe." When I was losing my voice, I started to hand the megaphone off to people. I would literally pull people out of the picket line if they were very active and I'd be like, "Come on, lead some chants. Here's the sheet!" That's something I improvised and we continued doing it.

I walked like thirteen miles on day one. I think that was the most strike-iest day that we had, if that makes sense. Just because it was the most similar to a normal picket line before we evolved into a music fest picket.

The picket lines were located based on where the public spaces on campus are. I know there was a conversation about how many pickets we should have—some people suggested five, others wanted one. The picket at Russell Field was very visible to the public, because it is very busy during the day and that's where some buses come into a major parking structure. So, Russell was more visible for the general public. Meanwhile, Hutchinson Field is located at a major intersection, where tons of traffic come in, and there is also a huge parking structure with buses coming. But what was extra special about Hutchinson is that it is right near to a lot of STEM departments. In consequence, the Hutchinson picket was especially visible for departments that were scab heavy, because there was a lot more retaliation and fearmongering; whereas in the humanities departments—closer to Russell—striking seemed to have a moral value.

Before the strike, if we—for whatever reason—were lost on what to do, we would normally ask Aarthi, who was one of the bargaining team members for Local 2865 and the lead organizer of UC Davis. But the week before the strike we had a long conversation about how we needed to stop asking Aarthi for help on everything. It's easy to lean on the person or persons who are more involved and who are also accessible. Aarthi is all of that, and she has a personal connection with most of us, but we realized it was not OK to ask that much of her, and that we needed to take more initiative. So, the first week of the strike was also a reorganizing of our internal organization.

Keeping Up Momentum

Kien Le

I think some of us expected the contract negotiation would end by the end of the first week. But I could tell that was not possible because of what I was seeing at the bargaining table. For me, we had to keep moving.

How do I bring people into the strike? One-on-one conversations are really important. You cannot make a call on social media like, "Guys, show up to this picket line at 8 a.m. tomorrow." It doesn't work like that. Technology can help, but it doesn't guarantee successful participation.

When you commit to go on strike, you must show up to the picket, you must do your part in order to make the strike successful. And, if you see your coworkers scabbing, you need to tell them to not do that, but you also need to talk to them, convince them to go on strike. You cannot just condemn them publicly: that's going to backfire at us.

One of the difficulties of organizing for the 2022 strike was the different levels of participation people are used to. Some people are really committed; others just don't know what's going on because it is their first time participating in collective actions. We need to bring both sides together. That was difficult because some people who are well-versed on strikes feel some kind of moral superiority, and instigate public shaming against someone who is scabbing, rather than trying to understand them. But that's not how we should work. The goal of organizing is to bring people in, not to push people away.

Emily Weintraut

As the strike went on, there was always the question of "What do we do next? We've done so much. How do we keep the picket line entertaining?" Which is interesting because most strikes I've seen before are just picket lines where you march around. I remember setting up day one, realizing we were going to have speakers with music and a dance party, marches, and a rally, and many other things I can't remember right now. And we kept on having different activities every day. But it wasn't so much that we needed to entertain our coworkers but rather that we needed to entertain *us* because you're doing the same thing for six weeks. Realistically, striking is not fun. I would much rather do my job. I enjoy what I do. I'm not going to do it for free, but I enjoy it. Most people here enjoy their jobs, and marching with picket signs is not the most fun.

We were building the picket line based on what we knew about pickets—you're picketing in a line; you're walking around and stuff like that. But then on day two, it was flagged to us that there are a lot of people with autism and sensory issues, and they were getting overwhelmed, so there was a makeshift sensory deprivation tent area set up away from the picket line, where people could sit quietly, close their eyes, and get away from the noise if needed. And I was dealing with another issue because people were talking about access needs on the picket line. So what I did was, first, I talked with an old roommate who is very involved in access needs and disability justice. I asked her, "What can we do? I'm hearing people complain about it, but I don't know what to do. I don't have any of these issues. How can we accommodate that?" Hearing people complain about things, but just complaining, was a rough tension point because we were willing to change or implement whatever, but people didn't want to get involved in doing it. Finally, I worked with a group of people, and we had a debrief to discuss what we needed to do and who was going to be responsible for implementation. There were things like that that created tension because in our union there are people who think, "Oh, union leadership is a third party that will do things for us." It's not. It's your coworker. If you want something to change, you have to tell someone something, get involved, don't just grumble about it. Get involved and you're going to get empathy from people. I was really frustrated because no one said anything in a proactive way, they complained. If you have a problem, can you help us do something? We are working sixteen-hour days, every day, and that's not enough. Can you please help us with this? We're union members too.

During the strike, we were actively trying to get people more involved. For example, to address the access needs on the picket lines, I made it a point to seek out people with access needs, so they would have a say on how those issues need to be solved. I get that people shouldn't have to tell you about stuff, but it's hard. I'm just a fucking person. I'm not educated enough on this matter. And yeah, when more people who had specific issues got involved in planning, the conversations changed so much and we were able to solve a lot of issues on the picket line! I think people felt more empowered and that was great! And they kept addressing access needs and contributing ideas after that. That was a result of us actively telling people, "You are leadership, please join."

On Russell Field there were different groups of workers doing stuff that was unplanned. For example, there was a group of grad students from cultural studies and Native American studies, and some undergrads with signs that said "Land Back." If I remember correctly, they did a couple of teach-ins and a dance lesson. Another group of people, people who wanted to cook, was in charge of the kitchen. They raised money for that. They were also grad students for the most part. There was also the group Cops Off Campus, which at UC Davis is a group of undergrads and other people in the community who called themselves anarchists—whether they are an anarchist group on campus or not, I'm not sure, but they had the symbols and stuff like that.

One main struggle with some of those groups was that we would have a plan for the hundreds of people who'd show up, and we'd think about safety every day. But certain groups, especially Cops Off Campus, would get frustrated that we weren't militant enough or doing enough road blocking whenever we marched. Legally speaking, we cannot just stop in an intersection, we need to keep moving. Actually, UC filed an unfair labor practice charge against our union because the UC claimed that Cops Off Campus was part of our union, and they were blocking the traffic near the Russell picket. And as a union, one of our legal strong points was that we had not committed a single unfair labor practice and the UC had committed over twenty. We are legally the good guys here. And the university knew that Cops Off Campus was not part of our UAW strike, but they claimed that it was, which became a tension point.

Multiple times, Cops Off Campus was blocking a street, especially near Russell, and we would tell them, "We can't have the official union strike signs up here because we don't want to get an unfair labor practice filed, we don't want the university to think that this is our plan, and also because it's also a safety thing." I mean, we saw people get hit by cars multiple times throughout the strike, someone ran over someone's bike in the Cops Off Campus barricade.

The strategy of not blocking a street but continuing to move also prevented cops from coming, so it was also a safety measure, especially for marginalized workers. Because having the right to strike doesn't mean that you can't get in trouble if a cop comes around. So you want to protect workers, but especially the most marginalized workers. We had police liaisons there, and we had a plan to get all international students out if a cop showed up. Things can escalate easily and police will escalate things and we don't want to see that. We don't want to see anyone get hurt, get in trouble without a plan for it. And by blocking off the streets completely you get cops to come. It sucked to see people who claim that they were there out of solidarity to then start shitting on our union and shitting on our tactics of safety, that was really fucking irritating.

We had different kinds of chants. We had the normal ones at first, like, "One, two, three, four, we won't take it anymore. Five, six, seven, eight, UC must negotiate." And then we had, "No contract, no class, Gary May can kiss my ass."[1] I think that really helped a lot, grad students really like the ones with curse words in them. One big thing that really helped to unite people or bring morale up, was saying something with

---

1 Gary May was the UC Davis chancellor at the time of the strike.

a curse word. It's goofy, but laughing lifts morale. Another chant that prompted unity was, "Who's got the power? We've got the power! What kind of power? Union power!" And when we would have a lot of bystanders, we would get people's attention with, "What's outrageous? Poverty wages. What's disgusting? Union busting!"

We had a ton of support for the strike even before the strike began. I remember we were talking to local teachers' unions even before the strike began. And at Davis specifically, there were locals from the firefighters' union, and nurses' unions supporting us. Solidarity hit more as the strike went on. It became more emotional to see the continuing support. For example, across from where the Hutchinson picket was located, there's a health building, and I remember—around week three—someone came up during set up and they said, "Here's some donuts, we see you guys out here every day. We want you to know that we support you." And that broke me into tears. I also remember that on the march on University of California Office of the President in Oakland.[2] We had someone speaking on behalf of the Oakland Teachers' Union, and I—again—got emotional seeing the continuing support of teachers. That was the thing, I was expecting support on day one, but as it continued, it hit deeper and deeper.

I think since Queer Day, the picket lines evolved into some kind of a music fest. I remember literally being into picketing and just marching and chanting an hour in, and people coming up to me asking, "Is this what we're doing all day?" And I'd explain that picket lines look like that, and people would be disappointed, maybe frustrated. And I think mentally people really needed a rest from that because being on strike is mentally exhausting, but it's especially exhausting and demoralizing because of the treatment that we received from UC, and not knowing how long the strike was going to last, and the feeling that it could take forever. Also, people's bodies were hurting. I remember my muscles were aching after the first few days. I had completely lost my voice.

From the first week, we were continually discussing how to make the strike more sustainable, and as a result we changed picket strategies at the end of the very first week. We merged both picket lines into one,

---

2 On November 28, 2021, workers from several Northern California UC campuses convened in Oakland to march on the University of California Office of the President (UCOP) demanding a fair contract.

and morale was so much better. Everyone was together, united, and there were not rumors running about what had happened at this or that picket line. Also, when we had events, we didn't want the other picket line to miss the fun.

After deciding we'd have one picket, we chose Hutchinson Field because there we were more visible to our coworkers in STEM, so they could see that we were still out there, asking them to join us. And in fact, we did get a lot of people come and say, "I was worried, I didn't think there were going to be that many people on the picket line."

Joyce Chan

It was almost dreamlike, really. Every day you would come in, greet friends, sign in, and figure out what was the strategy for the day. And I loved it because I would just be with the people I loved and cared about, sharing food, having conversations that we normally wouldn't have if we were working. We got to know people on a deeper level. To an extent, that bond I created with my picket friends is still very much alive. There are some experiences that change you forever; the picket line was one of those.

When I spoke to news outlets, I always framed our strike as part of something bigger. We are not just a bunch of irate workers at the UCs in California, the most liberal state, who decided that they're upset and they don't want to take anymore. Our strike was the result of an overarching pattern that prioritizes profits over people. We're going to see more and more resurgence of unionizing. People realize that we can't live with the continual pressure to maximize profit and they'll have to do something about it just to live. This is a universal trend that we're seeing as the iron hand of capitalism becomes tighter and tighter on our necks. You either organize or you live a miserable life, that's my perspective.

That first week I also remember going on Twitter and just seeing everyone going like, "Holy shit, it's happening" [*laughs*]. Or like, "This is the first postdoc strike!" and just feeling I was a part of history.

What took most of our time on the day-to-day was marching, chanting, having conversations with people, using our voices a lot, using your feet a lot, building up that muscle. And then just getting used to having people around all, but I mean *all* the time. Aside from that, I was playing the ukulele with people who had drums that were made from pots and pans. Someone brought in a bongo, so I was just chilling with that guy the first couple of days, and then people brought in more and more instruments. We were just essentially jamming out and trying to find ways to maximize noise. And then we started crashing into different locations like the lectures of certain abusive principal investigators, and disrupting the delivery docks.

I would like to think that my ukulele played a big role on the day-to-day of our picket line [*laughs*]. I was known as the "ukulele lady," trying to boost morale, trying to hype people up.

Elsie Jacobson

I can't name just one outstanding moment of the first week of the strike. All the rallies were great, but the Friday rally where we shut down Wilshire Boulevard was outstanding. We blocked Westwood on our own! The cops showed up after, and they were just standing there! And it's crazy to have that kind of power.

For those readers who don't know, Westwood Boulevard is a fairly major road that meets with UCLA, and intersects with Wilshire Boulevard, which is a ten-lane road. It's a major thoroughfare. So, we did the most intense strategizing we've done for a march, and because we always prioritize safety for everyone, we had so many safety marshals. There were so many of us that it was very safe! We began marching and there were marshals at the front, marshals at the back, and all along the sides. And as we went down Westwood Boulevard, we'd stop at the lights and then as soon as the lights were in our favor, we would get as many people across the intersection as possible. And we were yelling down the line. It was a wildly coordinated march!

When we got to Wilshire Boulevard, there were like two thousand people, and we formed a circle in the middle of the Westwood and Wilshire intersection. But there were so many of us that we actually couldn't move! We tried, we were really trying to keep the circle moving because it is not legal to stop when you are marching, but it was just impossible to move. It was an absolute traffic jam! However, because there were so many of us, the police couldn't do anything about it! I truly believe people felt the power, they were like, "We can run this city!"

And at the time, the UC had been stalling on bargaining with the grad students. The same morning we marched over Wilshire and

Westwood, UC said they weren't going to bargain with the grad students over the weekend. But after our march and other marches that same day on other campuses, UC had to bargain through the weekend. I think often the power and the result can be kind of indirect, but when things like that happen where it's like, "There is no doubt this action had a direct impact." There was a very clear cause and effect.

I think the Wilshire march and its impact on the bargaining had an important role in pushing us into the second week because before it happened, even I was like, "I don't know how long we will last, because so many people will have a hard time going for one week." And again, with all the conversations I had before the strike, we'd be talking on a day-by-day basis: "Can you do one day? Can you do two days? Can you do three days?" I was worried that the first day would be great and then it would decline, but the participation held pretty steady through the week in terms of numbers and people in our picket! And then, Friday of the first week was the biggest day ever!

In terms of the development of the strike, there is no doubt that accessibility was a huge thing that we worked really hard to build! One of my favorite parts of the picket was making it accessible for everyone.

In-person accessibility was something that we wanted to be really good about. Obviously, we had all the hybrid and remote options, but doing in-person activities is really important and we didn't want to have a disabled person or anyone with access needs feeling like they couldn't participate in the in-person picket. That's why we worked together to make the picket line more and more accessible. For example, each day that passed we would have more camping chairs, and at the beginning of the strike the camping chairs were in one area away from the picket, and then we moved some into the middle of the picket so the people who couldn't march could still be in the middle of the action.

We formed a strong community of disabled workers to make sure our picket was accessible. Before the strike we created a committee and during the strike I was officially the in-person access needs coordinator. It was a very informal committee, everyone that had an access need could join the group, and that's why I think it was really smooth. It was workers supporting workers and looking after each other. It all started with me emailing people asking what they needed but, of course, not a ton of people responded to those emails. With those who responded, we would share our plan to accommodate their specific request, and we would ask them to join us on the picket line on the first day of the strike. And once on the picket, we'd sit down, have a chat about what accommodations they needed to be comfortable and how we could make that work. And then everyone who needed an accommodation started contributing to making everyone safe. Honestly, so many accommodations are not even that hard as long as you have a proper conversation about it and make people feel comfortable to ask what they need.

There were people who went back to work after week one. But among the people who stayed out, the positive environment stayed alive the whole time, and there was not a sense of anger or frustration with the people who did leave.

I can't speak much on behalf of the grad students, but the number of postdocs on the picket line dropped pretty rapidly the second and third weeks. Honestly, I think that the difference between the first week and the second and third week was the joint events, where all of the different picket lines would converge for one rally or event. During the first week, the joint things were really, really amazing. And then we diverged a bit and then the joint things were not necessarily what people had expected them to be. I'll try to explain this. Our picket was really organized; we are scientists and we like to have order and structure. Something that I think was specific to us is that we were working as hard as possible because we wanted to make progress as fast as possible so we could go back to work! We wanted the strike to successfully end and then go back to our research because, again, the only reason to do a postdoc is because you really like doing research. I think someone once said that our Gonda Building picket was crafts and discipline [*laughs*]. Whereas some of the other north campus pickets were like arts and chaos.

Another place where ideas diverged was trying to stop deliveries on campus. I thought it was a great idea, but our priority should have been our picket lines, and we didn't have a majority on the picket line, and on top we were supposed to stop deliveries. That didn't make sense to me. To me, the most important thing was to get ourselves withholding our labor because our labor is so valuable to the university! But people were signing up to do side quests and we'd have people coming up and asking for people from our picket to join them. And we were like, "We can't, our picket is shrinking." Ours was the most public picket—across the road from Ronald Reagan Hospital—and I felt we needed to keep up the energy and feeling of community to keep nonorganizer workers on the picket.

Throughout the strike there were walk-throughs happening. We did our best to try and go and talk to the people that were still working, which was really challenging because—how can I explain it? Look, the people that came out, came out and they stayed as long as they felt that they could stay. And trying to get out the people who didn't go out at the beginning was very difficult. And by that point, I was honestly pretty worn out, and my energy was focused on holding down the fort at the picket. So, I wasn't personally part of those efforts, but there were other people doing walk-throughs and organizing. Ultimately, what we were trying to do was less getting people to come out to the line every day, and more trying to get people to come to the big actions and come to the rallies, that's why we refocused the walk-throughs to be before the rallies and the big marches. I mean, we did have new people joining throughout the whole strike! People were signing up for strike pay all the way up and until the end of week three, which was kind of wild. We had one professor of biostatistics canceling classes toward the end of week one, and we had a bunch of teaching assistants come down and be like, "Oh well, I guess we're not teaching anymore!" And they signed for strike pay and joined the picket.

Every unionized worker in my lab was out the first week. But undergrads were doing research in many labs, in some cases as nonunion paid workers. However, without the grad students, the postdocs, and the academic researchers, not a lot happened! The strike was pretty, pretty devastating for research operations! Having whole labs shut down felt a little bit like what happened at the start of the pandemic when all the labs shut down for a few months.

That first week I also heard a lot of stories of people having a hard time working because we were so loud [*laughs*]! I heard the story of someone who had a committee meeting and they had to move to another building because it was so loud, they couldn't hear anything.

We had media all the first week at our picket line, and the articles that were coming out every day were unanimously positive. It felt like the public was in support and even the nonstriking academic workers were still in support of us. I think the public supported us unanimously, based on the reactions of every nonacademic worker, bystander, or person who approached us at the picket line. Whenever people found out how grad students and postdocs and academic researchers are treated, they were like, "What? That's crazy. Aren't you guys doing really important stuff?"

UC and the principal investigators didn't really respond much during the first week of the strike. Most principal investigators knew they weren't supposed to interfere or ask if people were on strike. UC made that clear. When I told my principal investigator I was striking, she said I was hurting my own career, which was silly because our union helps both principal investigators and the university. She wasn't happy, but didn't try to stop me.

Responses varied depending on your job title. Postdocs had it easier since we're just workers, but for grad students, it was more complicated. Their research contributes to both their degree and their paid work. Some principal investigators told them, "You can stop working on the paid stuff, but you should keep doing your PhD research," even though it's all the same. One grad student was told if he didn't finish a paper by Christmas, they wouldn't write him a reference letter, which was just a pressure tactic. It was really frustrating.

During week one, something that we did that was really cool was the debrief at the end of every day. It started as a debrief for the most involved organizers and then it morphed into being a debrief for everyone. So, at the end of every day, we'd all sit on the steps and people would share personal stories about why they're on strike and what brought them there and what experiences they had. We also would talk about how the day went and what things didn't work so well and what things could be better, and then what worked well and we wanted to have again. And then we would ask everyone to text their friends and colleagues to come out tomorrow!

Aarthi Sekar

The picket line was coordinated on a daily basis. There were groups of leaders that would organize different aspects of the picket line. For example, some folks really took the lead on coordinating the marches for the day. There were a group of leaders and organizers who would be making sure that department meetings on the picket line had an agenda. There would also be a group of members and leaders that would coordinate the picket entertainment, like the pole dancers and the DJs and the local community groups who wanted to perform music, or the

The Stanford University marching band spells out 'UAW' at the Berkeley-Stanford football game during the strike

speakers. There were people, members, organizers, leaders that were the ones that took the lead on all of those different efforts and coordinated them on a daily basis. And that created such a tight bond among that group of folks that is still very, very in place today.

There were reporters on the field from the local newspapers, the *Davis Enterprise* and *Vanguard*, and from the local NPR station, and the articles were very, very favorable in support of our strike. I mean, there were also social media posts that were getting amplified by the community. And as a spokesperson since before the strike, I noticed media took us more seriously. There was a shift in the attitude. I think seeing our numbers and seeing our force on the picket line that day and that week, the media really were like, "Wait, this is a real situation." There were a lot of questions about what does it mean to get paid as PhD students, like, "Are you just getting paid to study?" And we'd say, "No, literally our research is what turns out all the grant money and the funding. However, every single thing that we do is UC patented, we don't own anything."

By and large, faculty members were still unsure about the strike. We didn't have faculty support come out until the second week of the strike. And UC was nowhere to be seen except for the labor relations golf cart that was following us around all day at every picket site and every march. And if we went up to them and asked them in a very polite way why they were there, they would say, "We're just here to help support," which was a lie, because if they wanted to help support, they would have helped push negotiations along, not just spying on us very clearly. They were counting our numbers and reporting back to UC.

That first week was really good. But the end of that first week, though, was tough because I was an academic student employee bargaining team member and the bargaining process had been far too long since we met with UC, for Local 2865. And by the end of that first week—even though our strike and our picket line was so strong and our leaders were organizing and keeping up the energy on that picket line, our leaders were just incredible at organizing and executing that—as a bargaining team member, I was having difficulties answering questions on why isn't UC meeting us at the table.

Right from the beginning of the strike, the relationships between groups of workers from humanities and STEM fields were a little bit tough. We started off as having two big pickets, one picket was largely populated by folks in the humanities, Russell Field, and the other, Hutchinson Field, was largely populated by the STEM workers. And although there was a really strong group of STEM workers, it was not as large as the humanities force, and early on in the strike there was a tough conversation that needed to happen about how to work together to reach out to our coworkers who are scabbing or aren't on the picket. The separation between STEM and humanities needed to be bridged because by and large, the majority of the workers who were scabbing were in the STEM and the biological sciences, which was due to a difference of work experience. One of the things is that the fear of retaliation in the biological sciences and the STEM fields is much, much higher; most of the principal investigators didn't want to engage in any conversation about the strike, or if they did, it was negative. So, it was the bullying and the fear of principal investigators that kept a lot of people out of the picket line.

On the contrary, the humanities folks would talk about how members of their faculty were very supportive, talking about how the strike was a historic experience. So, as workers on strike, we really did need the support *and the stomach* of the humanities folks to give the courage and the confidence to a lot of the STEM striking workers.

And that support did happen when we merged pickets, and it definitely helped.

There were also contrasts between workers depending on what kind of labor we perform. Going on strike as a teaching assistant means you are withholding instructional labor that UC touts and provides for undergraduates, and then takes all the credit and makes a profit off of it. Also, withholding your work as a teaching assistant is concrete because you teach a course and you grade a midterm or a final. But there's something else because the students are dear to us. That's where the challenge lies within because we feel that by going on strike we are letting down the undergraduates who are taking a class.

On the other hand, withholding research as a graduate student researcher feels a lot more nebulous, like, "Okay, if I withhold my data for the next few weeks, what's going to happen? What's the immediate consequence?" It's difficult to place an immediate consequence. And so it's a realization that it has to be all of us stopping our research labor, not going into work, and going to the picket line instead. The impact of withholding research on the university is harder to understand until you're actually on strike. But when the administration sees thousands of researchers on picket lines, and principal investigators are complaining that they can't do their experiments to fulfill their grant requirements because their labs are empty, that poses a huge crisis they need to resolve.

A consequence of how the disparities between academic cultures impacted our strike was that, although we started the strike with two picket lines, we merged into a big single one the very first week. That first week, the more science-based picket had less people than the more humanities-based picket. And thanks to the science-based picket meetings we learned that the reason why some of our coworkers were scabbing was because they were afraid to leave their research spaces. So we figured that it was important for us to be visibly present in the science area to encourage and empower our coworkers to come out on strike with us. So, at that point forward, starting mid-first week, we became one big picket at Hutchison Field.

Dez Manuel Fonseca

Even though the rallies got smaller after the first day, during the rest of that first week they maintained almost the same size, huge rallies.

I've never seen rallies that big at UCLA! And that's not to talk down any other movements, but just the size and power that we had was huge. So, the mood was good from November 14 to 18. Even further, from the beginning of the strike until Thanksgiving break, things were really positive on the picket lines.

But if you talked to the bargaining team members, you'd find there was concern because, basically, *the university was stalling*. We didn't want them to stall because it is a union-busting tactic. Although, at the same time, we used stalling as a mobilization tactic to keep people engaged, keep them angry at the UC, and build militancy against the university.

Another thing we realized at the end of phase one was that our strike wasn't going to be like the Clark University strike.[3] We had two examples: the Clark University strike, which is a small research university with like a thousand students, where they were on strike for over a week and got raises up to 90 percent over three or four years, but were starting from a lower base pay. And we also had the Columbia strike, which is an example of a more prolonged, protracted strike, which won less wage increases, but they were already at a higher level of pay than we were.[4] So, right before Thanksgiving break, we knew our strike wasn't going to be like Clark's.

Before Thanksgiving we had big rallies every day. But by day four, I became aware that the university was going to keep stalling, and that our original plan wasn't going to be enough to quickly get us a fair contract without a more prolonged strike. So, on that particular day, I was just walking around campus, talking to workers, and I saw a construction site and I went and we had a conversation. I told them, "Hey, I don't know if you know this, we're on strike, we've got picket lines. What would it take for you to respect our picket line?" And the construction workers immediately expressed their solidarity, they told me that we had to get a picket where the construction site was, get a

---

3 Unionized graduate workers in Teamsters Local 170 at Clark University in Worcester, Massachusetts, went on strike from October 3, 2022, to October 7, 2022, when a tentative agreement was reached.

4 Unionized graduate workers in UAW Local 2110 at Columbia University went on strike on March 15, 2021, until May 13, 2021, and then again on November 3, 2021, until January 7, 2022, when a tentative agreement was reached.

group of ten to twenty workers there, and they would walk off because they don't cross picket lines.

The first construction picket was chaotic since it happened midday. While talking to some workers on break, they mentioned that ten to twenty people on the picket line would get them to walk off. I, Todd, and Rachel immediately started running to different pickets to gather support. We finally gathered around one hundred people to walk over to the construction site at the Luskin School of Public Affairs, maybe it was too many people. That's how the construction pickets began. Looking back, the action was very disruptive, because we were taking people away from our picket lines. But we wanted to try it out, and it was a success. On the following days, we did a few other locations too and we fought with UC's labor relations officials through those solidarity pickets.

A day or so later, we got some construction workers to show up, honk, and turn their cars around in support. We also targeted delivery docks—dining halls, the hospital, research docks. To get that, I waited all day to talk to drivers, asking if they were unionized and if they'd respect picket lines. We learned which Teamster locals had sympathy strike language—I think it was 848 or 44. I'd ask, "What local are you in? Call your shop steward and send a picture of the picket." Some drivers, like US Foods workers, turned around immediately! I remember their names—Danny, Octavio, Luis—guys who'd honk and show support every day.

We—workers—organized the construction picket lines; it wasn't a top-down directive, it happened because we were empowered to develop the strategy on the picket lines. Eventually we moved the construction pickets to early in the morning, and we learned that Clark University went on strike with the Teamsters, so they had some pickets that started at five in the morning, and others that were twenty-four-hour pickets.

The night before we set up our first early morning picket, I couldn't sleep. There were several nights I didn't sleep because we were trying out new things, picketing the medical center, picketing construction sites, and because you never know if people are going to be mad, try to run you over, or if the police or labor relations are going to come and intimidate you. But eventually, the construction pickets became pretty regular.

Delivery and construction pickets were my main thing during the strike, and they took a lot of work. We were running back and forth, making sure people had water, food, and got replaced since they'd been out there at four in the morning. I was on the walkie-talkie, checking in on folks, organizing mutual aid runs, getting cars to drop off food, and planning for the next day. None of it was random—we had a plan that changed as we learned more and so did UC. Todd had his iPad, mapping out picket spots and how many people we needed at each. We were redirecting trucks and figuring out new routes every day as UC adjusted. I spent hours talking with workers from different union locals and my coworkers about bargaining, organizing rallies, and finding speakers to keep folks fired up. Honestly, I was busy with the construction pickets, but I was busy with everything!

I'd say we had faculty support during the strike. At least in my field, history, they did support us. They didn't retaliate against us; they understood the demands and stood on the sidelines and let us do our thing instead of working with the university. They were pretty neutral, and understandably so, because we didn't do any work to have their active support. We had so many workers to organize—forty-eight thousand across the state—that our main priority was not and could not be organizing faculty. Because of this, faculty's support would vary, but overall it was negligible. I say "negligible" not to say I'm upset. I'm not. I say it just to point out that our power came from us, and other unions that had the ability to proactively stand in solidarity with us.

The general public sympathy that we got, we got it because we were broke as hell! All I had to do, talking to a construction worker, was tell them how much money we made and we'd get immediate support! It was like snapping fingers. I talked to people with Trump stickers, talked to people with Democrat stickers on their helmets, it didn't matter. People recognized that we're at a so-called prestigious university, and we would say how much money we make, we explained to them that we do most of the teaching and that was enough.

Kenzo Esquivel

The turnout in the first week was steady, not as big as day one, but that's expected. Looking back, I think we should've involved more new people in leadership, though a lot of folks naturally stepped up, offering to do events. Organic leadership just happened. Musicians who had never played together became the strike band. We had yoga, salsa, picketing, marches, political education, de-escalation workshops, and even cornhole and chill areas. I have only fond memories of week one.

As I said, I was a spokesperson, I interacted with media throughout the strike. I actually remember pretty distinctly that on day one of the strike a TV reporter asked me, "How is the university going to work without you guys?" And I responded, "That's the point. It's not going to work, you nailed it!"

There was another line of questions about our wages because our funding structures are convoluted as fuck. It's hard to understand for us as graduate workers how and when we get paid. So, for an outsider to have all these words like graduate student researcher, graduate student instructor, fellowship, what the heck do they mean? Finding a way to communicate and justify our demands, but also put in the context of the critical labor that we provide for the institution did end up making sense to most folks.

Interacting with the community was interesting. I remember, maybe it was week one or two of the strike, there was one aggrieved gentleman who was saying, "You all are so privileged to be going to a place like UC Berkeley, you are probably so well off." So, when we told him our situation, this gentleman was genuinely shocked about how little we make a year. And I think that there was this real reckoning, especially at a system with as much prestige as the University of California, with the fact that, historically, the people who have been able to access an education like this have come from relatively privileged backgrounds. Our task was to communicate the fact that we were fighting for a living wage in order to make the system more accessible to everyone. I got involved in this to create a fundamentally different type of university that welcomes people that don't have generational wealth or previous family experience in institutions of higher education.

During week one, teachers from public schools showed up at the picket line after they got out of their classroom. They joined us a few times. And there were other community members that came out every once in a while. I also can name the three faculty members who showed up from my department on the picket line [*laughs*], although they came only a few times. Librarians and lecturers, who couldn't go on strike with us because of a clause in their contracts, brought us donuts and snacks. Actually, food donations were another key form of solidarity. I remember even undergrads dropped off boxes of granola bars, and people in general would swing by with different goodies.

By the end of the first week I was feeling pretty good. Even through Thanksgiving, I was worried about whether we could come back with enough gusto or momentum, or if we would lose some momentum after the break. After the Thanksgiving break, our numbers were diminishing, so we needed to think, strategize, and organize around that fact. But it didn't feel like an insurmountable challenge, and it felt like it was a product of our break. And then the fact that the strike was going to be longer than what some people had initially bargained for was another organizing challenge. It wasn't until the drop of the COLA [cost-of-living adjustment] language and the drop to asking for $43,000 that I started to feel nervous about our strike. And even then, I maintained a level of artificial confidence, and a sense that we could still win.

The overall trend was the gradual diminishing of how many people were out in the picket line. At the beginning, the structure of strike pay helped to keep people coming to the picket line consistently, but once it felt like the university was not going to dock pay, people felt they didn't have to come quite as often to the picket. But there were still moments where more people showed up. For example, every once in a while, we would host department check-ins and meetups to touch base with people, and on those occasions, people came out more because they knew other folks were going to be there.

Weeks three and four we tried to be more intentional to have a designated team to do walk-throughs or stand in front of doors to have conversations with people as they were going back into the labs. Logistically, it was a challenge to ensure we have enough people to do both things: maintain the picket and do walk-throughs. But we found out that the struggle was more people not coming back from the Thanksgiving break rather than going back into the lab.

When there was scabbing, part of my thought was that we needed to have conversations with the workers who were scabbing about the pressures they were facing and the ways in which it was still important for them to be engaged despite that retaliatory behavior. For me, our narrative had to be, "We are having an impact. Principal investigators are freaking out. They are retaliating because they're recognizing the importance of our labor and the ways in which we are critical to the functioning of their labs and the research output of this university."

Impressions of Bargaining

Elsie Jacobson

I was involved with the disability and accommodations aspect of the contract for bargaining since we began the bargaining process back in 2021. I remember there was a survey to capture what postdocs wanted, and this survey was used by the bargaining team as a basis for the high priority list of demands that we wanted to win. That list of priorities was later distributed to working groups to make progress conducting research and drafting proposals on each of the different topics.

For the disability articles, we worked with postdocs from other campuses to figure out key issues for the contract. A small core group coordinated the discussion about what we wanted, and people came to meetings and talked about their experiences and the changes they wanted. A big topic was remote work as an accommodation. While we agreed remote work is crucial, someone pointed out that universities shouldn't use it as an excuse to avoid making physical spaces accessible. In the end, we proposed individualized accommodations based on need.

When we presented this to UC's labor relations administrators, they pushed back, citing the cost of things like building elevators, they said, "We have to have 'reasonable' in the article because what happens if someone needs an elevator in a building, would we have to build an elevator? They are really expensive!" Well yes! You can't put someone away from the rest of their lab because they can't walk up stairs! Labor relations' dismissive attitude made it clear that we'd have to organize and apply pressure to win anything.

The experience with labor relations helped me to focus on organizing because it was very clear that no matter what we said, no matter how we wrote the proposal, they weren't going to give us anything unless we made them do it!

Maddy Duong

I expected the strike would bring some changes, but I wasn't sure exactly what. I felt our power, especially with so many people on the BOMMM and strike authorization vote, but I didn't really calculate what that would mean for results. I knew we wouldn't get everything we asked for. I understood enough about bargaining to know you don't always end up with what you start with.

Before the strike, I didn't know much about what was happening at the bargaining table. I knew UC was committing a lot of unfair labor practices, which is why we went on strike, and they were making excuses to not meet with us. During the strike, I saw bargaining happening more often—sometimes in the middle of the night, crazy times, even multiple times a day. But UC's slow movement in the first week really got people on the picket line agitated. People were like, "UC says they can't book a room? There's plenty of rooms at UCI!" Their excuses fired us up, but I think UC was trying to drag things out, thinking we'd give up.

Aarthi Sekar

In the lead-up to, and the first days of, the strike, I was thinking that we would win *something* on all of our demands. And throughout the first week, I felt really hopeful. But going into the second week, not being able to explain to my coworkers why UC wasn't meeting us was really hard. Maybe as an elected representative, I felt like it was really hard for me to answer questions on why we have not met yet. And yes, it was a strategic move on UC's part, and that's what I would say, and most members would completely get it. But then it was, "How do we strategically really ramp up the pressure on UC, and make sure we're organizing our picket line to be even bigger on the second week so that UC comes and meets us at the bargaining table?"

Curtis Rumrill

It was clear, since before the strike began, that there was a contingent that planned to use the strike as an opportunity to take power in a very cynical manner. They were modeling it on the Columbia strike, and their goal was to vote down the first tentative agreement, no matter what it was, and demand the resignation of the bargaining committee in shame after having recommended ratification on that tentative agreement.

They used specific talking points, highlighting the Columbia strike as a model for our own and praising Columbia graduates for their radicalism. And their strategy was to vote no on our first tentative agreement because that's how you win better. And finally, they instigated an environment hostile to union leadership. They claimed that the picket requirements were onerous and the picket lines didn't matter in the first place and that the leadership is overly focused on the picket lines. That's when the Academic Workers for a Democratic Union caucus was rebranded as the Rank and File caucus.[5]

I never got in on their Discord channel, but I did end up in a Rank and File-adjacent student-parents group. But that was less vitriolic than the screenshots I saw from the Rank and File Discord. The messaging they were sending was, "Vote down your tentative agreement, remove the bargaining team." Those two missions were hand in hand. And I think it was also really clear from the beginning that they were attempting to set up an inevitability of voting down the tentative agreement because their slogans were, "$54K or we won't go away," and "No COLA, no contract." Essentially, they were saying, "If you don't get your initial set of bargaining demands, then you can't ratify the contract." This sets up the conditions for a no vote. Because they *know* that part of settling the contract in any eventuality will be moving off of the initial set of demands, finding some sense of compromise somewhere. But they framed the entire question of whether or not to ratify on the question, "Did we get our initial set of demands?"

I think the bargaining team was hampered by the fear of giving the Rank and File caucus anything to run with. Every time the bargaining committee made a strategic decision in bargaining, the ten bargaining team members who wanted to advance bargaining had to plan on incurring a certain amount of fallout from this faction. And there were nine members—called the BT 9—who voted as a block against it, and went out to claim that the union was selling us out.[6]

The fear of Rank and File resulted in a poor position to begin the strike. We were essentially at our initial bargaining positions when we began the strike. And when you go into a strike, you want to have narrowed the issues down to the priorities that you think you can win and still give yourself some room to bargain and see how things play out with power. It's also essential to make quick and agile decisions by setting aside proposals that are unrealistic, or very principled but

5 Academic Workers for a Democratic Union was a caucus active in UAW 2865 from the mid-2000s to 2018.

6 The academic student employees and student researchers bargaining teams were each composed of twenty workers (two from each campus).

unlikely to be achieved, in the current contract negotiations. But the division in the bargaining team had put us in a position where we had not made substantial progress before the strike. I think some of the Rank and File-adjacent side of the bargaining team sincerely misunderstood how bargaining worked and thought that if you held out on your initial positions longer, that increased the possibility of getting something on those issues when the strike was rolling because they believed that a strike inevitably gains power as it goes on. The reality is it's more like a war of attrition.

UC was not taking us seriously, so they had no idea what they were actually going to have to agree on to settle the contract. And it took them a long time to get there, because for a long time our bargaining team was so far out there with our demands, it didn't seem like there was a path to a contract. But I think they would have gotten there a lot quicker had we actually bargained smart. The boss was entrenched because they had not really grappled with the size of concessions they were going to have to make in this contract.

I think retrospectively, deeper networks of member education around how bargaining works needed to happen. I think to an extent it was a mistake by leadership not to focus more on that, but more so I think it was just a lack of capacity, especially given that the combined bargaining units are enormous.

Bird's Eye View

Emily Weintraut

I would split up the six weeks of the strike according to the energy we had in the picket lines, the heat of the internal debates about strategy, how bargaining was developing, and UC's strategy. With all of this in mind, the strongest and the most exciting time that we ever had was day one. Day one—hands down—had the best turnout, the best energy. After that, we got a boost of energy back when we went from two picket lines to one. I think those were the biggest moments in terms of energy.

By week three we had lost some energy because some people stayed home longer from Thanksgiving and the number of people on the pickets started to dwindle. That same week, internal divisions climbed. It was a constant battle to appease people because there were very different perspectives on strategy. For example, I would talk to people in my department and surrounding areas about escalation, and they would say, "I don't want to escalate! Oh my God, that's scary to me!" But when you talked to some people in other departments, no matter what escalation we did, it wasn't enough for them. And that internal division became a bit more prevalent starting week three.

The lowest energy week was the last week of the picket line. I get lost timeline-wise now, maybe it was week five. There was a lot of misinformation spread about the caucuses and bargaining. At the picket line, some of us were battling misinformation about legal processes. For example, some people were advocating for partial striking, to which we—the people I organize with and myself—were responding, "No, don't do partial strike. You could lose your job over that. And there's really nothing that our union can legally do."

It was interesting because at first the picket line was like, "Let's all be here together." It was very strong. But as it went on, it was less about active picketing and more about some people wanting to do one specific escalation and us trying to provide accurate information. And I think that we were unprepared for the amount of information that people would want but not pursue for themselves.

Other huge energy days were Queer Day—which was in the first week—and when we went to Sacramento, at the start of week four. Actually, we did huge events at the beginning of the strike, and then we were running out of ideas of what else to do; we were being repetitive, and that's not good for the energy. I wish we would have done more themed days like Queer Day because those boosted the energy a lot.

Dez Manuel Fonseca

I'd say the strike had four phases. The first one is from day one of the strike to the beginning of Thanksgiving break; characteristically, things were really positive on the picket lines, and we had marches and big rallies every day. Also, that's when Todd and I and a few other people started organizing construction and delivery pickets, trying to find other unionized workers on campus that—because of their contract—would support the picket lines or walk off the job at strike locations.

The second phase started when we dropped the cost-of-living adjustment, or COLA, language. I use quote marks when I say "COLA" because the raises we got are more than any cost-of-living adjustment could ever realistically be. And if there was ever 20 percent inflation, we have bigger problems than a labor negotiation. When we dropped that language, we got a lot of division, and it got more intense when we dropped down the wages demand from $54,000 to $43,000. And—for other reasons—people were leaving the picket line. So, we knew the strike was not expanding at that point. The characteristic of the second phase was the beginning of the internal debate.

Third phase was escalation and direct actions—which some people were against. At UCLA we occupied the Luskin Center for a whole day, we did direct actions outside the regents' houses in Southern California, and we had the Regents Romp. I'm going to talk about all of this later. And finally, the fourth phase was ratification and the debate over it, which started probably a week or two before ratification itself.

CHAPTER 4

Past Becomes Present

Aarthi Sekar leads a rally in Sacramento with workers from all the northern UC campuses.

A Brief History of Caucuses

Curtis Rumrill

My first hint that there were division problems in our union, especially in Local 2865, came when I saw the low numbers from the 2018 ratification vote, which happened after a bargaining process led by a bargaining team that came from two different caucuses. In this ratification vote, participation was abysmally low, and evenly split between yes and no. Personally, the thin majority supporting the contract made me think, "This is a weak union, there's weak participation, and no clear sense of leadership." Also, these vote numbers made me lean toward a yes vote on the contract because a local that is that deeply dysfunctional can't sustain a strike.

After the 2018 contract ratification, there was a group that opposed it and launched what's known as the Mussman appeal, raising questions about the legitimacy of the vote. I was invited to a rally for the Mussman appeal by an organizer from the Berkeley Tenants Union, thinking it could help me to understand the problems in our union. However, the rally turned out to be a coffee cake in the comp lit grad lounge instead of a rally because only twenty-five people from across the state attended. It was at this event that I first encountered Academic Workers for a Democratic Union, the caucus that had previously held influence over the union but had just been voted out of office.

The Mussman appeal aimed to contest the ratification by claiming procedural issues, such as concerns about access to certain lists. Despite their efforts, they ultimately lost the Mussman appeal. They had been campaigning for nearly a year to force a revote on a contract that had already been ratified. It wasn't entirely clear what their plan was after that, as the employer was unlikely to return to negotiations just because the membership deemed the initial ratification invalid, but that was their agenda.

Academic Workers for a Democratic Union's goals of democratization and strong demands are *good things*. But, as time went on, something that isn't uncommon in academic unions ended up happening. The union attracted a lot of ideologically leftist people who were not disciplined organizers. Most of the leadership came from humanities departments who were mistrustful of the idea of hiring staff for organizing. Plus, they were pessimistic about the prospects for organizing. Their power base was in the humanities and they weren't keen on organizing beyond that. They sincerely believed that outside of the humanities, graduate workers were inherently conservative and would interfere with the union being a progressive and radical organization. I think they sincerely believed it was important for left-leaning humanities departments to keep control of the union and that STEM departments were too conservative to be involved in the union or go on strike.

The tensions surrounding the organizing strategy go back to the 2014 contract. In 2014, Academic Workers for a Democratic Union was in power and they went into bargaining and they did two limited-duration strikes that happened *before* the boss gave the last, best, and final offer. And coincident with the second strike, the boss moved a little bit more on wages. They were very low participation strikes with overall a thousand members statewide who voted to authorize the strike—although I'm not sure about the exact number. And being generous, I think around 10 percent of the bargaining unit participated in the strike. They had almost no disruptive power. Therefore, it'd be an overstatement to say that the strikes organized by Academic Workers for a Democratic Union had any impact on what actually happened at the bargaining table. When the boss made their last, best, and final offer, it was slightly better than what had been on the table before the strike and the bargaining committee recommended unanimously for ratification, which was a condition of the offer. And the contract was ratified by something like 97 percent of the members who voted.

In the wake of that contract, some Academic Workers for a Democratic Union leaders started a conversation about what a supermajority strike would look like, and what it would take to actually get substantial gains in the upcoming bargaining process. There was a tension in the Academic Workers for a Democratic Union approach to strategy, where they believed that radical actions with low participation, like a wildcat strike or a long-haul strike, would have a snowball effect, and would bring and radicalize more members to build power. However, a group of Academic Workers for a Democratic Union leaders began advocating for a different perspective, emphasizing the need for a supermajority of members committed to participating in the strike from the beginning to derive real power. Eventually, this last group decided to form its own caucus and run their own slate for elections in order to build for mass participation strikes. So, with these former Academic Workers for a Democratic Union leaders, the importance of organizing outside the humanities departments to achieve real wins gained traction. This viewpoint clashed with the leaders that remained in Academic Workers for a Democratic Union who believed that STEM workers are inherently antiunion or antistrike and inherently conservative and will blunt the radicalism of the union.

The new caucus was named Organizing for Student-Worker Power and they organized really well for the next set of officer elections and won a lot of seats, particularly in UC Berkeley, San Diego, and LA. They started focusing on organizing in STEM and left humanities almost alone because the assumption was "the humanities are good, they've got leaders that are going to bring them out on strike when we go on strike, we need to go and organize in STEM." So they spent the time between 2016 and the ratification of the 2018 contract organizing hard in STEM and came to the conclusion that there wasn't enough support to go on strike in 2018 because the statewide union membership was around 30 percent in 2017.

The question of membership levels became starker with the 2018 *Janus v. AFSCME* Supreme Court ruling. Prior to this moment, there wasn't a huge distinction between membership and nonmembership, and a lot of people were paying agency fees because they wanted to take the cheaper option.[1] But after this Supreme Court ruling, either you were a full member of the union or you didn't pay anything, which creates a much larger incentive for folks to not be union members. It wasn't ever because there was antiunion sentiment in our local that membership fell to 30 percent, it was a pure lack of organizing. There was no organizing or member education happening. Folks didn't know they had a union or they didn't know what it meant to have a union. So the question of whether they should fill out a membership form and pay dues felt like a personal decision with no real impact on their working conditions.

The union members who advocated for a no vote during the 2018 ratification ran an aggressive campaign with very heated rhetoric. The vote no campaign did press statements describing the contract as horrible and as a major loss for the union, even though it's essentially identical to the last contract they happily ratified and promoted, plus some marginal economic gains due to fee remissions. The difference

1 An agency fee is the fee that nonunion members must pay when they work under a collective bargain contract. According to the Communication Workers of America, "An agency fee payer is a worker who has chosen not to join the union (or has resigned his membership) but who must, under the agency shop/union security language in the collective bargaining agreement, pay agency fees (equivalent to dues) as a condition of employment." CWA, *Union Operators Procedures Manual*, https://www.cwa-union.org/sites/default/files/part_xvii_union_security_agreements.pdf.

was simply who was in power. Academic Workers for a Democratic Union lost the ability to control the bargaining team and the new caucus, called Organizing for Student-Worker Power, narrowly gained the ability to make the decisions at bargaining. Academic Workers for a Democratic Union then aggressively claimed this was a coup, and used the word "coup" over and over again to describe democratic elections that they lost. Which is indicative of the kind of inflation that they use in their rhetoric. They were not tied to truthfulness in what they would say. There was a level of exaggeration and hyperbole in the way that they described things that happened from here going forward.

2019–20 Wildcat Strike

Dez Manuel Fonseca

I think historically some spaces were more marked by division than others. The people who attended the statewide organizing committee understood those divisions. But I didn't understand that the debates I saw during the summer were rooted in longstanding divisions; now, looking back, I understand what the divisions were.

Those divisions were linked to the Santa Cruz wildcat strike. The leaders of the Santa Cruz wildcat weren't as concerned with the legal protections as the leaders from other campuses who had been making longer-term plans for a broader strike. And after the wildcat, the different interpretations of what had happened deepened the division.

For me, personally, the wildcat was something I looked at closely before coming to UCLA. When I was making my decision about grad school, I saw the wildcat happening and I thought that shit was cool as hell... little did I know about it!

Kenzo Esquivel

I got more involved with the union around the time of the Santa Cruz wildcat strike in 2019–20. Workers at UC Santa Cruz went on strike without union sanction, demanding a cost-of-living adjustment. The movement started there but spread across other campuses, and even gained some national attention.

At one point, there was a call for solidarity strikes. My department, a larger science one, talked a lot about joining, even though it wouldn't impact us directly. Most of the support at Berkeley came from the humanities.

People in my department supported the wildcat because they understood how bad the situation was for Santa Cruz workers. The argument was, "These are comrades in need, and even without union protection, there's strength in numbers." But it created tension because they knew the risks of retaliation and didn't want to endanger the union.

Santa Cruz workers did a great job mobilizing the media, which pushed my department to help, even though it was a minority movement at Berkeley. We felt a responsibility to show that larger STEM departments also supported the wildcat, hoping to inspire others.

During all this, I got more involved. I was a first-year at Berkeley, attending organizing committee meetings, and relaying updates to my department. I became known as the "union person," though I resisted that title because I wanted everyone to feel part of the union. Alexa then asked if I wanted to run for head steward. I joined the slate and ran for the position because it aligned with my values. I was already doing the work, so I figured, why not do it in a more official capacity?

At the time, I don't think I was super onboard with the wildcat program. I was definitely sympathetic, but going into my role as head steward, I conceptualized myself as walking a tightrope between these two stances, that of the wildcat strikers and the union establishment. I knew we—meaning Local 2865—couldn't support the strike officially; however, I felt we could find ways to leverage that moment to have more unity. I think I've always had more of a foot in our official union establishment.

The wildcat strike time was really difficult for my department. There were different factions that felt differently about it. And although we tried to keep a safe environment for people to participate in a solidarity strike without feeling ostracized, a lot of people came out of that period feeling fatigued and unsure of their relationship with our union. That became more evident during the recent strike, which was *sanctioned*. I remember, in the lead-up to the 2022 strike, conversations with folks who had been around since the wildcat, and who were very hesitant because of the turmoil within our department and our union during the wildcat. There was a level of trauma associated with that time and with the fact that it was abruptly stopped in its tracks by the pandemic, which shut down any possibility of filing and moving toward an unfair labor practice strike.

Earlier I said humanities and STEM departments responded

differently to the Santa Cruz wildcat. In general, I think STEM and humanities disciplines have some core differences. And this can translate to how we get involved in our union. In the STEM or STEM-heavy departments, there is more flexibility for not teaching and doing your own dissertation research under a graduate student researcher position. And there are often higher levels of pay for departments that have higher external funding. That's not necessarily true across the board but it is a pattern. On the other side, I think humanities and social sciences were more likely to solidarize with the wildcat because humanities and social scientists think a lot more about issues like inequity, social structures, and social movements, and have a vocabulary and a theoretical structure around them. Scientists generally do not have a curricular training in those issues—though they still can, and often do, develop a framework to face social issues. Even in my department—which is mixed—there is a distinction in talking to a scientist about joining the struggle and talking to someone who has more familiarity and a language to speak about it. That's not a hard or fast thing; so many of our incredible leaders are from STEM disciplines. But there are these more structural elements. In my college—the College of Natural Resources—we have departments that are funded at significantly higher levels for their graduate students based on the types of research that they do. A few years before I started in my program, the social scientists in my department were making less on average than the natural scientists. So, there wasn't even intradepartmental equity across fields. And this happens because social scientists have much smaller pools of funding that they can pull from to support their students.

Curtis Rumrill

The Santa Cruz wildcat of 2019 was a test of the Academic Workers for a Democratic Union hypothesis, which states that if you have a small number of workers on strike with really good optics and very idealistic demands, other workers will join them en masse, eventually leading to the necessary power to win all of your demands. However, it is a little bit difficult to assess what ended up happening because of the pandemic, although I think the pandemic was ultimately a convenient excuse for them to give up the strike which at that point seemed hopeless.

Once the wildcat was rolling, they withheld grades past the grading deadline at the end of the fall 2019 term and the beginning of the spring semester of 2020. And then the University of California Office of the President started threatening to fire strikers for withholding grades. At that point, the majority of them turned in grades. Of the two-hundred-some that were initially on strike, eighty-some stayed on strike and refused to turn in grades under the threat of termination. At that point, the Academic Workers for a Democratic Union caucus started organizing rallies across the state in support of the Santa Cruz workers who were being threatened with termination, asking for everybody else to go on strike in solidarity if they got fired. And when those eighty workers were fired, Academic Workers for a Democratic Union organized departments to declare themselves "strike ready," meaning that the majority of the workers in that department said they are willing to go on strike. "Strike ready" doesn't mean they have a plan or an understanding of what it means to go on strike; it means they said they are strike ready.

They effectively mobilized the workers who were already inclined or willing to go on strike. Although it's questionable what any of them were ready to do when their own departments or schools threatened to fire them. At UC Berkeley, of the thirteen departments that initially went on strike, all but three of them quietly crossed the picket line within a month. African American studies, performance studies, and ethnic studies were left out on strike, thinking that everyone else was still on strike, only to discover that nearly all of the other humanities departments went back to work almost immediately. And that was the end of the wildcat strike at UC Berkeley. On a statewide level, the wildcat strike was essentially called off under the auspices of "we can't continue this under the pandemic."

We never got to see a statewide wildcat strike because within a couple of weeks after it was declared, the pandemic lockdown started. But there was no reason that the wildcat strike could not have continued because everybody just moved to online teaching and according to them, picket lines weren't important for the strength of a strike. The idea that they couldn't have continued a virtual strike in the face of the pandemic doesn't seem true. The reality was that they had built no real infrastructure for their strike. They just had not done the organizing to build real bonds of solidarity to bring people through any kind of strike.

The level of mistrust of union leadership after the wildcat strike was much higher than it was prior to the wildcat strike. And it really foreshadowed what we saw in our strike, in 2022. The folks who pushed for the wildcat were effective in propagating this message of union corruption and bureaucracy—which is essentially the right-wing trope of what unions are. And it is deeply *inaccurate* for our union. Thanks to the efforts of dedicated member organizers, our union operates as a genuinely member-driven organization with a robust system of direct democracy.

My department, the music department, was *not* inclined to join the wildcat strike even before I weighed in on it. Folks organically felt like it was something that was being forced on them and were not interested in losing their jobs or their academic careers for this because it didn't seem like it was well planned.

CHAPTER 5

What's Appalling? UC Stalling!

Workers assemble at UC San Diego

Rise of Internal Divisions

Aarthi Sekar

By the second half of the strike we started holding spokes councils.[1] We also had department representatives who—for their part—were having

1 A spokes council is a meeting format where representatives from different groups or departments come together to share information, discuss concerns, and coordinate actions. Each representative speaks on behalf of their group, which has had its own internal discussions beforehand, ensuring that diverse voices are heard and decisions reflect the wider group's perspectives.

meetings within their departments about how they felt, about where the strike was going, about how many of their coworkers were actually on strike or scabbing, and about people's opinion on lasting a few more weeks or into winter quarter. These departments' representatives would share what their conversations were like during the spokes councils. We would also have department meetings on the picket line and people would share how they were feeling and what their expectations were. We were constantly trying to have avenues in which we were bringing people together to have these really important conversations.

As a bargaining team member, if I wasn't bargaining, I was on the picket line. And if there were department meetings happening, I would float around to all the different circles and sit in and ask and see if they had any questions about what was going on with bargaining or anything I could help answer. I was at every single spokes meeting. We would hold impromptu, sort of Q&A sessions, and I would be there to answer questions as best as I could.

Divisions started showing up more when we really had to have strategic conversations about how to move negotiations forward when UC was refusing to budge from its low base wage offer, which they said was their best offer on the table for a wages proposal. UC was *not budging* and they were not showing any efforts to meet us at the bargaining table in good faith. Up until that moment, the general sense was that we were all united.

But, again, we needed to move forward because people cannot be on strike forever. In this context, one of the first moments where we started seeing division among workers was when we removed the clause on median income from the wages proposal. And that was early week two for academic student employees and late week one for student researchers. The second moment that prompted division—which was really tough—was when we amended the wages proposal from a $54,000 annual base wage to a $43,000 annual base wage. It was on Wednesday November 30. $54,000 was always pitched as the big goal to reach for, but with the understanding that it's a negotiation. Besides, this decision was made because UC wasn't budging from where they had been for months, which was $28,000.

I'd say there was miscommunication and misunderstanding about the bargaining team's decision. There was miscommunication and misunderstanding on removing language tying future salary increases to changes in the statewide median rental prices. Some of our coworkers felt it meant we were no longer fighting for a cost-of-living adjustment, or COLA, which was a problem because COLA was an important part of why they were out on strike. And when that clause tying together future salary increases to median rental prices was removed, some folks felt that it meant we were no longer taking into consideration fighting for a cost-of-living adjustment, which was not the case. The wages proposal, without the clause on median rent, took into consideration what the cost of living would be in all of the regions where the campuses are.

I think I could have done a better job conveying that negotiations are about *negotiating* and that we had put in extra language around wages to pad our proposals and take into consideration COLA. This is because we foresaw that we would need to be strategic about moving our chess pieces.

The misunderstanding came from false information, ironically spread by some members of the bargaining team. Why? I'm still trying to understand, but it may come down to ideological differences on what a strike means. Some believed a longer, indefinite strike made us stronger. However, from my conversations with coworkers, it was clear people were tired of striking. They wanted to continue but also wanted negotiations to move forward, not just stall while striking indefinitely.

Moving negotiations forward required actual bargaining, and the misinformation framed amending our wages proposal as "conceding." But we didn't concede. Conceding means losing something we already had, which didn't happen. We negotiated and adjusted the proposal to move closer to UC's position. *There were no concessions.*

On a statewide level, it seemed that the division ran deeper on other campuses than it did at Davis. We had division at Davis, yes, but having a big picket line and a big debrief at the end of the day really helped to keep everybody in the same space talking to each other and the division didn't feel as deep. And also, it was resoundingly clear that people at Davis wanted negotiations to move forward.

It felt like the ideological division was worse in places like Berkeley and LA, just from speaking to coworkers. I heard that Merced and Riverside felt differently about our ability to strike for a long time. And I may be wrong about that because—to be honest—I didn't talk with many of the workers on those campuses.

At first, communication between the bargaining team and the picket lines wasn't great. We didn't have a system for quick updates after each session. We gave brief updates on the picket line, but early on, there wasn't much to share since UC wasn't meeting with us. While we discussed removing the median rent clause in caucus, we didn't communicate the amendment right away—not to hide it, but because we hadn't figured out the best way to do so. Eventually, we improved communication by creating a WhatsApp group, holding office hours on the picket line, sending regular email updates, and hosting Zoom town halls. This made things much better.

We had different chats. One of the chats was almost a news feed where the bargaining team posted updates; it worked really well. We also had a strike captains' chat where it was really hard to engage effectively with all the questions and explanations in a way that felt complete and satisfactory because it was a lot to keep track of. I don't know if chats were the most effective way to communicate. I have the feeling that sometimes the chat dynamics may have caused more confusion or may have been ineffective for communicating what was happening.

Overall, the online activity was way more active than in-person activity. Maybe people felt a lot more free to say whatever they wanted in online spaces like chats and social media, and in person they wouldn't. And that was not good. It was in online spaces where people were getting individually called out to answer questions on command, which was basically bullying. And if you didn't answer immediately, then they'd say you were ignoring them. But the reason why I wasn't answering every single question was because I was busy. Maybe I was in bargaining sessions or I was on the picket line or I was—I don't know—actively organizing or answering somebody else's question.

I remember the Wednesday evening of week three, when we—the bargaining team—voted on the amendment to the wages proposal, we were trying our best to be communicative, open, and transparent about what was happening at the bargaining table. And there was a WhatsApp chat blowing up with messages calling us out, telling us that we were conceding and that we were working against the interests of workers. It was nonstop, just a barrage of comments saying that we were failing as bargaining team representatives. That was really tough. That group of voices got really loud on online spaces like chats and Twitter posts, but it wasn't really organized on the picket line. The pushback happened online.

I guess people called me out online because they didn't want to say it to my face; had they done it to my face, they would have seen I'm a human being with real feelings and emotions, and that I'm their coworker. I'm not UC. The balance between online and in-person organizing is something I would change for the future. I don't know if having an open chat is the most effective because I did have good in-person conversations with people who were calling me out in the chats, for example.

I think there was a difference in experience or perception of the strike because a lot of the people who argued that the amendments were concessions were not talking to the folks who were returning to labs; they hadn't been organizing with them before the strike so they weren't positioned to support the people who were facing retaliation from their principal investigators and were really scared about staying away from research. What I mean is that a lot of the people who were saying that the bargaining team had conceded were from the humanities side of campus, more, not all of them—there were people within math and physics that felt we were conceding. But a lot of the people who were ready to go back to work, and ready for the bargaining team to make a move in negotiations so we could end the strike and have a contract, were within the large sciences. And many of them, like the biological sciences workers, were planning on going back to work, if they weren't already at work.

Additionally, I would say that the leaders that showed up at 7 a.m. and stayed until 10 p.m. or 11 p.m. felt very strongly about making sure the contract negotiations were moving forward. And not a lot of the people who felt like we were making concessions were arriving as early or staying as late; they would make parts of it, maybe they would show up in the morning and unload or trip to the evening debrief, but they weren't the ones that were putting in every single waking hour into the strike. Not most of them, at least.

There was also a difference on how long we were organizing in our union. As I said previously, there was *so much organizing* on the ground that happened before the strike, months and months prior to the strike getting departments out to all the rallies and actions, like the BOMMM [Big October Monthly Membership Meeting] and the strike authorization vote. I can safely say that a lot of the people who were calling us out for "conceding" to UC, and who were advocating for a long-haul strike, joined our union during the strike and were not part of the previous efforts. So once on strike they weren't familiar with how to organize more of their coworkers to come out; that wasn't their focus. Meanwhile, the folks who wanted negotiations to move forward were mostly people who had organized for months—if not years—prior to the strike. And every day, the goal of the picket line debrief was how to get more people out to the picket so the strike is stronger because that needed to be the focus so we could have an effective strike to win big on the demands we all wanted.

By the end of the third week, the media was starting to get that dissent was happening within the UC strike. The media was able to catch wind of the infighting because so much of the calling out of elected leadership as "corrupt," or spreading misinformation and falsely accusing bargaining team members of conceding to UC, was happening in social media—like Twitter—and it just caught fire in the way it can only do in the world of social media! I mean, everybody was reading it and everybody thought that what was spread on social media was the reality of the situation! In reality, the vast majority of the people on the picket lines would tell you a different story. It was a small but loud faction at Davis that was trying to dominate the narrative with divisive language.

Kenzo Esquivel

The most obvious first turning point of the strike is when we dropped the COLA language. Maybe it didn't feel like a huge turning point per se, but it was the first crack. The major turning point was when the bargaining teams lowered the salary from $54,000 to—I guess—$43,000.

There were divisions that were becoming apparent in a way that during the BOMMM were history or memories, and when the COLA language was dropped there was a response from folks who were—if we're thinking historically—aligned with the wildcat efforts at Santa Cruz. But at that time, there were still a lot of people who were saying things like, "We were never going to win everything. If we're still going to be asking for $54,000, even if we don't have one word of specific language tying our income to the cost of living, I'm comfortable calling that a cost-of-living adjustment." To me, that framing was rhetorical. But at the same time, there was a faction of people that started to emerge for whom dropping the COLA language was a big thing. But generally speaking, the upset about dropping the COLA language felt somewhat fringe.

When the drop from $54,000 to $43,000 happened, that was when the conversation shifted significantly. The progression from hearing about the drop to the drop happening felt like it happened very quickly for me. For me, it was a question both of the move itself, and perhaps more importantly, the process by which the move happened. For such a big move, it felt important that we bring people into the fold and try to build an understanding of the rationale behind the move before we let it happen. But the way that I recall it, the first time I'd seen or heard about a potential drop was in a Google form that was being circulated by someone at a different campus to urge the bargaining team to not make that drop. I remember being in the picket line when I got that form, like a petition. Later that day, maybe a few hours later, we had our daily poststrike or debrief meeting, and one of the bargaining team members brought it up in a discussion that was only allocated five minutes in our schedule. That was the first time that I had officially heard about dropping from $54,000 to $43,000. In theory, the purpose of the debrief was to talk about logistics. We never constructed an actual strategic organizing space. Earlier in the strike, we had decided that not all workers needed to go to the debrief because they were just to report and hear how things were going on. Anyway, I remember I spoke against the move, saying that I thought that it was too big of a drop. And the next day there were people on campus who were thanking me for saying what they were feeling.

Then, it was the evening after that meeting that we all got a text on the WhatsApp bargaining updates thread saying that the bargaining teams were meeting with UC's labor relations representatives that night to discuss this point.

The fact that the drop progressed from hearing it from an external source, to hearing about it for the first time in the debrief meeting, even though in theory debriefs were supposed to be logistical, to the bargaining team making movement on the decision that evening, it felt bad to me. I think it felt bad for a lot of people. It was the first time that it felt like that crack was really getting bigger.

The caucus became pretty contentious after the drop of the COLA language. I feel like negativity was brewing. The evening of the caucus before the $54,000 drop, there were tech issues during the Zoom which certainly weren't helping, and it all happened so fast and the overwhelming majority of people who showed up to that caucus meeting were speaking against the move. And ultimately, the bargaining team decided that that was the move that they were going to make. It was the first time I broke down in tears during the strike; I was really heartbroken about how it all went down.

It felt weird to see the move being made even though it did not reflect what was being shared in the caucus, which I think was the only formal process we had to get feedback or give input at the time. It also was weird feeling fairly isolated as a dissenter at Berkeley. Being a dissenter wasn't a position I had ever conceptualized myself in; I had always seen myself as someone who was sympathetic to the wildcat cause and wanted to support my department, but would still be wearing my union elected cap. So it was the first time that I was disillusioned and felt alienated by our leadership. I felt like I was blue-pilled or whatever the Matrix thing is where I was suddenly seeing a lot of things in a different lens.

It was also a personal turning point. Before that caucus, I had conversations with people who were skeptical of our bargaining team members and were pessimistic about settling from the start, or who didn't have faith in our leadership. And I was a defender. I was the optimist. And so, it was really challenging being forced into the position of acknowledging there were other things I was not seeing.

I know that it was a turning point for a lot of the people who thought that the dropping of the COLA language wasn't that important because we were still asking for $54,000. It was a big turning point for my department. My department is a little bit more plugged in and maybe more independent thinking. That is not to say that others are mindless followers, but we are willing to dissent maybe a little bit more.

In some ways, the big turning points didn't affect my involvement in the strike. At least for me, personally, I was still doing the shifts that I was signed up for, I continued to do media interviews. Although, personally, doing media started feeling a bit harder because I felt we were entering a new phase, and in some ways, the fire in my gut had diminished; but I still put on a face, tried to stay motivated, and tried to keep folks coming out.

At the same time, this was a moment where I knew I disagreed with our leadership, but I didn't feel completely alienated or unable to continue organizing alongside these folks. It was a moment where it felt like I needed to voice the strategic differences that I had. It also was a moment where I had difficult conversations with folks that I had brought into the fold, into organizing. Those conversations were the ones I struggled with the most. I specifically remember a worker who I had referred to our communications team—they shared their own personal struggles with finding housing, having a kid in the Bay Area, and being a student who had been profiled on campus. Their story articulated very well why *I* was in this fight. After the drop to $43,000, they came to me and told me they felt *used*, and that their story was used without an intention to actually support student parents. They told me they have lost trust in the leadership.

From my understanding, prior to my time in the UC system, there were folks in leadership in our union who were more ideologically aligned with the faction that emerged out of COLA and Santa Cruz. And our recent union era has been more focused on building membership and organizing for student-worker power—it is more focused on on-the-ground organizing, in creating actual infrastructure and power that could enable us to win bigger things. And if you look at the historical trajectory of our union density and our union membership, it has gone up under recent leadership over the last years. So, there is real proof that the current leadership knows how to organize. But at some point, it started to feel like we were no longer investing our collective efforts in the strike to organizing our coworkers. But these things—organizing and theory—don't have to be mutually opposing. The folks who were aligned with the wildcat in 2019 were good at writing up flyers and pamphlets, and discussing and putting their ideas in writing, but not very good at broadening their base. Whereas the leadership elected in 2018 was very organized and focused on building membership. These are different skill sets that people are bringing, and if we could figure out how to talk to each other, we could create the perfect storm and bring the university to its knees. That's the dream I have for the future.

Curtis Rumrill

The drop from $54,000 to $43,000 on wages was a decision that did not happen opaquely. The majority of the democratically elected bargaining team decided after serious conversations with member leaders. It happened the way that bargaining typically happens, which is bargaining team members go to the leaders and all of their different departments and units and have conversations with them about what the next move is going to be. We moved off of $54,000 because it was an insane number in the sense that it would be a 100 percent raise—not something winnable in one contract—and $43,000 was still high. Leadership prepared for that, but the move was too fast and there was not real consensus built around it before it happened. And in the fallout from that, we lost good, reasonable people that wanted to win and understood that bargaining is a system of compromises and a reflection of our power, and yet were so shocked by an $11,000 move. The thing is, we should have been bargaining on wages incrementally over time, since before the strike, and getting closer to something that was real. That's what gave the Rank and File caucus political leverage, because up to that point they had only marginal fringe support and it was really contained in the humanities, but after that move they became a community. To be clear, I think that the bargaining move was not the issue—the issue was the bargaining history that preceded that move.

Rank and File put out lots of fliers. And they had a strike update newsletter where they claimed credit for the entire strike. They claim that the only reason the strike was happening was because of the *incredible* [*irony*] wildcat strike that had happened. Also, they were consistently calling the leadership corrupt, bureaucratic, and working against our interests. And they did this thing of showing up to meetings and disrupting them and making the meetings not function. And that served to polarize, but not to organize.

Just like in the wildcat strike, they did really well on social media and with earned media. But in all my years of organizing, I came to understand that that never translates to significant real power. Media can be a little bit of additional leverage, but it means nothing if you don't have the membership organizing behind it. And that was resoundingly proven with the wildcat strike because their media was incredible and their social media was really good. And it was proven with the vote no campaign. They did a good job with the electronic communications, but they did a poor job, generally speaking, with member-to-member communication. They never understood the importance of how you build a union and strike.

UC Berkeley bargaining team members Samuel Chan, Tanzil Chowdhury, Tarini Hardikar, and Jess Banks discuss bargaining in front of a large rally

Joyce Chan

I was expecting that the vibe of week one would last for at least two weeks. Maybe I was extremely naive, but I was satisfied with how things were developing, and I was confused about the inflammatory conversations that were happening. Maybe I was satisfied because I'm a postdoc, and the postdocs who were involved in our union were supportive of how things were developing. Or maybe it was because I came from an institution that *didn't* have a union, so, to me, any sort of union work was incredible. I was just very, very pleased with what we had.

During the strike, we went through the whole range of emotions ranging from the most jubilant, joyous, energized, where it felt like we were capable of doing anything, to points of fear and uncertainty. It was definitely a lot of peer- and self-reflection, thinking about where we stand, thinking about how we engage with people, thinking about our boundaries, about respect, thinking about the different ways that we show solidarity. We were learning.

Personally, an eye-opening and intimidating moment for me during the strike was when I spoke at an access needs rally that we held in the Ridge Walk Academic Complex, when the bargaining team was discussing whether or not to tentatively agree to the offer for postdocs and academic researchers. In that rally, there were rightfully angry people who are disabled sharing their anger because they felt like their demands as disabled persons were ignored or left out in the contract. It was an intimidating moment because in my heart I knew that the people who drafted the contract article were also disabled, and they had been working hard since before I came into the picture, but I also understood the anger of the people who were present in the rally because disabled people are put through horrific experiences, and it is frustrating to feel like we are being put on the back burner all the time. And then I dug deeper into the articles that our bargaining team was voting on during bargaining, and I understood the enormity of what they were working with, and I saw that access needs weren't cut out of the contract. The problem was how very convoluted our contract language is. Personally, I think there is power in our contract, but we need to enforce it; it's not like we got zero net gain in terms of access needs.

Kien Le

I never expected to win the amount we proposed at the beginning of bargaining. We always have to ask higher than what we wanted, so we can start going down. I think most people understand that. The move from $54,000 to $43,000 was called a "concession"—it's not a concession, it's a strategy. It's not conceding something we already had—our proposal was still much higher than what we had. I still agree that we should have made that move.

But some department leaders disagreed and disrespected that decision, so they turned members against each other. For me, that was not productive at all. I feel like disagreements or conflict is fundamental for every democratic organization. That's how democracy works. Internal disagreements are productive if we keep them among us; if we turn them into a display and harass bargaining team members on the picket line, I don't think they are helpful at all.

Maddy Duong

In the early days of the strike I didn't feel like there were people who didn't trust or were suspicious of the bargaining team members. I didn't even know that people would feel that way until they did. Around midweek two there was a split among workers because of the decisions that were being made by the bargaining team, being the removal of the cost of living adjustment language. Unfortunately, it seemed like there was nothing we could do to solve it because the people who had strong disagreements with the bargaining team just left the picket. So we couldn't have conversations about it. This is a moment that for me is a turning point in the strike because the atmosphere among workers changed.

Emily Weintraut

What did I know about bargaining? I knew very little at all. Maybe that's because I'm a person who overall trusts the bargaining team. I thought, "I know the Davis bargaining team. I know what their values are. I trust them to advocate for me." So, I never tried to go to a bargaining caucus or look into a bargaining Zoom.[2] I felt like, "It's just going to be the UC doing something stupid and then us trying to fight back." For me, that pretty much is what every single bargaining session is.

My perspective about what we would get from the strike changed over time. First, when I heard the number $54,000 for wages, I did the math so badly that I kept thinking we were asking for a $10,000 raise, but actually $54,000 would have been a $20,000 raise. So, I kept picturing my life on a $10,000 annual raise. I don't know how that number got in my head, but it was wrong. When I would tell my coworkers about the $54,000 number, most of the time they would be shocked, and say something like, "Yeah, we're not going to get that!" In all the walkthroughs I did, most people didn't have that big expectation.

Some of the workers who set their hopes on the $54,000 were in the more "radical departments." In other departments, for example, in my own department, most people expected it to go down. And nonetheless, we got close to $10,000 a year of increases. Starting in October 2023, I think it's an extra $700 a month for most people in my area, which is huge, and that's not even counting the October 2024 raise. And when I was talking to people about the contract, a lot of them were shocked because that would be a life changing thing for them. Their hearts weren't set on the $54,000 because the amount we ended up winning was still life changing.

The drop from $54,000 to $43,000 was the perfect storm that made things *horrible*. That day it was raining and we had to do an inside picket,

2 In bargaining, a *caucus* refers to a meeting that takes place during a bargaining session when one or both sides call for a break for internal discussion.

so everyone was very close together. A lot of people really took it out on two of the bargaining team members, Aarthi and Ximena, because the other two members, Marshall and Diana, were both in Irvine because bargaining had shifted from Zoom to in person. So, some people were screaming at them and there were honestly disgusting things said to them. And the way they were treated was very gross. I don't think it's justifiable. I think we were all shocked.

When in shock, a lot of people are prone to speaking and acting immediately, and that was the case that day. Meanwhile, the bargaining team was trying to explain the move, "This is a strategic drop. There is precedent that a big move works to push the boss." And the UC was not moving time after time and time again on wages. So, the bargaining team said, "We have seen in the past, we saw it with the Local 5810 contracts, that when they made a big jump, the UC came and met them and that helped them resolve everything."

Some of the people who were in shock and upset were also out there every day on the picket line, and they might have thought that the drop didn't make any sense because they thought and argued, "We're all out here." But in reality, our numbers were dwindling on the picket line; it was getting untenable for people to be on strike because their academic progress is tied to their academic work.

I think the drop was further upsetting when the UC continued to not meet it. And then people were like, "The bargaining team did this so the UC would meet us, but the UC didn't meet us at all!" and would blame our own team. Well, if you were to ask me, I'd say, "You should be blaming the UC. We made a strategic decision that was a risk, but everything we had done to that point was a risk—this risk just didn't pan out immediately how we thought it would."

A strike is withholding your labor and being on the picket line. But withholding research is different from withholding teaching and grading as a teaching assistant. Teaching assistants who also do a lot of research—especially in STEM—are not as emotionally tied to teaching. I can speak for myself because at that point I was doing a big lecture hall of over five hundred people. I wasn't personally connected with any of my students. In contrast, when I did a lab course, I was very attached to my students because there were less than twenty of them and I knew them well. But for some people who only teach, the job is really emotional; they argue that they don't want to hurt their students with a low-quality education.

When it's your own research, that's your own career progress, which makes it harder for a lot of people. Again, I can use myself as an example because even two months after the strike ended, I am constantly thinking, "Holy shit, I'm six weeks behind!" And I feel bad about being behind, but I know it is on UC.

And then, withholding your labor is different depending on what discipline you are in. What people from humanities have told me is that a lot of them report to their bosses infrequently; they are not giving constant updates on their research. On the other hand, a lot of people in STEM will meet weekly or every other week to report data back and stuff like that. So withholding your research it's a bit different because you either have or don't have your boss asking for updates constantly. On the other hand, people from humanities are not in labs, but they are writing, which makes it harder for them to withhold their labor mentally because, like, "No one's seeing this. How is withholding my labor, my dissertation, affecting anyone but me?"

I understand that the humanities areas have less guaranteed funding sometimes, and I say "sometimes" because I come from a STEM department where we don't have summer funding for a lot of people, and we don't have reliable teaching assistantships for everyone. Honestly, my funding is as precarious as theirs. But it is easy to think that just because you're in STEM, you have guaranteed funding, that's not the case. I literally did not have funding for three or four months and I had to get extra jobs.

Dez Manuel Fonseca

I remember that toward Thanksgiving break, there was a reevaluation of not just strategy, but "What's next?" Week one, we realized that we were going to have to go after Thanksgiving break, and the strike date was planned to give us that break to put pressure on the university to get it done before the break, but also to give us a break if we needed to go another week, two weeks, three weeks, four weeks.

As I said earlier when I talked about phases, division showed up when we dropped the cost-of-living adjustment. When we dropped that language, some workers began a strategy of shaming the bargaining team members who backed that decision. That shaming got more intense after the $43,000 drop. And look, even though I understood why we had to go down and I thought it was a smart move, I didn't want that drop to happen. I felt that that move should have happened earlier, we shouldn't have gone into the BOMMM with the $54,000 demand still on the table. So when we went down, because it happened all at once during the strike, it felt like a quick decision.

The general mood changed because the bargaining team dropped the language that tied wage increases to median increases in rent prices. Another thing that affected the mood was the changes in the community safety article.[3] And particular workers—mostly Black workers like myself—were upset because that was a really important demand. So just the recognition that we weren't going to make much, if any, progress on it, changed the mood. And I had—or tried to have—a lot of conversations about that issue with my coworkers because I was involved in the drafting of that article.

It was really tough. Week three and week four was the worst of it, actually. And this was coming off the euphoria of week one and before the strategic reorientation of weeks four and five, when we began having town halls and the bargaining team responded to the dissenting arguments on a unified campus-wide level.

We always imagined that UC would make better offers than they did, and you could say we were kind of naive, but UC was acting like a private corporation. We were thinking, "Shit, maybe they will come off the bat on week one with a decent offer to demobilize the strike." But UC came back with shitty offer, after shitty offer, after shitty offer, which mobilized some people, but also demobilized others. It was especially demobilizing for student researchers who at the onset were hesitant to strike and were willing to strike just the first few days, hoping we would get a good offer immediately. Those people were really anxious to go back to the lab once they saw that a good offer wasn't going to be easy because—unlike academic student employees—they didn't have the protections of a contract yet.

I'm sure some people have talked about the—I'm going to say it in the intrigue voice they used—"Wednesday night massacre," which is how the people against negotiation called that November 30 when the bargaining team voted to move down from $54,000 to $43,000. Then

---

3 The community safety article was initially proposed by the academic student employees' and student researchers' bargaining teams with provisions related to campus policing. It was eventually withdrawn.

the mood just got . . . at my picket line, the mood got real sour every day. And it got smaller, but it didn't get too small, but definitely smaller. It also got colder and rainier into December, and we should take that into consideration. I think it was week three, I remember seeing somebody doing chants, "We're coming back for the $54,000 demand," or doing a teach-in talking about the Cops Off Campus demand—which was the community safety article—and getting applause. So, there was a noteworthy amount of dissent. But also, a lot of people were afraid to voice dissent to dissent, which is ironic.

Calling it a "Wednesday night massacre" is ridiculous, and I should say that publicly. Before moving on, I want to address the drop from $54,000 to $43,000 and the language around "concessions" some were using. The idea that we made "concessions" disrespects the wider labor movement. It assumes all we have to do is make a demand to win, which is not true. Collective power is needed, and it is also important to have good strategies to fight the boss. If making a demand is enough to win it, then the labor movement wouldn't be a movement. Bargaining is a negotiation, and moving from original demands isn't "selling out." To call it a massacre when we still achieved an 80 percent wage increase is wrong.

Since I was in charge of the solidarity pickets, I was around many of our different picket lines, and I saw different cultures. At UCLA there were different cultures at different picket lines; I'm sure that existed at other campuses as well. So, the picket line I was at—Bunche Hall—was the most contentious one. And I would say it was the most contentious because it was social sciences and humanities, people who think theoretically about a lot of the issues that were coming up in their day-to-day work.

The national coverage the strike got was not as widespread as it should have been, given that it was the largest strike in the history of higher education in this country. I feel fine about what was written, which is strange because usually that's not how I feel about the mainstream press, the bourgeois press. It was the scale that I'm upset with. It should have been more coverage, more analysis. They'd take the basics: the length of the strike, the public support in the strike, and the end result of the strike, which was the contract. There was a period where big newspapers like *LA Times*, *The Nation*, *The Economist* covered some of the dissent, and I think that had a role on the dynamics of the ratification vote. But, at the same time, I don't necessarily blame the press for this coverage; it wasn't super nuanced. I mean, the people writing about the strike *weren't there* unless it was an opinion piece written by workers. And the press—like *LA Times, The Nation, Jacobin*—weren't necessarily writing pieces about how incredible this strike was or how remarkable the contract itself actually was when compared to other union contracts. But all that I'm saying is an observation more so than a particular disillusionment. I think covering that dissent, however large or small it was, it's more coverage. It's like the union version of "If it bleeds, it leads."

I'll repeat what I've said: I knew nothing about bargaining before getting involved in the union. I learned some things in summer 2022, but I wasn't an expert. One of my biggest regrets is that I was telling people that we should get a raise to a minimum of $40,000 and no less, even though I now recognize that wasn't possible. I also regret slogans like "$54K or we won't go away," because they were unrealistic.

We should've bargained over wages earlier, before October, so the drop to $43,000 wouldn't have been so controversial. Workers weren't ready because there wasn't a unified strategy across campuses.

Now that we have experienced bargaining, I would explain it super succinctly: Bargaining is just negotiation over your rate of exploitation—you can win and be exploited less, or lose and be exploited more. It's not revolutionary; it's a compromise the state gives us to reduce labor militancy. It's a tool to lessen exploitation, but it's not the only way unions make progress. We can win industry-standard protections and reforms, but bargaining isn't the end goal.

And how does bargaining work? Oh, man, that's a tough question! In our case, we elected workers to represent us at the bargaining table to negotiate against *highly paid* and *highly trained* lawyers whose fundamental job is to maintain a high rate of exploitation. We had sessions every other week all over the summer. We bargained all summer, but didn't end up making progress on economics until the strike started.

I don't think it's my place to criticize the people on the bargaining team. It was hard, time-consuming work. I didn't do it. I don't know if I could do it. I commend people on all sides for their dedication, for sticking it through, because they not only fought a boss like UC—a public institution that functions as private—they also had to be responsible to thousands of workers. That's tough. People put off self-care, lost a lot of progress in their own degrees. They made sacrifices.

From what I remember, the bargaining reps—two for Local 2865 and two for Student Researchers United—had different and simultaneous communication channels that developed in time. They held debriefs at every picket line to explain the decisions that they made at the table. There were also online chats that changed through time, there were one-on-one conversations, and toward the end of the strike we had town halls, which were a really good way of gathering the sentiment of the majority.

In the picket debriefs some people would get into the back and forth about contentious bargaining issues. There were two narratives about what happened on those debriefs. One side would say everybody was mad and *unanimously* against the decisions of the bargaining team; the other side would say that it was three or four people who dominated the conversation and a handful of people would agree with them, but most people were just awkwardly standing there because they lacked information or history to fully understand what was happening.

The open forum chats were also not the best way of communicating because they were dominated by the same four or five people who were being hostile and not believing in the goodwill of the bargaining team. And also because being online makes it difficult to know all the people who are participating and that adds up to the mistrustful environment. Eventually those chats transitioned to a Signal chat where only the bargaining team reps could post clear updates, and people liked that because the majority of workers just wanted updates.

I expected division in our union, but I wasn't sure how it would play out. There was already division in the bargaining team before the strike, which showed up in strategy and rhetoric. While the process was rocky, ratification helped regain some unity, and in a way, the division made us stronger—political debate is healthy. What surprised me was a small group being hostile, both online and in person, with unprincipled behavior like recording and posting to sow discord. Unfortunately, that gets noticed more than the majority's sentiment. Striking, bargaining, and building a union are all hard, so division isn't abnormal—it's part of the struggle.

In my department, debates mostly happened in group chats and on Twitter, though I only heard about the tweets secondhand. We had an eighty-person department chat and a three-hundred-person picket chat, but both were dominated by the loudest voices, which didn't reflect everyone's views. That's why one-on-one conversations are so important—they give a clearer sense of how people really feel.

In online spaces, I tried to present both sides of debates, like the COLA discussion. I agreed that dropping COLA language made sense at our negotiation stage but also pointed out that housing costs had risen 60 percent in some areas. This highlighted the challenge of organizing across different campuses with varying political economies.

Interestingly, while online chats were contentious, one-on-one conversations were much easier. Group discussions, especially on Zoom or in person, were hard to manage because the most upset voices dominated. This was especially true in my picket line, but other lines had better group discussions where people understood or were more open to listening about bargaining strategy.

I remember one mediated conversation in particular. It was pretty bad. Someone from one of these anonymous Twitter accounts that were built on dissent—and that's fine—*recorded a conversation* with two of our bargaining team members without their consent! People were yelling at them because some of the answers they gave weren't ideal answers, but you should know it's hard to stand in front of hundreds of your coworkers to explain decisions you make at a bargaining table, and you are bargaining for the first time. Their answers could have been worded better, but people recording and posting them online was unprincipled and pretty bad because anybody can see that—the boss, the media, the right wing, they all can see the internal dispute. And if you take that one snippet of what's happening on this one picket line at this one campus, you might think that our union was falling apart. But that was not the case, we were strong; we had incredible direct actions after that to prove it. I just think that broadcasting ourselves in the process of figuring things out should be part of a strategy and not a decision of just some workers.

After we went down from $54,000 to $43,000, around the end of the third week—I remember the postdocs had settled their tentative agreement—the university presented an offer. I don't even remember what the offer was, and we didn't agree to it, but there were bargaining caucuses—I never went to any of the caucuses—where five hundred people or a thousand people would show up, which is a lot of people, especially if all those people are angry. We have thirty-six thousand people that we are representing in Local 2865, and if the people who are the most upset are the people showing up, and if it's all of those people, and those are the people who are drawn to go to the bargaining caucuses, then it's not a representative sample, it's a self-selecting sample. And that's hard to navigate because, as I keep saying, it was substantial, significant disagreement and dissent. I want this to be clear: I think most of the disagreement and dissent was substantial and significant.

The first time I saw division happen was during a Zoom meeting while I was in Cape Verde for research. The meeting was about explaining the protections of an unfair labor practice strike and debating what motivates people long-term. While the debate on fighting service unionism and engaging workers was important, active organizers started clashing over strategic differences. These disagreements, especially on what a militant strike should be, are vital to discuss. I personally want militant strikes that push for housing protections, but I believe we need a broad, strong union to achieve that.

Another disagreement was over "permissible and mandatory subjects of bargaining." At first, I thought housing was the most important issue, and we should bargain for it, but the university refused. Forcing their hand requires a massive, organized worker movement, even for mandatory subjects, let alone optional ones. Some didn't see the distinction between mandatory and permissible subjects as relevant.

Retaliation

Aarthi Sekar

The most common form of retaliation I was hearing about during the strike was this: principal investigators would threaten to give grad students a failing grade in required academic courses if they continued to withhold their research labor. In addition, departments were sending out emails saying, "If first-years continue being on strike, then we don't know whether funding will be available." There were also threats about position security or funding security for workers on strike. To sum up, departments were sending very vague emails implying that the workers would lose their job security.

We did our first march on the bosses on week three, especially in the departments of engineering and biological sciences that had sent out an email about the course number 299 research credits, which really scared the first-year students. And so we had a whole march on the bosses of workers who were on strike from the departments of genetics, plant biology, and neurosciences to deliver cease and desist letters saying that what these departments had done was an unfair labor practice. At this point the university had already racked up more than thirty unfair labor practice charges.

For a march on the boss, you would have a high number of workers who decided to take collective action to confront their boss about the inappropriate and/or illegal behavior violating the rights of workers. Our march on the bosses looked like this: graduate workers of all the departments that got these emails got together, they had their signs, they printed out the cease and desist letters, they went up to the administrators' offices and delivered the cease and desist letter to the dean. The dean of biological sciences, for example, got his letter taped to his door and read out loud in front of his office. These actions happened all over campus, and they were really important for all workers to see that when we come together in large numbers and take action, admin listens to us because they have to. It was showing power in numbers that countered the fear and disengagement UC was trying to provoke.

Emily Weintraut

We faced different kinds of retaliations in the lead-up to and during the strike. Generally speaking, people were afraid of their principal investigators and that fear stopped people from striking or led them to go partial striking.

By the end of the strike, the biggest form of retaliation was professors failing people in the 299 and 298 courses, because if people were to fail those credits, they'd be put on academic probation. Some principal investigators and some departments sent letters saying people would fail those courses if they didn't fulfill their "student" job for the quarter. The trouble is, both courses are affiliated with our work as student researchers. So, it is illegal for the UC to fail us for those credits because they're tied to our labor and we have the legal right to withhold our labor. Failing people in one course is retaliation. Tying our academic progress to our labor makes it easy to retaliate and conceal retaliation. That retaliation strategy is also kind of cynical and funny because the 299 and 298 courses are pass/fail, and the people who were failed did more than 50 percent of their work because the strike didn't happen until the back end of the quarter, so they should have passed. That proves that people were failed because their principal investigators wanted to retaliate against them for withholding their labor.

As a union, as soon as we knew about the failing threats, we fought back—we filed an unfair labor practice complaint against the letters sent by principal investigators and departments, and we also delivered them, along with a cease and desist letter. We also did marches on the boss and a big information campaign.

Although I didn't participate in all the marches on the boss because being on the picket line was my main task, I knew about all of them. We called them satellite pickets and we held them whenever we delivered the cease and desist letters. Also, we would march to specific areas on specific days to give speeches so that people inside specific buildings would hear us. We liked to march where buildings are very close together because the echo sounded amazing. The echo from those marches is pretty clear in my memory.

Maddy Duong

Then numbers began to dwindle and people were feeling tired. People were starting to feel afraid. I remember one picket shift where people were talking about the retaliation letters that they were receiving and being worried about their relationship with their principal investigators and stuff like that. But the relationship between the workers was always good for the people that remained at the picket. People were feeling really distraught, but the environment wasn't ever negative. I think some people were feeling really anxious about their relationship with their principal investigators, but they only ever shared it to be like, "Oh, you know, I'm dealing with that too, but we're here together."

Along the strike, we held actions against the principal investigators who were retaliatory against workers on strike. These direct actions against retaliatory professors were empowering for the workers who worked for those professors. That's what I noticed. And I think other people would identify with that like, "Oh, wow! I'm also dealing with the same thing, but they're still out here, so we're all in this together."

Kien Le

I also heard that at the picket in front of the biomedical science building or whatever, the students were singing and dancing some random song, totally stupid. And the professor called the cops on them, and ten policemen showed up. It was so absurd having a professor call the cops on strikers. Why would you do that to your students?

Kenzo Esquivel

Basically, throughout the strike, in my department there were no reported cases of retaliation. I think that our faculty may not have been super supportive or actively supportive, but they were not retaliatory. And in departments where the climate was more antagonistic, there were not—from what I can recall—a huge number of retaliatory behaviors reported in the first week. We started seeing that behavior from week three and on.

My department was slightly insulated from retaliation. At some point, we were trying to figure out cross-departmental swaps with departments facing harsher retaliation because the organizers in those departments were experiencing a growing sense of fatigue and exhaustion. But this exhaustion never resulted in a broader change of strategy to put public pressure on the principal investigators who were retaliating against workers, like what UC San Diego was doing, where certain Twitter accounts were naming specific principal investigators for intimidating workers, and they got hundreds of retweets. I thought that was an interesting strategy because a march on the boss feels pretty localized. The public pressure against principal investigators we had in UC Berkeley happened in fits and spurts in certain places, but never as a coordinated strategy. At the same time, it felt like we didn't have an organized structure to figure out who were the people scabbing so we could have one-on-one conversations, difficult conversations as they might be, to maintain their involvement in the strike.

My perception of retaliation was informed by what I heard from people in other departments. It sounded like principal investigators were starting to directly pressure people to come back into research activity. One particular thing I heard about was principal investigators offering postdocs who had ratified their contract to take over the research of the graduate students, which would compromise the ownership or the ability of grads to use that research for their own dissertation. So, principal investigators were threatening grads with removing them from their projects. Later, I started hearing about principal investigators threatening to fail grads for research credits. But none of these retaliatory practices were happening in my own department.

I wasn't aware of many marches on the bosses, but hopefully they were happening. As I was mentioning earlier, I think that moving forward, it's critical for us to have a plan about what to do when retaliation happens because I heard more about retaliation and less about how to fight back against it.

Strikadian Rhythms

Emily Weintraut

I planned for the strike initially. I bought microwavable breakfast burritos in bulk. I would have my two thermoses, one to keep my tea warm for the full day, and one for the morning. I also went grocery shopping so that I could bring sandwiches for myself every day on the picket line. I'm not good at making myself lunch, but I had to really do that. When it came to dinner, most days I got takeout or ate out, just because with all the organizing, I didn't have time to cook. And then I had to spend more money because I was so burnt out that I couldn't go to the grocery store after a week or so on strike. I spent a lot of money.

I didn't have time to do my laundry, but that was okay because it was so cold that I would not really care about what I was wearing underneath my coat. I would also wear my UAW hat every single day, so I had to wash my hair less. I would have the same boots just because we were in a field. I didn't have a personal life when I was on strike. It was strike and organizing all day. When I'd get home, maybe I'd talk to my mom, try to distract myself on TikTok, and that was it.

As the strike continued beyond week one, people were realizing that getting a good contract wasn't going to be fast. People in my department were saying things like, "I can't believe the UC is so okay with how horribly the education is going right now with us on strike. How are they not rushing to the negotiations table?" So, it was demoralizing to see the absolute greed by the university. And that was something that we hadn't experienced. And, yes, as a union we were preparing for a strike; but as an individual, I really did not see it taking that much time. And it was a very big shock to me.

From week one and on, I arrived late to set up for the picket line every single day. I'm not a morning person. I would try to be there on time every single day, but we would start the set up at 7 a.m., and I was exhausted. Especially during the first parts of the strike, I would be organizing, phone banking, and doing strike pay and access needs accommodations, and once I got back home, either I was in meetings or figuring out logistics, so I'd be working until midnight. That's why having to be somewhere at 7 a.m. was almost impossible, I was *fucking exhausted*! I was working sixteen hours a day on strike!

Maddy Duong

During the strike, my everyday life was difficult. I was barely home. I was home less than when I was working full-time. Picketing itself is pretty hard! It is really energy depleting. With "picketing" I mean being at the picket or whatever that entailed, like rallies, actions, marches, et cetera. And by the third week I was pulling extra time on weekends to debrief and organize. Striking is, by far, way more work than just going to work because it's not just all day that you're picketing. You're also going to the debriefs after the picket, you're going on the weekend to talk about the bigger action for the next week, you're doing phone banking. So, how did I do it? I was eating strike pizza, strike donuts. I'm somebody that cooks pretty often and I was not doing any cooking at all. My self-care definitely was not a priority during that time. But I managed it; it was fine. You can wear the same shirt pretty much every day [*laughs*], nobody really cares, everybody else was doing it [*laughs*]. The days when it was hard, I was like, "This is so hard, I would give anything to just chill and not think about the strike." But also, I think I was so in it because I really believed in what we were doing. I never thought of just stopping. I had to see it through, but there were definitely moments where I was missing normal life.

Me myself, I never had second thoughts about the strike. I was pretty committed to it. I remember that on Thanksgiving I went home to see my mom, and I was only talking about unions and striking—I must have been really annoying. That's when I realized that I really hated the day-to-day of my job [*laughs*] because once I was on strike I felt like, "Well, I'm pretty tired, but I actually love going to our strike every day," I felt like we were doing something, and like we were doing something important, like actively inflicting change.

Kenzo Esquivel

We were all pretty tired. I was definitely not working out; that dropped off for sure. I live with my partner—who is not a grad worker—so beforehand they asked me, "What do you need from me? I'll make dinners; I'll get all the things you need." Having their support was critical, honestly. They did all the grocery shopping and made little snack bags for me. I had additional external support in maintaining some semblance of balance and health. But even so, the strike was pretty mentally consuming. There was always something to be thinking about or something to be doing, like texting or following up with someone. It was a lot. And at a certain point I drew a bit of a boundary with how much I was able to sustainably do.

And there was a group of folks who, after our debrief meetings, would go back to the office and fix signs and whatnot. But at a certain point, I was like, "I can't be doing that too."

Aarthi Sekar

Week one was the big kickoff week, a lot of energy. Week two was Thanksgiving, so a lot of people left for break. But also, week two was when bargaining started getting more intense. And what I mean by intense is we—as the bargaining team—were really trying to push forward the contract negotiations by amending our proposals, and one of the more contentious things that we amended was the wages proposal.

Then, I would say that week three was a tough week, coming back from Thanksgiving, but we had a really good group of leaders and we were actively trying to push negotiations forward. This was also the week that we did make an amendment reducing our original wage proposal from $54,000 to $43,000.

We definitely lost many strikers by week three and definitely into week four. By week five there were not very many people at all.

Overall, by the third week we had less of a presence in terms of the amount of people that were on the picket line, but the people who were there were the ones who were really committed to doing everything for the picket line. And there were people who came every single day since week one. But we did lose a lot of people over Thanksgiving break. A lot of the people we lost were especially researchers who felt the pressure of going back in and doing research because their principal investigator or their department were pressuring them.

One of the groups of leaders that had really solidified and become an incredibly well-oiled machine that was very in sync with each other by the third week was a group that called themselves "Cunties," in a very affirming way. The Cunties were key and responsible for making sure that the picket line operated on a daily basis. These were leaders at Davis that got up at seven in the morning, unloaded the U-Haul, set up the strike table, set up all the materials, got a group of yellow-vested folks together to lead the marches, and coordinated the entire day's picket.

When we amended our wage proposal, by and large, many, many people were incredibly supportive because it meant that we were actually moving negotiations forward. But there was a group that was really pushing back, and calling out the bargaining team members, saying that we were conceding and we weren't holding our ground and that the strike could keep going indefinitely.

However, people were expressing that they were getting tired; that was the reality on the ground. I spoke with several leaders and when I asked them how they were doing at week three, they broke down in tears. And these were leaders who—like I mentioned before—were there from 7 a.m. to 10 p.m. or 11 p.m., or who went home and continued organizing well into the night. Those people were getting really exhausted. For example, there were leaders out of the plant biology graduate group who were so committed to getting the picket line organized and bringing their coworkers out to the picket line, but some of them were breaking. I remember one leader who was having a really hard time because she genuinely missed her work as researcher, but she was on strike because she believed in what we were fighting for. But by week three, without a lot of movement from the UC on the wages side, she was expressing what a hard time she was having. And I understood that because being on strike is a huge sacrifice and, also, it's exhausting. It's emotionally and mentally draining and people were sharing that with me on the picket line. And that was really, really big week three.

Week three, I noticed that the state of emotional vulnerability of those out on the picket line really increased. Being on strike is *not a vacation*. Being on strike is *very hard work*. It's a huge sacrifice. My coworkers were explicitly stating that they couldn't keep it up for too much longer. They missed doing what they love, which is research or teaching. Exhaustion was definitely setting in around midweek three. They were also worried about the relationship with their principal investigators and whoever they work with. Over the course of the strike, I had talked to hundreds of people and I can definitely say that after midweek three, people were really wanting to see the end of this strike.

Along the six weeks of the strike I didn't know what day of the week it was or what date it was. I mean, I knew only because I had to know for bargaining. So when I was heading to bargaining, I was realizing what day it was in the context of the strike. But my emotional self, not my intellectual self, didn't know. You know, the moment that you get up in the morning and you think is this Monday or Sunday, there is a difference in how you feel, but for me that was not there. My body felt the same. Every morning, I thought, "I'm exhausted, but I'm up and I'm going to go because I have to go and I have to get myself out of bed and I have to do whatever needs to be done." And it didn't matter if it was Sunday or Thursday or whatever, it was all the same. Every day felt the same in that I was getting up to fight for survival. It was survival mode. Time was unreal. It was all blurred together. The strike—all six weeks—was an amorphous cloud of time that was happening. One day blended into another, which blended into another. That's why it is so hard for me to think of the strike in sections. I always have to go from start to finish.

Also, there was no self-care. I barely was able to wash my clothes and I didn't have time to cook. The reason I was even able to wash my clothes was because I only wore three sets of clothing for the entire strike, so it was really easy for me to wash my clothes because I would wear one set of clothes and I would throw the other two in the washer and dryer, and then they would just sit in a pile in my room and I would just rotate the three sets of clothing I had. I did not cook. My house was disgusting. I mean, I didn't even really have dishes in the sink because I wasn't eating at home, but I didn't clean my bathroom, didn't wash the floors. I came home and I slept. I took my clothes off and I crawled into bed. If I brushed my teeth, it was a bonus. That was how I lived. I took a shower in the morning. I put on one of my sets of clothes and then I called it a day. I ate out all the time—the cheapest food that could be bought—because that's all I could do. But then again, this is where the community stepped in because everybody was so kind about buying each other food. I'm eternally grateful for all of my friends who supported me and kept me fed.

All the Davis bargaining team and many other leaders were experiencing the same. I don't know if it was the same across campuses. I remember in an action in Sacramento—this is so funny—somebody said, "Oh, the Berkeley bargaining team members look really sharp!" because they looked clean and were wearing ironed clothes. And it was implied that the Davis bargaining team did not look really good. We all looked awful! All of the bargaining team of Davis looked unshowered, disheveled, not sleeping, barely eating. I mean, Marshall—one of the bargaining team members—lost fifteen pounds. It was a lot.

Dez Manuel Fonseca

How did time feel during the strike? Oh, man! Every day went by *super quickly*. But time did not because the weeks went by too slowly. It felt like I was there for longer than I was. I was on the picket line for about thirty days because I went back home on December 14, the day of the Regents Romp, which also was finals week. I had bought my plane tickets early in advance so they're cheaper because, again, we make too little and that's one of the reasons we were on strike. So, I ended up going before ratification. But anyway, I feel those thirty days were a long—and I mean long—thirty days. But also every day went by really fast. I don't know what phenomenon that was.

During those thirty days, I did nothing but strike every day. My roommate *knows*. I probably slept four to six hours a day, but sometimes I didn't sleep at all, or I was half conscious throughout the night worrying or planning or stressing. I was waking up at as early as 2:30 in the morning to go out and to get coffee and donuts with a core group of five to ten workers, making sure that those early morning actions went well. I ate maybe one meal a day and then just lived off of clementines and donuts and granola bars and cough drops. I stopped exercising completely. I lost probably ten, fifteen pounds. My throat was killing me the first week. I stopped chanting after the first week because I couldn't do it anymore. It was really, really intense.

I know some of my coworkers had experiences similar to mine. I was not alone in that. It also definitely was not the most common experience—it's one I shared with a small, dedicated group. I'd say at UCLA, rough ballpark, fifty to one hundred people experienced something similar. Most people were not doing that. It was a core group of organizers who sacrificed sleep and food. And that's not to say that everybody else wasn't tired: everybody was tired, everybody. Especially once the picket moved to organizing remotely during the last week. We were making fliers, everybody had work to do, but there was a certain level of dedication and time commitment that a core group of organizers definitely felt, and I'm really grateful for them.

Some people took breaks, some didn't. A friend of mine didn't sleep in his own house throughout the strike, he slept at somebody else's house because it was walking distance from campus. I had to bum rides from people because I don't have a car. I'm very grateful for people that would leave or pick me up in the morning. I'm very grateful for all those people that did early morning carpools and also stayed late to clean up the signs and store the supplies, do the debrief, and the debrief after the debrief. On our campus, twenty people were doing *all those things*, but other people did their part.

CHAPTER 6

The Second Wind

Striking workers block an intersection at UC Irvine

Escalation and Direct Action

Emily Weintraut

Once we passed the hype of being on strike, the actions that brought us together and filled us with excitement were escalatory actions and love-based events. Besides Queer Day, other actions that prompted unity were the few days before Thanksgiving, when we had a lot of events that were about sharing with each other. And once we began escalation, there are three events that stand out to me: the Mrak Hall occupation, the protest outside Gary May's mansion, and the Sacramento rally. Actually, every escalatory action united us and refocused our attention on who is the enemy here—it is UC, not a particular bargaining team member, nor the person who doesn't want to participate in anarchist actions.

One of the first escalatory actions we did was protesting outside the mansion of Chancellor Gary May. It was on Wednesday afternoon of week three, November 30. After being on our regular picket line, we marched through a route carefully planned to get more attention from the general public, but when we were marching over, Gary May left his house, and we were obviously hoping to find him and confront him. So, when he left, the vibe changed, but it was also invigorating, we even had a chant, "Fe fi fo fum, Gary May here we come." That was really fun and uniting. When we got to his street, first we marched around his neighborhood and some of us talked to his neighbors; they were very supportive of us. We stayed outside his house for a while; people were having a good time playing kickball, listening to music, dancing, chalking the roads. We were all having a very good time being in the mini park across from Gary May's mansion. Getting people to leave so that we could pack up everything was hard—and we needed to pack because the action was in the afternoon and it was getting dark. We were like, "Guys, we need to leave. We need to put stuff in the U-Haul. We got to go." That's how fun and reinvigorating it was.

The next escalatory action was when we got inside the administration building for UC Davis, Mrak Hall. On December 2 we wanted to go into Mrak Hall right when the picket line started. The international UAW staff member that worked with us, Carla, had specifically done a business-casual cosplay [*laughs*]. She called it her "admin cosplay" to sneak in because Mrak was locked up since day one of the strike. And she did in fact get in, and hid in the bathroom and waited for us. Meanwhile, we split into groups and walked separately, trying to be incognito. We planned out taking different routes to get in. However, as Carla was holding the door for us, she got kicked out by an officer. But that was not the end because Paul and Ximena—both of them were bargaining team members—went up to the doors, one of them forced their way in, and we all got in. We stormed in! It was great! And the cops bodychecked a couple of people and literally tried to throw them out. They got very physical with some people.

While we were in Mrak Hall, the people who were upset about bargaining tried to tell everyone why the bargaining team was acting wrong. They were also giving incorrect information, saying that, for example, asking the state to declare an impasse isn't bad. Impasse is an optional phase of California public sector bargaining where the state declares the parties have reached an impasse and appoints a fact finder and a mediator to negotiate a contract. One thing that scared us about an impasse is that when you got to a third-party arbitrator, they will typically make a settlement based on precedent. And the precedent for our union in the past was that we would get 3 to 6 percent raises yearly, maybe a 9 percent raise max. This is just one of many examples of the complexities of bargaining that we were trying to work out on the fly every day.

The Mrak Hall action summarizes something that happened on other occasions. First we were united, and then particular groups of workers and undergrads showed up and took our action as a platform for their fights—they would set up a table and pass out fliers, trying to shift attention from the strike. That's how we would lose unity. For me, during the strike the focus needed to be on our fight as workers of the UC; there are so many struggles in the world, and as an individual, I agree with so many things that these groups brought up, but we were there to fight against UC.

The night of December 2, just after our Mrak action, UC made a new offer on wages, which the bargaining team discussed on every campus for a week or so. And while we were discussing that offer, we escalated, we did some direct actions and civil disobedience. The first of those actions, for us in Davis, was the rally in Sacramento on Monday, December 5. During the march, I was in the truck that had the sound system leading chants along with Aarthi. We marched around downtown Sacramento; it was amazing because we had a fluid picket line, which for me means we were able to march and change the route of our march, just like we did when we decided to go to the University of California Office of the President [UCOP].

We were supposed to have a lot of state legislators speaking on the steps of the capitol to show their support for our strike. But we ended up having to nix the speakers for the most part because a group of our coworkers had gotten into UCOP in Sacramento, and we had to quickly march over to show them our support. That shift in plans was interesting because we showed these legislators that we were doing a lot, and we also showed UCOP that we were willing to come to the capitol and hold them directly accountable and pressure them. We surrounded the UCOP building, blocked the streets, and got tons of support from community members.

Dez Manuel Fonseca

UC's offer on December 2 was the first offer that some of us workers took seriously. If you tell me that offer was presented at 1 a.m., I believe you. I wasn't tapped into bargaining because I had to wake up at three in the morning every day to go to a delivery or construction-site picket. So, I got updates about bargaining, but it wasn't my main focus. I was strategically focused on building the strike and building disruption.

There was a debate over whether the bargaining team should tentatively agree to this offer or not. At that time, I was uncertain about what to do, if we should tentatively agree to it, if I would vote yes or no. And the offer itself—in the context of what it means to negotiate with an employer in 2022—was a strong one. If you were to take that contract and the percentages of wage increases and match it up to other contracts that unions and workers negotiated, the offer from December 2 was a strong one. And that shows the power that we had. And also, the fact that we were so hesitant and didn't want to tentatively agree to it, the fact that we didn't think our membership would ratify it, highlights how strong our power was at that moment. So even back to December 2, I was thinking about ratification. Thinking about a tentative agreement.

And the decision about the December 2 offer was twofold: the bargaining team wouldn't tentatively agree, but we would escalate because what we had been doing wasn't getting the results we wanted. And that's not to say that the offers didn't get better, but we weren't getting what we wanted to settle for. So we decided to channel our power through direct actions.

And just like some events of the strike led to disagreement and dissent, others prompted unity. Escalation and direct actions brought many of us together. The Luskin Center occupation at UCLA was absolutely huge! I wish we would have stayed longer; we should have stayed overnight, indefinitely, but it was the difficulties of organizing such a thing. Next time—let me say this to the mic so it records clearly—*next time we'll do an indefinite occupation*! That way the UC won't stall as much. I think in a lot of the direct actions, not to say that the divisions went away, but people were able to work together toward common cause.

People got really excited about showing up to one of the regents' houses early in the morning, a wake-up call to the decision-makers, to the people who can put their pressure on the UC to get these annoying kids, these annoying workers, out of their front yard. That was a concrete action that we thought could feed back onto the bargaining table and get UC to bargain seriously with us. Those direct actions are real sources of unity and coming together where people who had been disagreeing with each other were kicking it with each other in the hotel we took over. It provided a breath of fresh air. The next huge direct action was the Regents Romp outside of the Luskin on December 14 or 15, but I had already flown back home.

The point of escalation and the direct actions—to say it succinctly—was to put pressure on the key decision-makers. The Luskin Center, which is a hotel and a convention center, is a primary source of profit for the university. I'm sure they bring in thousands of dollars a day in revenue. Our occupation had the objective of disrupting the revenue streams and putting pressure on the administrators to show them that we're not going away. It wasn't enough to chant "one day longer, one day stronger, we'll be back." We had to constantly be a presence and bring out 100, 150, *hundreds* of people to a disruptive action where we're risking arrest, to show them we're really serious about this.

On the other hand, the direct actions came at a point where we had rejected the December 2 offer, which we seriously had considered tentatively agreeing to. And the rationale behind rejecting that offer was that "we'll reject this, but we have to escalate. We can't just keep doing the same thing because it hasn't been getting the results that we want to this point." We had a group of people who were really against a tentative agreement to the December 2 offer, and I'd tell them that we could reject it, but we had to go all in because the fear of an impasse was also something to consider. The postdocs had been bargaining for a year. We had been bargaining for six months, and—if you ask me—we were essentially at an impasse because of all the stalling. We weren't coming closer to an agreement. Before we began the direct actions, I was saying, "We've got to be really annoying. We got to look like insane people who just won't leave these regents alone. We have to make them beg us to stop. And the only way they can stop us is by bringing us a fair contract that we can put to a vote for our members."

When we started the direct actions, I helped organize a few. Some people were scoping out neighborhoods, others were printing those big hilarious, "fatheads" signs with the regents' pictures on them, you know, the funny large cardboard face signs used in parties and protests. People were thinking about how we were going to get inside, figuring out the physical layout of a neighborhood, or the chancellor's office, or their mansion. I was doing a lot of outreach membership turnout. My role for a lot of the direct actions was getting people involved, spreading the word, but doing so in a clandestine manner—which looking back is a funny thing—trying to make sure that the university didn't figure out that we were planning these direct actions and try to circumvent them. Some people were police liaisons. I sometimes functioned like a coordinator, making sure that all the different parts of this plan were connected and keeping track of what people were doing.

One of the first direct actions that I remember was a demonstration in front of a regent's house at five in the morning. I was on the megaphone from five to eight in the morning, chanting outside this man's house.

Later we occupied the Luskin Center. There, we had three different entrances where we sneaked people to prepare the occupation, and I was in charge of sneaking people through the back door. The front two entrances were kind of the main ones to get a mass of workers inside at once, and the back door was for smaller groups of fifty or twenty people. I was on the walkie-talkie with people outside telling them if there was a guard nearby. And the guards were committing crimes, barring us from the doors. They were assaulting people! I almost got assaulted by a guard. I was just opening a door, he said "You can't open the door." I said, "What are the doors for then if I can't open them?"

Kien Le

When we rejected the December 2 offer and started really escalating, I was in Vietnam already. And I had this crazy fear of missing out when I heard about all of the crazy shit that my coworkers had done during the last few weeks of the strike. They did the famous kayaktion. I helped planning that overseas. We went to the house of a megadonor and had a picket; we also had a picket in front of the Irvine Company, which is the largest landlord here in Orange County. Escalation works because we get public support, but also it brings more people in.

Maddy Duong

As we were ratifying the contract for postdocs and academic researchers, and the graduate students were still in the bargaining process, we all escalated actions, we disrupted more directly, and did some civil disobedience. It was week four. Those actions were awesome!

One of the direct actions we did was the kayaktion on December 8. I planned it! We went to the house of one major donor of UC and the Irvine Company, where we had a picket.[1] That day was amazing. Personally, I was so tired because I was in the same kayak as the person who was taking videos and pictures for the media, which meant I was the only person fucking kayaking [*laughs*], and the water was choppy that day. But anyways, it was an incredible and fun action.

The direct actions—escalation—were an easy way to get more numbers too! Because doing the repetitive picket line stuff was not really enticing to people. People stopped coming. But if we did some organizing around a certain action like shouting down a street on a particular day, then we would get a big turnout.

Elsie Jacobson

In the late weeks of the strike, we escalated our actions. Those escalations were risky in terms of law enforcement, which was very intentional! People were intentionally trying to get arrested. So, for me, it was hard to be heavily involved because I cannot risk that as an international postdoc. If I get arrested, I'll get deported [*laughs*]. And so, I was definitely involved in supporting all those more escalatory actions, but my task was to always maintain a strong picket to keep the pressure on the university.

Among the escalatory actions, the occupation of the Luskin building was obviously the canonical one; it was an amazing action. The Luskin Hotel and Conference Center is a very, very expensive building

1 The kayaktion took place on December 8, 2022. It consisted of twenty-one workers disrupting the home of Donald Bren, one of UC's major donors, located on a private island. The day prior, workers picketed the Irvine Company, owned by the same donor, as part of this disruption strategy.

that UCLA decided to build instead of paying academic workers fairly and treating us with the respect that we deserve. And so, as a protest, we decided to occupy the Luskin. This was our strategy: A team of workers from around campus, including many leaders from our picket, went down earlier in the day, and they were inside, hanging out in the lobby and waiting to let people in once the march arrived. This team was sneaking in sleeping bags all day because our aim was to stay the night. And while they were doing that, we had a big march in the afternoon. In the march, there were groups of people assigned to basically storm the building, and be let in by the people who were already inside. All this was completely secret! So, you only knew about the plan if you were involved in the plan, that way there was no chance for the UC to expect us; and they didn't expect us. This kind of secrecy was new for all of us, so we were making jokes in the morning, like, "Oh, are you on the inside or on the outside?" We didn't talk about this plan in any group chats, instead, we just said it was a march. It must have been such a weird experience for people who were staying in the hotel. Imagine being a visiting professor in that hotel! I didn't take part in the occupation, but I was right at the front of the march with the banners and—I get pretty excited just remembering this—just getting to the front and then seeing people storm inside, that was an amazing experience! The bike cops, the security guards were completely overwhelmed, unable to do anything—just running around. And people were still just going in the back of the hotel too. It was crazy.

Later in the strike, there was another action in the Luskin Center on December 14. So much happened that I almost forgot about it. Outside the building, Tom Morello from the band Rage Against the Machine was playing. And while they were playing, a group of workers occupied the inside and disrupted the regents meeting. This time, the strategy was to book rooms as guests and spend all morning inside. It was pretty awesome too!

Kenzo Esquivel

And yeah, I remember the pivot to civil disobedience stuff, and I remember it feeling rather abrupt. There was a point of strategic contention when the civil disobedience stuff started where, on one hand, I agreed that we needed to escalate and create more public pressure on the UC, but at the same time, I felt like suddenly the entire organization of our organizing committee pivoted toward organizing and plugging people into civil disobedience.

For me, we could create public spectacles, but we shouldn't put all of our eggs in that basket. So at this point I volunteered to run one of our organizing committee debriefs to pose the question of what was the role that civil disobedience would be playing, and I also tried to posit that we needed to not devote every ounce of our people power into civil disobedience because civil disobedience needed to be paired with a vision of how to continue to bring people into the movement and to be part of a broader organizing strategy to keep pressure up.

In my opinion, the core power of our strike comes from the withholding of our labor en masse, and it relies not only on mass participation, but also the withholding of our labor. And I think it also comes from the amount of social pressure that we're able to put on the university and its administration. To me, there are many different ways that our power can be flexed, but ultimately it comes down to people doing various tasks to apply pressure to the university, whether that's making them feel acute pain and not having us in the classroom, not having us at the lab bench, or tarnishing their reputation. For me personally, it still feels like an important point to be applying pressure and making the university feel the heat, and I think it's a less concrete and less primary part of flexing our power, but I do think that it is an articulation of our power. And, for me, that is contingent on having mass membership and mass involvement who are able to be doing all of these different things at once, because I also think that there's so many core elements of running and keeping that strike strong that needed to be happening.

Postdocs and Academic Researchers Ratify Their Contracts

Joyce Chan

Personally, the reason that definitely inclined me toward the vote yes side was—I mean, honestly it was because that's where the organizers who had been organizing for a very long time were. But more importantly, what was putting me off from the vote no side was the tactics they used. I was seeing my friends and the people I cared about getting hurt or intimidated by the people who were actively advocating for not ratifying the contract. I was also not a fan of all the misinformation or the shouting down that I was seeing on Twitter, which was coming from the vote no side. All of this made it difficult to take them seriously, even when their fears were legit and even when they have legitimately been through traumatizing experiences. I mean, that's not to say that we haven't either. But there's been, I think, more taking to social media about it as their form of organizing so that it gets amplified a lot more, especially on Twitter.

The night of December 9, when the ratification vote results were announced, I was back in San Diego from Taiwan—I had to go to Taiwan for a week or so because I had a family emergency, but I stayed engaged from afar. The results were announced in the evening. And the main thing on my mind that night was how to make sure that our contract ratification wasn't read as if we were breaking solidarity with the graduate students. In my mind, if anything, ratifying the contract for postdocs and academic researchers meant that we could focus more on helping graduate students get something that they want. So, when we got the contract ratified, I felt relieved! I thought, "Okay, that's two units down. Two more units to go."

Even though I went on strike being kind of naive, thinking we could get everything, I did not feel conflicted about ratifying the contract. But I guess the difference between me and many other people is that I was looped into the conversations about bargaining, and how informed you are helps you so much to navigate your decisions in this process.

I actually felt relieved when we got to ratify our contract. I mean, it wasn't an immediate raise to $70,000, it phased in over the life of the contract, but it was a sizable amount that would pull people up even higher in terms of being able to live more sustainably. And it'll only keep growing in the next bargaining period, especially with the steps. I was relieved because the strike was taking longer than I expected. As we were building up to the strike, we were seeing this as a one-week or two-week, not more than three-week sort of deal. So it took a lot of people by surprise how the UC didn't take the strike seriously—I for sure was surprised. They didn't take it as seriously as we felt they would! Which was very puzzling.

In general, I can't say the postdocs I interacted with were all satisfied with the wages we got, but at the same time, when we ratified, they were almost all ready to go for anything higher than the $54,000 baseline. To put it up front, this is a very sensitive topic because it concerns a broader systematic problem in academia: there is a very leaky pipeline to become a postdoc. So, some gains speak more to people who identify as disabled, but not many disabled people make it that far to become a postdoc. So, the demands related to disability were a very contentious topic for graduate students, but not so much for postdocs because for systemic reasons there are fewer postdocs who need accommodations. And for postdocs, because of their demographics, the parental benefits were more important.

Once the postdocs' contract was ratified, I stayed on the picket line until the picket lines got dissolved—around the beginning of week five. What I said and what I told people was that "I'm not leaving the picket line until graduate students get something that they like." And then as soon as that picket line disappeared, I was like, "Okay, the picket line is no longer here, it's time to put my efforts elsewhere." So, I was doing 25 percent of my work, just getting stuff up and running, and helping grads with walk-throughs and phone banking and whatever else was needed.

Maddy Duong

After ratification of the academic researcher and postdoc contracts, I did feel proud of the work that we had done. I also felt ownership. And yes, I felt good. I felt I had gained some new connections. And I felt pretty optimistic about organizing beyond the strike. I was like, "Oh, okay, unions are the place to be if you want to do some cool stuff for workers." So, when the ratification vote results were announced I was pretty happy. It was like 90 percent for postdocs. It was also really high, not as high, but pretty high for academic researchers. So, I felt happy. The numbers confirmed people can live and work under this contract.

Elsie Jacobson

Between the moment the offer for postdocs was tentatively agreed and ratification, we had a lot of discussions because we didn't win everything we asked for, and not everyone was happy with where we were. But honestly, a lot of it was just figuring out what the contract actually meant, and that took us a while! For starters, we focused on salary because it was a huge thing for a lot of people. In the new contract the starting salary goes up to $60,000 in April and then in October it goes up to $65,000. And some people were like, "We were asking for $70,000; that doesn't seem like a lot, it's really spread out." There was definitely some dissatisfaction. But when someone made the wages calculator—which incorporated not just the base pay for a first year starting, but what are you going to get paid over the next five years when you include both step increases and annual raises—people were like, "Oh shit! This is actually an amazing deal [*laughs*]."

The complexity of the contract was part of the discussions because there are so many aspects to it, and it has campus-specific things, like the transit stuff where the bargaining team had to be more vague and ambiguous because of the different public transit options at different campuses. For us, the more we talked about the contract, the more we learned and the happier we were. So by the time we were ratifying it, it was just easy. I mean, it was not easy in the sense that we didn't have to work really hard. We worked really hard to talk to as many postdocs as possible so that they would vote to ratify because we wanted a large majority to make that decision. But ultimately, at UCLA, we didn't find any postdocs that were serious about voting no. Overall, people seemed really happy with the contract.

There were two weeks to discuss the offer before ratification. We had two whole weeks, between November 28 when the tentative agreement was announced and December 9 when the vote closed, which is *quite a long time* once you realize it was all we were doing because we were on strike. On other occasions, when we had two weeks to do a thing—like the strike authorization vote of 2021—we were working full-time. So, having two weeks to do it was totally fine. For sure there were spaces where people were having conversations about voting no. The issue was that those spaces seemed to have a really strange understanding of what would happen after a no vote. I'm specifically referring to people who were on Twitter a lot. I found it very frustrating how people were tweeting things like, "This is a crap contract, you should vote against it." Or advocating for partial striking and saying, "We could stay on strike, but just like kind of keep doing research." It was frustrating. People who were advocating to vote no were saying things like, "We should stay on strike, but keep doing research, but withhold the data from your principal investigator." That *is not striking*! Or they were talking about things that didn't make sense like, "The strike will continue, but postdocs can do research because we'll just get pulled along by the teacher assistants and the fact that they're withholding grades and not teaching." And somehow—I don't understand how!—that strategy would get us a stronger contract. I had very long conversations with some postdocs at different campuses who told me that they thought there were leaders ready to join the strike.

I recall one conversation in particular where I said, "You know, just 15 percent of postdocs are on strike." And this person responded, "Well, what about all the 85 percent of postdocs? There must be some leaders in there that are ready to go." To me, it was like, "If there were leaders that were ready to go, they would have been on strike already!" This reasoning seemed a bit disconnected from the reality of the situation and from the organizing efforts, which is that we did the best we could and right now we should take these wins and move forward. This particular conversation happened with someone who I met on Twitter, but contacted by phone. I think Twitter is not a good place to have a conversation. So, I was just like, "Maybe we should talk about this on the phone." And we did, and it was a productive conversation.

The Twitter arguments were not just ignoring the twenty years of grad worker organizing history that led to this moment, but also the bargaining efforts of the postdoc bargaining team that—by that point—had been going on for a year and a half. It seemed to me like some people who were advocating for the vote no campaign had just got involved.

And just for the record, I'm not really a Twitter user, but in the second half of the strike, I became very active on Twitter because it seemed like the voices on Twitter were so overwhelmingly negative. So I felt it was really important to counteract their narrative and not necessarily to convince a specific person, but to show everyone on Twitter that there is an active debate and that there are two sides of it.

I also know that a few people who were loudly advocating for voting no had been attending conferences during the strike instead of striking fully. Meanwhile, we had been sacrificing absolutely everything! I didn't email my principal investigator once for four weeks and I didn't think about the X chromosome for four weeks. And then to have someone who went to a conference saying that *now* they are ready to go, is like, "Well, you kind of missed the time to do it, if this was so important, maybe you shouldn't have gone to that conference."

The hardest conversations I had in the lead-up to ratification were with people from other campuses. At my campus, UCLA, none, zero, of the conversations were like that. In fact, some of the people who had been a little hesitant about the contract initially, came out really strongly to vote yes when they saw that the no voters seemed to not have a strong plan and seemed to be advocating for things like partial striking.

At UCLA there was actually an academic researcher who I talked to who wanted to vote no. And I couldn't, I couldn't even finish the conversation with them because I was so angry and frustrated because they had been at a writing retreat, they had not contributed to the strike beyond not being in their lab. I know for a fact that they were not contributing one bit to any of it! They came to *half a meeting*, and they didn't contribute. And I called them on the phone during ratification and I was like, "I noticed you haven't voted on the ratification." And they were like, "I am thinking about voting no, maybe we can get better." And I was completely speechless. I actually handed the phone to someone else. It was just shocking to me because I had tried to get that person involved as well—I really tried to get more academic researchers organizing with us. And it felt like this person just didn't care at all until it was time to vote.

Another subject of discussion for postdocs and academic researchers was the fact that we had to ratify the contract before the student researchers. It was definitely a concern because none of us wanted to leave the grads behind. Like I said before, part of my motivation for getting involved in our union was the Student Researchers United campaign. And I actually think that if you had asked postdocs what was their reason to be on strike, we would have said, "It's for the grads." And academic researchers were like, "Well, I was just a postdoc and I really want something better for them." Really, there was a lot of cross-unit solidarity.

So, when we were talking to the bargaining team about the decision to ratify our contract before the grads, they told us that UC was using us as a stalling tactic. UC's labor relations officials were saying, "It's so hard to negotiate with four units at the same time." So they just kept negotiating with the postdocs every day and ignoring the grads. So it was really important to get us off the table so that all of our pressure could be on the university negotiating with the grads.

When we ratified, the grads at our picket were really, really happy that we got a contract. Again, in our picket at UCLA, it was all completely fine. But in the statewide conversation, there was a lot more discussion and frustration. That was actually when we got the first sort of negative press for the strike. We saw articles saying, "The postdocs abandoned the grad students," which is really upsetting because it's not at all what happened—it was part of the joint strategy that the bargaining teams of all units had agreed on. And actually, a part of the joint strategy was that there were contract articles that all units bargained on together and there were articles that were bargained on separately. When we—postdocs—ratified our contract, *every single one* of the joint articles had been finished and had been tentatively agreed. And what was remaining were the unit-specific things.

So, it was, like, really upsetting to me to see our ratification mischaracterized like we had abandoned the grads because all of the decisions were made in solidarity. And also, we stayed on the picket lines for an extra two weeks after ratification. Under normal conditions, if it was just us on strike, we probably would have gone back to work while ratifying like most UAW locals do, but we didn't, we stayed on strike because we wanted to support the grads because it was really important to us. And we always, a hundred percent, felt the same solidarity from the grads. It was not surprising that they were in solidarity with us. Some of these grad students are going to do postdocs soon.

I have asked myself if the no voters had a point that I should have listened to more. But, when it came to it, I honestly, at no point saw any real vision for how a no vote could end up with a positive outcome. And this is not because I did not listen, and it's not because I wasn't reading what they were writing. I was listening to them and I was reading them. I mean, it would have been great if it had been less partisan. It sucks that we ended up with two really strong groups. I would have loved had the debate gone differently, but it just didn't feel that was possible because a lot of it happened on online platforms, and it is really hard to convince anyone of anything when you're not in person. And so, in person, everyone around was yes. And then the no voters were mainly in the online spaces.

During ratification, I was pretty sure that the vote was going to go yes, but I didn't know by how much and that was exhausting! So, when the results were announced, I was so wiped out that I was home, but most people were at a restaurant. I was just sitting here on my sofa, by myself, watching and refreshing my computer every two seconds, impatient and desperate. I am reliving that impatient feeling as I'm remembering it; it left a strong imprint in my memory! So, when the results came out, I was so happy! I called a friend to chat about it for a while. The numbers were just wild, so many people voted, and it was 90 percent yes. And I was so happy that a vast majority of postdocs supported this contract and supported what we were doing. So, yeah, it was—I think I'm going to cry now.

CHAPTER 7

Contract Contention

Jacqueline Perez and other UCLA workers are arrested after a sit-in in the office of a UC regent

Introduction

Dez Manuel Fonseca

In the last weeks of the strike, the picket lines were definitely smaller. I mean, you throw the same party every day, people stop coming. The question was, how did that correlate to our power? It's really hard to signify what changed in comparison to the beginning because the people who were committed, *were committed*! You knew they were committed from the beginning, and were still committed at the end. Our problem was building a majority and a wide strike. And we didn't necessarily have a way to quantify that aside from the picket shift sign ins. I have a friend in engineering, and they were the only person in their lab on strike out of eleven people. And they are a great organizer, always talking to people, but none of their coworkers would strike. They didn't have a union culture, and since they were student researchers, they didn't have protections. Maybe they were scared, they didn't know much, they wanted to do their work. One of my friends was doing walk-throughs during the strike and he found mad principal investigators in labs, people being retaliated against, people who just didn't know. We realized that it was probable we didn't even have a majority strike by the end week four, or by week five.

But the people that were active continued to be active. People who weren't there, I don't even know who they were or what they were doing. I don't know if they were working, and they were not going to tell us. What we knew—thanks to the picket shift sign ins—is that the pickets were smaller. The rallies were still good, but definitely smaller. And negotiations had not gone to where we wanted them to go.

Who were the people who stopped striking? The discourse was that it was student research people who mainly work in labs. Student researchers have not only a different job title, but different work because it is very tied to their own academic progress. In contrast, my work as a teaching assistant has nothing to do with my degree progress. If anything, my assistant teaching gets in the way of my degree progress. Some people stopped assistant teaching, went on strike, and dedicated their time to their research. They wouldn't technically have been scabbing because legally they wouldn't be working. For me, I feel my own research is work, but I'm legally being paid to teach.

The bosses of the student researchers, their principal investigators, control their present job and their future job opportunities, and although they're not allowed to, they can fire them. It's *illegal*, but if they fire you, you'd have to go to court and fight for months to get some of your job back, and people are scared of that. And I'm not one of them, so I felt like I had to listen to the people on my campus who are organizing student researchers who said that people were not striking anymore, and that people were going back to work, or that certain groups of people never went on strike. Yes, I did some organizing, some walk-throughs in engineering two weeks before the strike, but I wasn't one of the lead organizers there, I was just trying to support them. This is about trust, and I trust that they knew their workplace better than I, and what they were saying shifted my analysis of our capacity to keep striking because you don't want to strike past your capacity to keep striking.

Mediation

Emily Weintraut

I think once we reached the mediation point, it was quickly suggested that we use a particular mediator—who had been a good mediator for a health care union—because the state wanted UC and us to make a deal and end the strike. I also am of the mind that the support from the legislature helped to get a successful mediation process. Prestrike, there was a letter from some California legislators to the UC saying that the UC should bargain with workers to set a precedent for other universities. A lot of legislators signed off on that letter. We also had resounding support from community members statewide.

One of the reasons why we knew we were powerful going into mediation was because the UC is a public institution and the biggest employer in the state of California. Having forty-eight thousand workers out on strike stopped a lot of stuff from happening at an institution that is supposed to be seen as a prestigious university. For example, the university started to hire external graders, but they were grading as pass/fail. Because of it, undergrads are going to have academic issues when they try to go to graduate school; a pass/fail course is seen as a negative in graduate school because they want to see your good grades. So, I think the perception of UC's prestige has gone down because they forced us to strike for so long.

Dez Manuel Fonseca

I think the ultimate effect of escalation showed in mediation. The press coverage we had in California was really supportive, basically it always said, "The university is being intransigent and the strikers' demands are reasonable. They need to be paid more." And *legislators saw it* and the *governor saw it*. And Darrell Steinberg, the mayor of Sacramento, was one of the most prolabor negotiators we were going to get. And for me, the fact that we were in the middle of escalation during mediation showed the mediator that we were serious, and that he needed to treat us seriously.

There were people who were upset that we even accepted a mediator, that we were celebrating that it was a friendly mediator. There were people who said it was a handout from the governor and we don't need the governor's pity appointments—but we were going to have to negotiate with somebody! Sure, theoretically, I'm down with a general strike, but it wasn't happening. We had been on strike for forty days, and there were no signs that a general strike was possible. The strike was not spreading to other sectors. We had to win with the tools that were at our disposal. We were in a situation where people were going back to work. Nonetheless, the fact that we were having mediation while escalating helped to recoup some of the people that were going back to work, and that kept that pressure and our visibility high. We were and looked militant. So the governor and the mediator realized they had to take us seriously where the university wasn't taking us seriously.

Kenzo Esquivel

I was hopeful about the mediation process [*laughs*]. I didn't know what to expect out of the process, but I knew that the mediator had successfully negotiated a contract for a group of mental health workers who were on a *very prolonged* strike, kind of similar to us. And I was hopeful that having an external party in the room would not only help UC behave, but also help the bargaining team get it together and overcome the interpersonal tensions and disagreements that had arisen. I was cautiously optimistic. At our picket line, I maintained an optimistic disposition about what we might achieve with mediation.

And I continued talking and having meetings to present my standpoint with our bargaining team members. I didn't ever feel checked out. If anything, after it became clear I had disagreeing opinions, I felt like I was being tapped in more than before about how to approach certain situations, or think through proposals, or how to amend processes. My hope was to facilitate a space for the elected leadership and the Rank and File coalition to exist together and have productive discussions. But that never quite coalesced—the skepticism and distrust ran too deep.

I was home in Chicago when ratification happened. I was pretty upset when I found out that we were putting the contract to a vote to ratify it. I was upset because my hope through the mediation process was like, "Okay, the university is finally moving. If we can just meet in the middle between where we are and what this offer is, if we can get one or two more passes back and forth, that's a contract that I feel I can support." And the fact that the mediation process in and of itself was becoming this "we have to take this or it's all gone," felt bad. It felt like it was artificially creating this really high-stakes moment that felt like we were just trying to push something through. It was frustrating.

Mediators, I guess, aren't supposed to take a side, but the fact that we were being cornered by him saying that he would walk away, and that the deal would also walk away, felt artificial. From my perspective, if the mediator walked away, we would be back to where we were before, which was a tense place but without this external person. Because, if mediation worked in our favor, great, but at the end of the day, the mediator has no power. We have the power.

I also think that it's not necessarily uncommon for mediators to threaten to walk away and they maybe won't walk away. They also have some stake in trying to keep all parties happy and to settle a deal. So, maybe he was being strategic, and perhaps he wouldn't have actually walked away.

My thought was, "We now know that this deal is possible. Yeah, the university can back down from it because we can't legally lock it, but we now know that the university has the resources to make this offer." Why let this external person in the room now lock us into that offer? Now we know the university can make this deal, and the way that we hold them to it or get something better is by continuing to build the power that we need through our strike.

But again, the speed with which these things were happening made it clear to me that our bargaining team was probably going to send this out for ratification. And that's what happened. There was a sense of urgency that we needed to wrap things up because we were going to lose strike power. We had divergent conceptions of what our strike power was in terms of people on the picket line or withholding of our labor or some combination thereof. There was a sense that we didn't have the same picket line pressure because people were going home or were already home for break. And for this reason, we needed to make good while we could because we no longer had that specific articulation of strike power. Whereas, for me, I was of the mind that the UC system was freaking out because we were getting so close to the grading deadline, and if we were to push them a little bit more, we could get something that people would be excited and happy about, and in a way that unified us. That's another thing I was thinking about, "Is this contract going to be one that further sows division or is it going to be one that we can come out feeling unified and proud about, and immediately off the bat start building toward a unified vision for how we do this better next time." That actually felt like the highest-stakes thing to me, not necessarily the specific language that we got, but whether we actually had a functional union at the end of it.

My ideal situation was to get one or two more offers passed back and forth after the mediator's "last offer" that we ended up ratifying, and we wrap it. I was of the mind that it was going to be an incredibly difficult position to be in if we were coming back to the new semester on strike. To say it plain and clear: it was pretty clear to me, even from my department, that sustaining the strike after the break would have been a step too far. But I also felt like as we were approaching the grading deadline, and I believed that the university wouldn't want to deal with even a minority strike, which would still be disruptive. Though it was never actually very clear what our numbers would have been, there were attempts to count how many grades would be left ungraded.

So, going back to ratification, before everyone dispersed for break, our departmental strike organizing team decided to actively engage with the vote no campaign if we needed to. We didn't necessarily think we were going to win the vote, but that it was important to hold true to what we had been saying and what we had been fighting for. And, again, being one of the bigger STEM departments, it felt extra significant. I think it felt important to me that we didn't let it slide and have a yes vote that didn't actually feel representative of what the actual temperature on campus was. And at Berkeley, the vote was overwhelmingly yes, which was what I anticipated.

Part of why it also felt important is that it comes back to what I believe are the basics of organizing, which are phone banking and having conversations with workers who have been less engaged, and get them thinking critically about what it meant for us to be on strike, and what they were fighting for, and to make their own decisions about it. But not to get a call or a text from our official union channels to be like, "Make sure to vote yes today," and have that be the only vantage point that they were exposed to. From my perspective, the campaign to vote yes on ratification was just promoting the yes vote, almost like pushing them; and in contrast, we were answering questions, outlining what voting yes or no would mean. And we did that by organizing phone banks outside of our official channels.

Democracy

Aarthi Sekar

Over the course of this strike we—the bargaining team members, staff organizers, and member leaders—were actively trying to work on creating more democracy every step of the way. It was everyone's first strike, and we were learning together—baby's first strike. I learned that it was important to create a space for conversations in a way that allowed every person to speak. Because in some spaces, some voices are naturally louder than others, and not everyone gets a say.

The spokes council method was effective in making sure everyone got the same amount of time and had a set of questions that they surveyed their coworkers on and got to share that with everyone else. It was also good for folks in other departments to hear how people were feeling. People in biochemistry and molecular biology were hearing how folks in anthropology were feeling and vice versa. Chemistry was hearing how plant biology was feeling, or how math was feeling. I also learned that it was important that meetings happened on a regular basis, and right after any discussion took place in bargaining or mediation. It was important that these meetings got called right away, and that as many people were informed, even though it's not a perfect strategy. Perfect is the enemy of the good.

Emily Weintraut

Our union always tries to be democratic. What makes things seem less democratic is that not all people participate. In our organizing meetings and in each one-on-one conversation, we emphasize that we're not just happy with increasing the union membership; we want people to be active union members who vote in elections *and* organize. We've had elections for union positions where we don't have an election because there's just one person running, and sometimes we have vacant seats. That's why it frustrates me when people say that our union is undemocratic. It would be more democratic if more people got involved and we had more elected positions filled. I do a lot of organizing. I would absolutely love for people to step up, take on more leadership, and take away responsibilities from me.

For me, democracy also means trying to represent all of us rather than just sharing my political beliefs and opinions to my turf. So even if I think our strategy should be *x* or *y*, if we as a union agree on something, I organize based on our collective agreements instead of spreading my beliefs. That's what I do when I have one-on-one conversations, and I think that's what most organizers do.

We had a union meeting every time we had bargaining. But those meetings are a very small group of people who are very involved in organizing or the bargaining process. A caucus on Zoom is a microcosm; it is not at all going to be representative of the majority because a lot of our union members are more passive or they're doing other stuff and they don't join the Zoom meetings. Like myself! I'm so into organizing, but I didn't go to caucuses prestrike because I trusted the bargaining team we elected, and I knew they would be checking in as much as possible.

During bargaining, I thought that people were unreasonably complaining about some things. For instance, the bargaining team members needed to meet together to figure out strategy, and doing it in front of a large group of people in caucus is not always the most effective method to accomplish that. I was of the mind that the bargaining team needed to have a plan to present at an open meeting with membership to discuss it. For me, the fact that they were democratically elected allowed them to do that. But there were people who complained about the "closed-doors meetings" that the bargaining team was having.

Realistically, I think our union locals are literally some of the most democratic and open locals in the country. Most unionized people do not have bargaining as open as we did with the Zoom-cast bargaining sessions and caucuses before and after. In mediation, the mediator would not allow us to Zoom-cast his conversations, but that was a condition of the mediation.

After the strike, what are we doing? We are doing membership drives to get people to be part of our union. The more people we get voting, the better. We got so many people to vote on the contract, we have historic participation numbers, and we want to continue to build power. We are also doing contract enforcement. I'm dealing with multiple abuse grievances and harassment grievances. In contrast, some of the more vocal people who voted against ratifying seem to have given up. From my point of view, if you care about our working conditions, you would continue organizing. It's frustrating because all I do is talk to people. And then, a lot of the people with dissenting opinions assume that they speak for the majority, but they don't talk to anyone outside their own departments. I talked to so many people all across campus. I've talked to people who complain about STEM workers not coming on the picket line, but who aren't sympathetic to how scared STEM workers are. Once, during the strike, the people who were against the Davis bargaining team stormed into a STEM building, and workers from that building are still getting retaliation because of that action. And it's that lack of empathy and understanding that leads to division.

We accomplished so much with the strike! And because we're getting this huge wage increase, we can get smaller percent increases in the future that will still amount to meaningful raises. I don't think we'll be able to get a 55 percent wage increase next time, but let's say, as an example, we ask for a 6 percent increase, that would be much bigger than 6 percent before our strike. We now have a huge foundation.

What actually worries me is that some people want to go back to how things were in our union around 2018. It worries me because things were not focused on member-to-member organizing. We are going to get a worse contract if we alienate people. What we need is to build power and do contract enforcement. So long as we continue to organize, we are going to get a fucking good contract next time.

Dez Manuel Fonseca

Toward the end of the strike, we started having town halls, which when they first got organized were very messy. But eventually they were seen as the best way to gather the sentiment of the majority of people who were on strike. And during the whole strike, the bargaining team reps were going around talking to people and being real-life people, and that was good because even if they'd have a conversation that engaged in a debate and some people didn't agree, they were elected to do a job and ultimately they can make the decisions on one level as a bargaining team. And if the workers didn't want to ratify those decisions, the mechanisms—ratification—were in place and they ended up working.

Rejecting the offer from December 2 was the correct decision our leadership made; moving forward to mediation was also the correct decision for me. We entered mediation on our own terms: knowing that we had public support and that we had state support, legislative support, and we still had an active membership committed to striking. So finally, we got the offer that ended up being tentatively agreed to and later ratified. It was a great offer.

Actually, let me recapitulate the facts. By the end of week five we—workers through the bargaining team—got a supposal, which is the verbal offer, out of mediation. And from what I understand, the bargaining team asked for a day or two to bring that supposal back to our workers and have town halls where we could gauge people's feelings about tentatively agreeing, counteroffering, or rejecting it. So before the vote on the tentative agreement, we had multiple town halls. From what I remember, the clear majority sentiment of all the UCLA workers was either tentatively agree to it and take it to ratification or make a counteroffer. And I personally—and other people I talked with—didn't think that a counteroffer made sense.

But in my department—remember, my department is history, so it's humanities—I couldn't gauge the majority feeling because only ten to twenty people showed up to our town hall! And my takeaway from that town hall was that we should tentatively agree. Some people, a handful of people loudly—or maybe passionately—opposed the tentative agreement and said that they were committed to keep striking and other people were more uncertain. But the vast majority of people didn't respond. And we also had a poll, but only seven people responded, three of them said "tentatively agree," two said "don't tentatively agree," and two said, "I don't know." But we are ninety people in my department, so these results don't actually matter. And later, when we had a campus-wide town hall with different department reps explaining their department's opinion on whether to tentatively agree or not, I reported, "Uncertain, not sure how the department feels about it."

At that point, the way we actually could get a sentiment on what people were feeling was to tentatively agree to the offer so people could vote on it, because we could always keep pushing about counteroffer, counteroffer, counteroffer until we get somewhere. But the point is you're going to reach an impasse; there's a point where you're going to be weaker in your strike power, and we see this historically. And sure enough, in my department it wasn't until the offer was tentatively agreed to that we found out that the majority sentiment was for ratification in a close but pretty clear majority. So, just because your strike becomes longer, doesn't mean it is stronger. Even though we did have the chant "one day longer, one day stronger," that's not necessarily the case.

So, going back to my recapitulation, we had the departmental and campus town halls and then, once we tentatively agreed to the offer, we moved on to ratification. It was then when I announced in a group chat that I was voting yes on ratification, offered my rationale, and encouraged my coworkers to ratify. I don't like interfacing with the group chats. I had to learn to interface with the group chats in these moments of intense and heated discussion. Then we were sending out individualized messages.

During ratification I also helped organizing and figuring out what the best political analysis of the situation was, which ended up being that ratification was clearly and undeniably the best path forward for our union in two ways: to secure and consolidate the gains that we won out of striking and out of mediation, but also to strengthen our union moving forward. This contract would allow for us to build a stronger union and stronger strike threats because it was the first time that we were going to have student researchers with a contract.

The big shock from the December 2 offer was the proposal for a two-and-a-half-year contract, which is part of the reason why I thought it was a really strong contract. It was an incredibly strong contract and it's two and a half years. When we went into mediation, I thought they would give us a four- or five-year contract so we would lose our institutional memory as a union. And student researchers and academic student employees were on the same timeline so it would enable us to merge student researchers into Local 2865 in a manner where we could bargain together again. We can continue to build capacity and membership, and build off of that institutional knowledge and all the challenges, the successes, and failures that we faced, and move forward and consolidate in two years.

The offer meant 55 to 80 percent wage increases over two and a half years. It's unprecedented; it was unheard of in the state of labor in 2022. I endorsed that. I said the reasons for endorsing it. I sent out some emails to my department along with other workers, and there were folks organizing against ratification. It became an internal political struggle.

I panicked during ratification. That's the first thing I did! But seriously, my biggest task during ratification was doing analysis. I was reading the offer, weighing pros and cons, and understanding people's concerns. What were people scared of regarding ratification? Why were people against ratification? What were the arguments for it?

I was having conversations and explaining our analysis. I used messages, emails—there were a lot of emails! I'm sure a lot of our coworkers were really annoyed with the amount of emails they were getting from us. Again, we were having one-on-one conversations, having phone calls with people. And in those phone calls, I wasn't trying to convince people. I was trying to tell people that "Hey, here's the reason I voted the way I voted. I just want to know your concerns, if there is a reason why you don't want to ratify, here's my response."

And the concerns about ratification were different: people thought that the raises didn't kick in early enough, that our wage increases would be in October 2024—ten months after ratification—and people thought that they should have come in earlier. Other people were very upset about nonresident supplemental tuition. And finally, some of them thought that the wages were not high enough. And my stance is that we deserve everything, we deserve higher wages, we deserve to not have to pay nonresident supplemental tuition, we deserve to have all these things as soon as possible. But *look at the state of this country in 2022*. Look at the state of labor in this country; workers don't get the things that they really deserve. We have to scratch and claw for everything, grind for everything we get; nothing comes to us easy. And we fought really hard for these gains right here.

When I decided to ratify, I had an internal conflict. At first, I wanted to just silently or quietly vote yes and let it fall the way it did. That was a moment of political clarification and struggle for a lot of people. Silently voting yes and not organizing would have been the easy way out. But often it's the harder things to do that are the most rewarding. At that point, I had been organizing with our union for a really intense eight months in which I didn't go a week without thinking about our union, organizing our union. And if I thought that this is what was best for our union, then I had to fight for that.

During ratification conflict and tension felt bad, of course! But I don't think it had to inherently feel that way, and the fact that it felt that way doesn't mean that it was bad in and of itself. I think our experienced conflicts felt that way because ... well, there were people who had been organizing for so long on one path, unified, but we didn't necessarily have the best mechanisms for conflict resolution for thirty-six thousand, forty-eight thousand people. We didn't have a structure to make sure everybody *felt good*. And at the end of the day the strike was not about feeling good; I didn't go on strike to be happy. I went on strike to win material benefits and to improve the material conditions of my workplace. That's why the majority of people went on strike. They saw it as the clear political strategic mechanism to win material improvements whether that's wages, workplace protections, whether that's getting rid of nonresident supplemental tuition as a condition of our employment, whether that's eight weeks of fully paid family and medical leave. That's why we went on strike. We didn't go on strike to feel warm and fuzzy inside. And yes, when we won and sitting here today, *I do feel happy*! I feel joyous. And most of the moments during the strike I did feel happy. It did feel ecstatic or euphoric. Struggling against exploitation, struggling for progress and justice felt good, but that wasn't the reason. If feeling good was the goal, I wouldn't go on strike, I'd go to the beach!

In the back of my head, I knew that the political differences between workers were going to be made apparent during ratification. And maybe I'm putting too much emphasis on the internal conflicts that existed in group chats, that existed on Twitter and social media. But it was not the same in real life. People would go home and they would enter these caucuses or group chats, and go on Twitter and start doomscrolling. That was stressful and that stress would carry on into the next day. But I never had a falling out with somebody in person, except maybe two or three people, and I don't take that that seriously because I had a sense of camaraderie with people on both sides of ratification.

When it came down to it at the end of the sixth week, I voted yes and I endorsed ratification. I organized for ratification proudly. But some of the people I felt the closest camaraderie with quietly voted yes, quietly voted no, or loudly organized yes, or loudly organized no. And within the group that opposed ratification there's people I grew really close with during the strike, broke bread with, risked arrest with. And my role as a striker, as a strike captain, as a picket shift leader—which anybody could sign up to be—my role is to strengthen the strike and strengthen the picket and through that I built a lot of camaraderie. The people with whom I couldn't feel camaraderie were the people—a small handful of people—who disagreed with the decisions and what was being done, but weren't organizing.

A significant amount of people voted against the tentative agreement. But the difference between the two sides of the vote was almost the same amount of people who voted against. It was 65 percent for ratification, and 35 percent against, so the difference was 30 percent. I see this result clearly as a majority position, but I also see clearly a significant sentiment against ratification.

There were these weird tensions that exist generally in political organizing, where a lot of people fetishize horizontal or the "horizontal models of political organizing." But really people just want a general assembly or Rank and File committee: "Let's take a straw poll." But when you have a campus of—I don't know—around ten thousand people and you call for a general assembly, best case scenario five hundred people show up. And who are these people? They are a self-selecting group of people who have their own political analysis or political desires. And that's not even close to being representative of what the campus actually is. Meanwhile, the bargaining team is elected to represent majority sentiment, which is what we were looking for. I heard a strange argument against majoritarianism during the strike, which I understand in the context of the United States of America, white supremacy, settler colonialism, and what the demographics of the United States are. I understand this. And the idea that a majoritarian stance on something is going to center able-bodied, cisgender, straight, white men ... and I understand that analysis, and where it comes from, but I don't understand how people were then advocating for more direct democracy in our union. I don't know how a critique of majoritarianism and an embrace of direct democracy—basically a poll for every single decision that is made—can coexist. Should every single bargaining decision come down to a poll? One, that will take absolutely forever to organize to get mass participation on every single poll. Two, you are not going to get mass participation. Three, you don't want a vote that doesn't have majority participation, and if you are calling for a vote with direct democracy, it's going to be majoritarianism. So, it was an inconsistent argument.

I don't know what is the best way to ensure a democratic process, I think it has to be structured. It has to be structured! We have to have clear reporting structures from the department level to the interdepartmental level to a campus level to the statewide level.

Kenzo Esquivel

I think what happened with the $43,000 drop should move us to think about changing how we make decisions so that those decisions don't leave workers in the dust or out of the loop. When the COLA [cost of living adjustment] language was dropped, we saw the cracks, but at that point I felt it wasn't a problem, and there was a vocal group who disagreed with that decision. I still trusted our leadership to work in our best interest, and I was happy with that model of organization. It was when the $43,000 drop happened that I had a more fundamental shift, and it was then that I thought we needed to think critically about how to run our union as a democratic organization.

After the $43,000 drop, it was clear that in our union there were both ideological and strategic differences, but the high personal tensions boosted the opposition between elected leadership and the COLA faction. And it felt like we were not able to communicate in any sort of effective way. There was a lack of trust, and a sentiment of frustration that came from both sides. It was both sides that enabled that. And that was tied to our history and to specific people and certain ideations of who these people were and what they were trying to do. I remember having a conversation with some elected leaders on the bargaining team who articulated the issue as "some humanities people are going berserk. What do we do about it?" It wasn't like, "There is a *difference* in strategic opinion, how do we work with them to figure out a path forward?" And I do think that it went both ways. But, in a way, I think the COLA faction's response had to be something like that because there were no democratic processes by which they could try to articulate a difference in ideas or strategy. And we didn't carve out—at least at Berkeley—a space where ongoing conversations about organizing and strategy at the bargaining table, not just about strike logistics, could happen. There wasn't a space like that outside of, I guess, the conversations that were happening at the office when people were hanging out. There was a sense that the decision-making spaces weren't clear.

Later on, during ratification, the question of power dynamics between STEM and humanities departments arose because workers in STEM departments were ready to go back to work and end the harassment and retaliation that they faced. Whereas the humanities were fighting so that all workers make closer to what the STEM departments make. This introduces a question about democracy, because if you have the STEM departments ready to go back to work, and that outweighs smaller departments that feel like we have to keep on fighting, what's the democratic way forward?

I remember that, at a certain point in the later stages of the strike, as a way of trying to create more spaces for discussion outside of strike logistics, we started organizing town halls where we would have representatives from each department come and speak about what their department was feeling. And I remember that one of those meetings was organized in such a way that the largest department was followed by the smallest department, and then the second largest was followed by the second smallest, et cetera, so that in relaying the sentiments of these departments, it also became clear what the size of those departments were. And it felt like a tactic to try to underscore a sense that it was a vocal minority of small departments that were advocating to keep on striking, whereas the large departments felt like we had won enough with wages and we needed to ratify a contract to enforce protections in the lab.

In my opinion, we need a structure or a space where we can have contentious discussions, and still come out at the end of the day being crystal clear that our enemy is the boss and that we are in this together, and that despite any internal political disagreements it is critical for us to present a unified front. And a precondition of having a space that is functional in that purpose is having a sense of mutual respect, a sense of mutual trust, a sense that we are in this together. But our history as a union makes that really challenging because there were people who, going into the strike, already had skepticism and lack of trust of our elected leadership and the strategies that might be at play.

It is not only the history of our local union, but also that the structure of our union makes it difficult. The fact that we're spread across so many different campuses with different political environments, with different costs of living, and with different administrators is what makes our union so unique and so powerful, but also really, really challenging to organize.

Ratification

Aarthi Sekar

The fifth week, on Wednesday night, we found out we were not only heading into mediation on Thursday, but that our mediator was going to be the mayor of Sacramento—Darrell Steinberg—who was called on to serve by the governor of California. I think our rally in Sacramento put pressure on not only UC, but the state of California to say, "This strike has been going on for four and a half weeks. What is UC doing?"

Mediation—and the mediator—was a crucial turning point because once we entered mediation, we were able to negotiate more quickly and effectively than we had been able to previously. And what we won through the mediation process was so significant for how strong our contract is at this moment. And the only reason we were able to leverage that power at the mediation table was because, yes, we had a mediator that was handpicked by the governor of California. But we had the power to get *that* mediator because of our rally in Sacramento and because we had been on strike for four weeks! We had that power because thousands of us were withholding our labor. We had that power because we organized for three years—*decades*—to get to that point. Without all of that, we wouldn't have had that leverage through the mediation process. And the mediation process with Darrell Steinberg, the mayor of Sacramento, getting on calls with the UC president to negotiate terms of our contract—that not just expedited, but actually bypassed the disorganized methodology that UC's office of labor relations was employing for months, which had been a failure up until that point. And that was huge!

It wasn't that Steinberg just came in and got the contract settled. There was a lot of back and forth where he was going back and forth between the room with our bargaining team and then talking to President Drake. At one point he came in with a proposal that was similar to what we ended up agreeing on, except that, in that proposal, Merced and Riverside would have a lower base wage than the rest of the campuses. We were all taken aback by that. I remember thinking, "Excuse me?!" I saw Pao, a bargaining team member from Riverside, was looking around trying to figure out how everyone else was feeling. And then a chorus of us spoke up and basically all said, "No way, these are the campuses that have been historically underfunded and generally have more workers of color. We are going to stand united against further marginalization of these campuses." It was a three-minute conversation at most. Kavitha summarized what we were all expressing and said, let's bring Steinberg back in and tell him we don't accept that. There was a lot more back and forth after that, but we ended up getting them to agree to bring Merced and Riverside up to par. And that felt like a strong moment of unity.

Kien Le

The sixth week of the strike, when I asked people to vote on ratification, some people asked me, "Why didn't we win more?" Some people who never showed up to the picket, who never withdrew their labor, they were saying they were going to vote no because what was on the contract was not what they wanted. It was in that moment that I realized they think of the union as a service. And that is so wrong. A union is not a service. A union requires participation and participation can take many forms. And without participation, I don't think you can say you are not going to ratify a contract because you already removed yourself from the conversation by scabbing. I remember I was sad in that moment, because people who never went on strike were saying we didn't do enough, and that really hurt.

During ratification I realized there is a conceptual gap between workers. Some, when they cast their vote, it's purely personal: "I'm going to vote no because this contract doesn't satisfy my demands." I agree, you shouldn't be forced to vote for a contract that you don't think you deserve. Or they vote no for purely ideological—nonstrategic—reasons. But other people, when they cast their vote, they are thinking of the long run: "I want this to be over with because this has been going on for too long." I had many difficult conversations with my coworkers.

I tried convincing them that voting yes or no was not as important as the commitment to keep organizing: "If you just want to vote no on the basis of what you believe in, I cannot judge you for that. But however you want to cast your vote, please remember that there will be consequences and you need to accept that it doesn't matter if you vote yes, or if you vote no, and then stop showing up. If you do that, your vote will be meaningless." I truly believe that. If you stop showing up, your vote doesn't matter.

Funnily enough ... I had planned to vote no from the beginning. Generally, I just like to maintain this kind of radicalism. And before I was involved, it seemed like voting no was the radical thing to do. It was oppositional. But being oppositional without strategy, without assessing your power in the moment, is not actually radical. And the whole vote no campaign was so screwed up that I decided I could not be associated with them. I was just like, "You know what? I cannot respect people who never participate and then vote no." And my decision does not mean I don't think we deserve to win more, because we do; we deserve more. And, to be honest, some part of me wanted to see the tentative agreement voted down to see if we could turn this into a more massive action. But I also know reality, and I believe that wasn't going to happen. Their whole rhetoric of a long-haul minority strike that would win more ... I have never heard of a revolution that dwindles in numbers and organizational capacity and eventually succeeds. I never heard of that in my life. I don't understand why that rhetoric spread like crazy. Twitter is insane.

I feel the media really did a good job overall of covering the strike, even though there were amazing actions that not everyone was aware of. These reporters, they cannot be everywhere and talk to everyone all at once, so the coverage was superficial. They also didn't understand how we pulled ten campuses together for this strike. But there was a problem when, at some point, people start writing opposing editorials, op-eds for a leftist newspaper, and those pieces had many factual inaccuracies. So, it was bad when the op-eds spread misinformation; it impaired the success of the strike.

Emily Weintraut

I went back home in mid fifth week with a lot of mixed feelings. I had planned my vacation thinking the strike would be over by then. To be away from the strike during the last week and a half was difficult, I remember I cried a lot with my family. It was very rough to see people who, just because they didn't agree strategically, were being cruel to their—and *my*—coworkers. Once the bargaining team tentatively agreed to UC's offer, I finally got excited and—at the same time—I got nervous thinking how to encourage people to ratify it. The week of ratification was a lot of work and it was emotionally draining.

But when we got the contract, I could not stop talking about the union. I went out to get dinner with a friend who is a lecturer at a university, and she said something like, "I think there is a union where I work," and I was like, "You need to join your union!"

For me, ratification week meant phone banking all day. It sucked because given the time difference—there's a three-hour time difference between New Jersey and California—I was phone banking in the evenings when I wanted to be hanging out with my family.

I would typically have good conversations with the people who picked up the phone. But most of the times, I'd leave a voicemail giving basic information, "There's ratification going on. We're trying to get as many people to vote as possible. The link is in your inbox, please just vote." Then I would just send them a follow-up text.

It was good to clear up information for people, especially if they were graduate student researchers because the wages are so complicated. I would have a lot of conversations where I looked at what their department rates were and then told them exactly what wages they would be making. The actual proposal is very hard to understand for graduate student researchers because there are so many different steps and each campus is different. Phone banking, for the people who answered the phone, was good because I could break the proposal down for them.

I would also be crying after caucus calls during ratification because I was hearing some people say horrible things to our bargaining team or because those same people were trying to vote down the contract. I started to realize that some of the folks advocating against the contract were doing so from a place of privilege where they thought our wins weren't transformative. For most workers I knew, the extra $700 was transformative and life-changing. But for folks who come from higher-income backgrounds, they may not see it as the true win it was, so they wanted to keep fighting and keep risking all that we had accomplished.

The minute I heard that our contract was ratified, I shotgunned a Twisted Tea with my brother. It's horrifying to think I was on strike for six weeks because my employer gave such little shits. But, at the same time, I was on strike for six fucking weeks! And look at what we accomplished! Does the contract include everything I wanted? No. But there's still that joy for all that we won. And finally, Christmas is my favorite holiday, so our contract was the best gift I could have. There is no way I'm going to say in a calm voice, "I'm proud." No. I'm really *fucking proud* of everything we've done!

To be honest, I understand where the people who voted no on the contract come from. Our contract is not everything that I wanted. What I don't understand is the people who are counterorganizing by saying, "The UAW is doing all these horrible things to us," making our union sound like an outside organization, trying to sow divisions. And I don't agree, this is your union, our UAW! It is us! It pisses me off when people are trying to antagonize workers against their union. To me, that's counterorganizing. No, this contract is not everything I wanted. I struck hoping to get a thousand dollars extra every month. But you know what? In a couple of months, I'm going to be making $200 extra every month, and by October, I'm going to be making over $700 more *every month,* and in 2024 I will be making $1,000 more per month than I am now.[1] We also got *huge* abuse protections!

And there are not that many people who are counterorganizing. In Davis, I'd say they are around ten very active people. But they speak and act like they represent the Rank and File workers. They were complaining about how we didn't have enough escalation on the picket line, saying that Rank and File members wanted to escalate. But people in my department did not even want to go into Mrak! All they wanted to do was picket; they didn't want to block traffic. For some people, being on a picket line is the most radical thing they could be convinced to do.

Just because you're brave doesn't mean everyone else is on the same page. You need to empower people to be willing to escalate. You need to have one-on-one conversations to truly understand what your department wants, instead of just claiming that you know. I've spoken to people afraid to dissent because of how loud the so-called radicals are. It's frustrating to see people acting like revolutionaries without even talking to coworkers—organizing is hard enough, and they're making it harder.

---

1 The first raise in the academic student employee contract took effect on April 1, 2023. Subsequent raises took effect at the beginning of the fall terms for academic years 2023–24 and 2024–25.

Kenzo Esquivel
And why did I advocate for voting no? Well, the increases we got in our childcare subsidies or assistance are laughable. The cost of childcare is immense and it's now a little bit over $2,000 a semester that student parents are able to access from university funding. That may get them through a month of childcare costs. We "won" new language on dependent health care, which I knew was a huge issue for folks in my department, but once we actually dug into what the language meant, it felt like it actually didn't cover anyone new. From our understanding it was like, "You'd have to be making less than what we would get paid under the new contract to actually qualify for the university to cover your child's health care." For me, it ended up coming down to trying to build a sense of empathy and solidarity with those who were coming from the most marginalized backgrounds. Because I think that's what got me and a bunch of us into this fight. I'm glad that we made enough headway that some international students, some parents, felt good about the wins. But at least for the folks that we were talking to in our department, it didn't feel meaningful enough and that was enough for us to be like, "Well, we want to fight for more."

Once the ratification results were announced, I was disappointed. In some ways, I felt there was a moment I was like, "Maybe we were just like a crazy minority. Maybe we were just fighting in a way that made no sense and that we were totally off base." But there was also a sense of relief because it was over. I mean, it was incredibly draining physically and emotionally and mentally. And it was Christmas Eve or something crazy. I was at home. We had family guests and the vote numbers came out and, and I couldn't engage with being at home at all. I mean, I was home that whole week and I was just phone banking. I was organizing and I didn't spend as much time as I normally might just being at home and relaxing and rejuvenating. And so, with ratification, I could finally rest, start recovering, and start to think about moving forward.

In the week of ratification, workers in STEM departments argued that we needed the contract that had been ratified by the bargaining team because they were facing critical and risky situations in their laboratory lives. They were saying, "We need to ratify immediately to be able to fight for a workplace that feels safe." Personally, I struggle with that argument a little bit because, yes, I know harassment is real, but at the same time, there are legal systems on our side and we have the structure of our union to fight back even before ratification.

In my opinion, we needed to draw on the narrative that retaliation is expected because it is a reaction to the fact that our labor is meaningful. And also, I feel like there are ways in which our union could have had a more strategic response to those instances of retaliation because it is *illegal* to retaliate against workers for union activity. We had other mechanisms at our disposal to fight against harassment and respond to retaliation, other than ratifying the contract to start implementing new protections.

For me, the strike was a fight for everyone at UC to make enough so that at a base level ... for all workers to make close to what some engineering and STEM science departments are making. And there is no other way; either we get it into our contracts or we don't and that's the end of it. From my perspective, fighting against retaliation and addressing the problem of unequal pay or the low wages for some departments were things we could be tackling at the same time. But during ratification, it felt like these two things were at odds. This was exacerbated by the fact that the STEM departments—where retaliation was happening—are larger than the small humanities departments, and this brought up a question of power dynamics and democracy.

Dez Manuel Fonseca

When the ratification vote results were announced, I was having dinner with my dad at home. I told him about everything, and since he got his first union job around the same time, we were extra excited. We were talking about unions a lot.

To me, ratification was the way to win and secure a victory. It was a football or basketball metaphor: we won by five points; maybe some people wanted to win by fifty, but a win is a win. We won that battle, but the war between capital and labor is still ongoing, and it was never going to stop with our strike. So that's how I felt about ratification. It was winning this victory and positioning ourselves to have more victories in the future.

Then, I also felt a relief; I don't have to be on strike anymore! And I can't even put that into words. I was getting up every day in the early morning. During ratification, I was doing phone calls *all day*. And I knew that if we decided to vote against ratification, I would have been back there on the picket line because that's what I had committed to do no matter what.

During ratification I did a lot of research about the standards of labor in 2022, and I saw some reports that said that 2022 was a record-setting year for the labor movement in this country, which is like bouncing back from decades of austerity and neoliberalism. And in this record-setting year, the average raises won by unionized workers were 4 or 5 percent. Meanwhile, we got raises of 55 percent over a two-and-a-half-year period, and a raise of close to 20 percent within six months. That's never-before-seen stuff for academic workers.

It doesn't mean that we're not exploited. It doesn't mean that we're not underpaid. But there's no denying how remarkable, how historic, how unprecedented the wins we got are. And, to be honest, wages are only one part of the gains we won.

I mean, an extra thousand dollars a month, that almost covers rent for me. We almost won rent. And now we have to be a part of a larger struggle with tenants' unions to fight for rent control in LA, in California, in the country, as they just did in Pasadena. So the fight is definitely not over. But we made significant, significant gains to alleviate the rent burden for all of our workers.

Many academic workers didn't see themselves as workers and I think our strike also changed that. That's a big thing that our strike did: clarify the relationship between our labor and capital in the university, to show that the university is just trying to exploit our labor for capital accumulation and profit accumulation.

I'm proud of how much I learned about bargaining, labor, cross-unit solidarity, and all I was taught about how to organize a strike. I didn't know I had that skill! Overall, the thing I'm proudest about is being at the forefront of a big moment in a movement in higher education among grad students. Grad students, academic workers occupy a really strange, liminal position in this economy and in the labor movement because at one point being a grad student was a class ascendant position, and due to neoliberal austerity, this changed. But during this movement we've seen a shift in the academic workers' class consciousness. And it's not only happening here, but at MIT, at Columbia, at Yale, at John Hopkins, at Cornell, Caltech, USC. All of these workers are organizing *as workers* and not with these dreams of class ascendency, and they are organizing in solidarity with service workers in Starbucks, Chipotle, REI.

I'm proud our local has inspired other organizers and movements, showing that mass mobilization is not just possible but real. We should be proud, not to pat ourselves on the back, but to keep pushing for mass participation and struggle across the US. I see us as part of a broader movement to make the world better. I've shifted from viewing the strike as the final battle to seeing it as the opening spark.

For me, some of the most important wins aren't wins for me, like parental leave, but I'm super happy for anybody who has, or may want to start a family because now they have eight weeks of paid parental leave or medical leave. And we got nonresident supplemental tuition enshrined as a term and condition of our employment, which I believe makes it a mandatory subject of future bargaining with the university. In the interim, even though we still have to pay nonresident supplemental tuition, I'm excited to continue to organize against it on a legislative level. I'm excited for my fellow coworkers and friends who are student researchers because for the first time, they have workplace protections against bullying and harassment, and against unsafe working conditions. I can barely fathom what it's like to have that kind of overnight transition between not having a contract to having a contract, from not having ways to enforce protections to having a way to enforce protections, which is the union.

The strike had no consequences in the relationship between me and my advisor. We are cool! He is really supportive. And the relationships with my coworkers have strengthened because I now see them primarily as fellow organizers in the workplace rather than just being coworkers. Everybody is comrades more than coworkers.

I myself am not the same person as I was before the strike. I can tell you straightforward, politically, I'm not the same! If you're the same person as an organizer before the strike as after, I don't know what the point was of going into the struggle. You had to have matured a lot as an organizer. I definitely changed as an organizer and as a thinker.

The question of what was our leverage as workers at UC had different answers and it raised a lot of debate. One argument I was really sympathetic to is that grading is the point where we have a particular leverage because we, teaching assistants, are not auto workers that go to work in a factory every day. We're in UAW, but we don't have a thing that we produce clearly every day. However, at the end of the day, grades were not some infallible leverage point that we could exercise at our own will as workers; there were other external factors that made the threat at the time less strong than we hoped for.

Curtis Rumrill

The vote no campaign put in a significant amount of effort, and the same held true for the yes campaign. The best organizing that the no campaign ever did was their vote no organizing. They did essentially nothing before the strike. But, you know, they organized a very credible vote no. What they did felt like going through a boss campaign, with what usually are boss tactics. They sow mistrust; they had no qualms about lying. When you have a caucus that is deliberately attempting to sell mistrust with literally everything that happens, everything else becomes dysfunctional as a result.

On a personal level, during ratification, my five-year-old got COVID and he and I were quarantined in the bedroom upstairs while I was trying to get out the yes vote. Which was actually funner than it sounds [*laughs*]. We had a good time together.

I was deeply worried about the results of the vote. I was worried that the leadership was overly optimistic. I was so glad to be proven wrong about it. Mara and I, as union stewards from the music department, formed our yes organizing committee. We charted the organizing thing with getting out the vote, and my five-year-old looked at my chart and he said, "Look, it looks like the yeses are winning" [*laughs*]. I was like, "You can read a chart!"

I was very concerned about the prospect of a long-haul strike because I thought it was truly an opportunity to watch this strike go from something really inspiring to something very disastrous. Let's say the no vote prevailed; it wasn't going to win by a resounding majority, it would have been a slim minority. Let's say close to 49 percent of the bargaining unit was saying, "We're ready to be done with this strike and this deal is really good." It would be really hard to keep them from crossing the picket line. And we could expect UC to begin docking pay. And somehow that was supposed to equate to more power than the power that we had had with forty-eight thousand workers? Most likely we would have gone back in with what was on the table or worse, and with a completely broken organization. And the lesson would have been that "strikes don't work." So, that's what I felt was at stake in that vote.

When the ratification results were announced, my feeling was not elation, it was just relief. And even like a level of just sadness that all of that infighting had to happen. We should be going back victorious because the contract we won was massively better than anything we ever won. And we're still going back in with a fractured organization that is going to have to do a lot of work to recover from the toxicity of the Rank and File vote no campaign.

The childcare benefits we won are nice—I'm not going to complain about money—but not life changing. Do I think that the union sold student parents out? There were a set of decisions that were made that resulted in us not being able to get more on childcare and some of those were strategic mistakes. Some of those were mistakes that the bargaining team was forced into by bad actors. And in no circumstance do I think that anybody on the bargaining team wanted to fuck me. That's stupid. It's bullshit to say that student parents got sold out.

Joyce Chan

The week for ratifying the grad students' contract was more stressful. It was a more charged environment. I was mainly helping in the neurosciences department, and I want to shout out to the neurosciences organizing committee—which was composed primarily of graduate students—because they inspired me in many different ways. The biomedical science graduate students in general were inspiring just by being so informed and making all these amazing graphics and detailing the rationale of the contract. The organizers, especially the graduate students, have various gifts and talents, and I'm very proud of them. Every time I see grad students step up, I think of where I was when I was in grad school, and I'm beaming inside!

The ratification week for the grad students' contracts put me in a bad place mentally, and I mean *a really bad place*. I remember hearing some of our fellow graduate student union members on the bargaining team getting harassed or doxed, their addresses and personal information being leaked, some of them being framed as if they were physically assaulting people when this was entirely false. All of this was terrifying to me. I was actually scared. But I think prioritizing what is good for people in general helped me to work in spite of the fear, if not entirely overcome it.

CHAPTER 8

Outcomes and Autopsies

Postdocs and researchers at the first ever strike picket of Lawrence Berkeley National Lab

Strategy and Conflict

Aarthi Sekar

The internal debates that took place between bargaining team members over the course of bargaining were held in a way and in a space that was less and less productive with each iteration. As the strike went on, our conversations as elected representatives went downhill. One of the biggest reasons for that was that people on the bargaining team encouraged people to call out their fellow bargaining team members in public settings about their conversations, discussions, and votes during bargaining. There were bargaining team members who thought it was okay to broadcast publicly conversations that happened in spaces that were meant to be private, particularly from our employer. These bargaining team members made the debate spaces unsafe for discussion of the strategy to win a fair contract. They detracted from workers' ability to have good faith conversations because they spread so much mistrust. To sum up, having good discussions became almost impossible, although that's what we should have been doing instead of sowing division among workers.

It wasn't always like that among bargaining team members. When we were preparing the demands and during the first months of bargaining, we did have good discussions during caucus. As bargaining team members we would have meetings to discuss the proposals we were working on, and take the input from different members. We'd also invite specific people to give input about certain matters, and we were quite productive initially. But as it got closer to the strike, the caucuses became weaponized, and the way to address dissent about a proposal became attacking or calling out bargaining team members during caucus and in open forums and chats. So no conversation about how to actually negotiate was productive.

Then, the conversation shifted from being about strategy to being about personal attacks and many of these conversations took place on Zoom. Hundreds of people were on these Zooms, so it was essentially public shaming. I would just get called out in the chat. Some people were saying that I have no personal opinion because I am employed by UAW as staff, and therefore whatever I say has been groomed into me. They were ignoring the fact that I organize day and night and talk to hundreds of my coworkers and have been for a few years in order to fight for the fair contract that we deserve. As if I'm an automaton with no actual opinions of my own, being groomed by some secret club that's affiliated with the international UAW. Bullshit. If my opinions were groomed by UAW because I'm staff, does that mean that UC dictates the opinion of all academic workers because we are all workers for the UC? I asked them this, and I was met with silence. That's so ... not just *narrow minded*, but *privileged* for somebody to say that I (having had my own set of lived experiences as an academic worker in UC) don't have thoughts and opinions on what a fair contract should be, and that (as an organizer) I wouldn't know what my coworkers want to see in a contract. It's incredibly offensive and just sounds exactly like what antiunion employers say about union leadership in order to bust unions.

It is so easy to sow division and do the bosses' work for them. It is so easy to assume that there is this institution—our union—that has its own agenda. When in fact our local is composed of workers who have worked in the bargaining unit, and all of the bargaining team are *workers*. There is no secret external force dictating what's happening. We make our decisions collectively and democratically. I'm not making any secret back-alley dealings with international UAW folks. And honestly, there are people who work for international UAW who are literally just there to offer support with all of the organizing experience they've had. I barely knew what a union was when I started organizing the student researcher campaign.

Working with international UAW staff doesn't mean we agree on everything. I've had disagreements with people on staff many times [*laughs*]. For example, on how to convey a meeting or an approach to organizing. So many disagreements, I don't even know where to start. But I am heard and I listen to the other person and we have a conversation about the pros and cons of each of our opinions. We come together and work together collectively and take action.

Looking back, I wish that I had started talking about how bargaining works way earlier. I wish that I had had way more open conversations about what it means to be in negotiations and that it is an arduous process, and that it does mean that we have to amend our initial proposal and manage our expectations, and what that looks like. For the future I wish we have a more effective way of communicating what's happening in bargaining, starting from the very beginning. I also reckon that it's important to talk about bargaining from orientations because we didn't talk about it until it was right upon us.

Dez Manuel Fonseca

Before the strike, I knew little about what actually happens during one. I didn't understand the details of bargaining, strike threats, or the risks and protections involved. I was aware of strike-breaking tactics but hadn't participated in discussions about them. It wasn't until we were in the strike that I learned how it all worked.

My thinking changed constantly. For example, I initially thought we should delay bargaining, but by week two I realized we should have bargained earlier and not presented the $54,000 wage demand at the BOMMM [Big October Monthly Meeting]. Entering the strike, we were in a position of uncertainty, while the university, a multibillion-dollar institution, had more power and long-term experience in union busting. I also assumed workers would stay out until the grading deadline, skipping academic work and withholding labor indefinitely, but I took that for granted.

We had a big conversation, *a huge debate* over when our peak power was. Was it in the beginning when we had high numbers? Was it the end when we had the grading deadline? I think it ended up being somewhere in the middle. I also am of the mind that we did leverage the threat of grading very well because you don't want to go past the grading deadlines and find that *the university survives*. The idea that all we have to do is withhold a handful of grades—10 or 5 percent of grades—and we'd be good, that idea wasn't reality-proof. Because if we get to the grading deadlines and the university acts like they can survive with no problem, then what? Then we have no power! And not only that: it's a threat that in the future we can't utilize because we—and the university—saw that it didn't work.

At first, my position about the strike was, "The end of January is when we'll have more power." And although we didn't get there, my analysis of the situation is that we'd have been in a much worse place; we wouldn't have been able to get people back on strike. At UCLA, the majority of teaching appointments ended on December 14 or 18, and once you get past that, it's actually not even your job to grade anymore. You have no legal obligation to grade; you already got paid or you didn't get paid for that. That grading is no longer your responsibility, it's the university's or the department's responsibility to find people to do that grading. Once we got to that point, how could we exercise more power? It was a theoretical power which wasn't rooted on anything concrete we knew about the situation because we've never been there before. People kept talking about a grade strike—withholding grades—as if it's something we couldn't have always done, but teaching assistants could have always gone on a grade strike. Why didn't we do it? Why didn't it work before? Why didn't we do it in 2014 or 2018 during negotiations? Why didn't they win huge demands then if it's always just as simple as withholding grades?

Ultimately, I do think there was a particular leverage in the threat of withholding grades, and we used it. We—through the mediator—forced the university into giving us a lot of concessions, because the university did make concessions.

My perspective changed just through listening to people, honestly, listening to the student researchers or the people who worked with them: listening about how pressured they felt to go back to work.

At the start of the strike, I hadn't considered that after December 18, we weren't responsible for grading anymore. Without that, how do we maintain leverage? While we could pressure faculty not to grade, it all comes down to organizing. In my department, a small group met with faculty to see who wouldn't submit grades, but most said they would, feeling bad for students. I realized we couldn't extend the strike past the grading deadline—our power was in the threat, not its execution. As someone put it, "If the kidnapper executes the hostage, they lose their power." Next time, we need to organize better with instructors so they don't submit grades, and not assume they know how to respect the picket line.

Another subject in which I changed my mind was that in the beginning I thought that this strike was the final battle. The way I originally interacted with organizing and the building of the strike threat was: "I'll go all-in to help organize a stronger strike, win as much as possible, and then go back to being an academic." In my mind, I was moving back home after the strike! But during the strike, and through organizing, I realized this is a long process of spreading workers' consciousness, of building workers' mobilization, of building a strong union, of working together with other unions to revive the labor movement and to revive the political struggle in this country.

We need to analyze a lot of elements to understand how conflict played in our strike and how we can manage it better in the future. First, the discourse around conflict primarily existed in online spaces. I don't know the people that were engaging in this often-anonymized discourse. I don't know if they were or are organizing; I think a lot of them are, but certainly not all of them. And it's tough to strike a balance because we're still in a pandemic as we are talking, there are people who didn't feel safe going to in-person events.

And I don't know how I feel about the people who are really loud online and *don't say anything in person*. But I know that not much gets done online. In the context of labor, you can circulate a letter online, you can tweet something, you can collect petitions, but strength and solidarity come from unified action, and for that you need the one-on-one trust.

I guess—related to how to manage internal conflict and division—the one thing I would stress is the importance of building one-on-one relationships, either for building camaraderie or for having discussions. Maybe you can build one-on-one relations online, but it is not that common. It is important to build those relations because conflict can happen in person but from what I've seen it doesn't get exacerbated in unhealthy ways like it did online.

On the other hand, for better or worse, having online spaces is a dynamic that the labor movement, social movements, and political struggles in general have to deal with now. We didn't have to deal with this during the inception of the labor movement over one hundred years ago. It's a new dynamic for social movements. And our strike was at the forefront of it. Going back to the wildcat in 2020, this played out on social media very heavily. It's a new dynamic that we have to add to our toolbox. We also have to analyze and understand it because ultimately social media is not controlled by workers, it's controlled by the giant corporations that dictate what it is that we see and what we're exposed to and how we interact with people; it's not a worker-run platform in a way that an organizing meeting can be.

There is one last thing I want to talk about in regards to the intense and heated discussion we had among workers. The really bad-faith argumentation about the character and the intentions of workers should not happen again. The baseless conspiracy theories about people's characters and about their intentions, the name-calling, the threats that were levied particularly against members of the bargaining team, none of that should exist. And I say this just to make specific points about the ways that we, as organizers, communicate in the twenty-first century, and to think about the role of social media in particular, because I feel that the in-person disagreements were not as polarizing and confrontative as the ones online. I'm all for embracing conflict in person, embracing political tensions; but the conflict that played out on Twitter felt unhealthy, as was the resulting perception of this strike.

There's also something to be said about the usage of identity politics—again, at large, not just in our union. Identity politics were refracted in our union in ways that I think are worth talking about.

When I was phone banking . . . First, let me digress: some people are really against phone banking, against talking to our coworkers, which I don't understand because how else am I going to know what you think if not by calling you, texting you, asking you what you think? That's what organizing is; it's talking to people. But anyways, sometimes, when I was phone banking, I would be met with wild accusations. I'd say I'm voting for ratification and people would tell me—in really condescending ways—that they'd vote no because they don't want to betray Black workers and immigrant workers, or disabled workers. There was an assumption that ratification was being pushed by privileged workers. Look, I'm a Black worker, my parents are immigrants! It was absurd how people would lead with all these assumptions about their coworkers. It's one thing to lead with assumptions about powerful politicians, corporations, and people who have a vested interest in exploitation, but it's completely different saying all this about your coworkers who are just as exploited as you, and who face the same workplace conditions as you, and who are struggling for a fair UC and hopefully a fairer world, and browbeating and making holier-than-thou accusations based on identity, based on bad-faith assumptions. I know this is not unique to our union at all. I know our struggle reflected and refracted these dynamics in a really public and widespread way. It's not the end of the world; it's just something that we should note for next time.

Joyce Chan

To be honest, I thought UC would have been a lot smarter [*laughs*]. I thought that they would just see all these people gathered outside and think like, "The more we run this place like a business and prioritize money over people, the less workers we are going to have for our classes and our research long term and it's just going to hurt us." Or even being like, "This is the majority of people that feel this way. We should really be taking this seriously." They did not [*laughs*]. I think I wasn't surprised with their response, but I was surprised at how long they were sticking with that response or lack of response.

I kind of understand why some workers doubted the bargaining teams. I mean, it's hard because, as with most things, it turns out you can't really understand how a union works until you've been part of it or have been organizing. I think the similar thing could be said for bargaining on a much greater level—I still don't consider myself an expert, even after the many sessions I attended. And there is no sufficient official training for this! You learn "trial by fire," and I'm still very much in the early phase of learning how this all works.

Another thing to consider about bargaining is that the significance of the bargaining meetings wasn't very clear for everyone until people were literally looking at their outcomes to decide when they would stop striking, or if they should keep pushing, or if they were satisfied with what was on the table. I sense that bargaining was something that was originally not very much on people's radar, and when it was, it was blowing up! And unfortunately, at the time when everyone was finally paying attention to it, there was no way to really accommodate the scale of teaching sessions or trainings that were needed to understand how all this works. And I think it was just that deadly mix of, one, bargaining is very dry and very abstract; and, two, unless you're directly involved in the process you don't think about attending the meetings just because of how out of the way it seems until *that very moment* when everything depends on bargaining.

This is especially important considering that the big majority of postdocs at UCSD are international workers, particularly from China and India. I'm sure it would mean a lot to those workers to see someone with a similar identity in our union organizing or in an elected position. I feel they'd feel less scared if they knew they can communicate in their own language. I identify as Chinese/Taiwanese, but I was not born in China, neither have I ever lived there nor even speak the language all that well; it is not the same. If we were to have more diversity in organizing, maybe we would find out about other issues that people care about or different strategies that we might not have even conceived yet. I say all this as an Asian American who didn't see a lot of other Asian Americans in the postdoc side of our union. I know having more people like myself in our union would have helped me during my process of getting more involved.

Kenzo Esquivel

I fundamentally don't understand why the bargaining team members dropped from $54,000 to $43,000. What the bargaining team said, but I can't fully believe in my gut, is that at that point—three weeks into the strike—the university hadn't moved at all and we needed to show a good faith effort in wanting to find a solution. A critical part of their analysis was that we no longer had the leverage, as based on the turnout of our picket lines, to keep at the $54,000 level. That's what the bargaining team thought. But I still have a lot of feelings and questions around why and how that came to be. There was a critical piece of the bargaining team's logic that was embedded in an understanding of power that wasn't shared across the board. I think another thing that came to light that evening was that the bargaining team felt a level of time-bound pressure in the fact that the longer the strike went, the less leverage they felt we had. And so, I think that the need to move quickly started to become more acute, and ultimately it was chosen over a process of democratic involvement.

And up to that point, we hadn't had to think about big concessions or what we are willing or not willing to concede. And there was no infrastructure or process by which we were trying to gauge what types of moves would or wouldn't be acceptable. Consequently, it was really on the bargaining team to make these decisions. It was around this time when I was asked the question on the picket line, "What is our model of elective leadership and democracy in our union? Is it that we elect a group of people and we defer to their leadership and their judgment fully? Or are they speaking on our behalf, which has different implications for process?" And it was becoming increasingly clear that the model was the former, where we elect someone to make these strategic decisions and to understand the complexities of bargaining, and that we defer fully to their judgment.

The drop from $54,000 was a turning point where all of these questions about process and strategy, and the conceptualization of our power, came to light. And so, the move sparked all of these other questions that we just hadn't grappled with in a broad way. Perhaps in certain circles, in certain spaces, these types of discussions had been happening. And to their credit, the bargaining team members from Santa Cruz led several sessions leading up to the strike called "strike school," where we were trying to learn from the experiences of other people and organizers and unions that had been on strike before. But I only ever made it to one of those. In retrospect, again, we should have been engaging people in these questions way sooner.

I absolutely did not expect to win every single item we demanded. I think most people would agree that we were never going to achieve everything in a single strike. If I had to put a number on how low I would've accepted to go on wages, I'd say something around $40,000, but I would have wanted that to be a community-level discussion, which never happened.

A fundamental barrier to having a common organizing strategy was the fact that the institutional structure has allowed for different departments to have different experiences of the university. This needs to change. In the future we need to pay attention to keep on building a sense of collective solidarity, understanding the situation of different departments so we feel a collective responsibility. We need to build a sense of collective responsibility because there are clear divisions across departments; for example, the STEM departments face worse retaliation, but they are paid more.

From my perspective, our union hasn't focused on developing those cross-departmental relationships in a way that builds a sense of trust or any sort of empathy for the situation of students who are in a worse position, which, by and large, are the social sciences and humanities departments, because they are generally paid less.

I think that there is a lot of strength in organizing our own departments because you understand the structures, the people, and you have actual social ties. But it would be interesting to contemplate ways that we can branch out from that strategy and have folks building relationships outside of their normal disciplinary silos. Maybe this is something I think about a lot because my department is relatively interdisciplinary—we are wildlife biologists, engineers, humanists, social scientists—and naturally we have a level of conversation that allows this type of sentiment to be more present.

At the end of the day, there is something viscerally real that is informing the fears of retaliation or the fear of unionizing. And from my perspective, multiple organizing conversations and investing in those relationships to develop trust are required to build a sense that they need to be part of this movement and that this movement can serve them too. This is how I—when I was an undergrad—learned to do this: You develop one-on-one conversations to understand an individual's stake in the movement and you use that to move through points of tension or points of disagreements to relate why this broader cause is important for them personally. But this is not something you can articulate in a short time span.

I do think that the COLA [cost of living adjustment] Rank and File movement had a lot of ideological points that I don't necessarily disagree with, but it hadn't articulated an organizing strategy or engaged in a meaningful dialogue or relationship building beyond their departments or their communities. And because of this, it became very easy to assign blame to the folks who were organizing STEM departments with lower participation, like, "You need to be organizing your turf better. You need to take more responsibility to be having those types of conversations."

In weeks one through three of the strike, we saw COLA-related fliers and leaflets going out. They were handing out papers that outlined their vision and their thoughts. They weren't talking to people; there wasn't any meaningful engagement with other workers. It was presenting workers information with the hopes that they might read and decide to agree. Nonetheless, I do think that by the end of the strike, those same folks were thinking really hard about creating rap sheets or templates of how to have conversations with STEM workers, and they were thinking about what it means to do organizing work. And so, in my opinion, in the context of the strike, there was a shift in the organizing strategy in the COLA faction, which I think is a good sign.

I'm hopeful that both sides, elected leadership and the Rank and File movement, can talk to each other and build relationships. There is a real bridge that needs to be built to actually talk to each other and build relationships that are meaningful and not built on a sense of obligation or resentment, and actually try to engage with people's ideas and translate those ideas into action. But I also recognize the logistical difficulties in actually creating that space and time.

Another thought I had related to what I've just said, I think the size and statewide nature of our union is both a huge source of strength but also our downfall. It's incredible that we have a statewide union because of the extremely high number of people we are able to reach and the power that we are able to build. When I got to our union, organizing all campuses immediately struck me as one of the bigger challenges because each campus is unique in its organizing structures, the people at the helm, the history of the union, et cetera. At the same time, the fact that there are campus-by-campus resentments raises other challenges.

One of the things that grates on me is the fact that we agreed on a contract that gave UCLA and Berkeley higher wages based on nothing more than the fact that we made more because we are prestige campuses, which I think was an intentional strategy on the boss's part, because they know these divisions exist.

Previously, I said that somewhere along the way, people started to set an expectation for the strike to last around three weeks, even though I tried to caveat this with people in my department. Looking back on it, setting that time frame was probably a mistake. How else could we have shaped the conversations about the strike length? Well, again, there is an interesting division that arose between how we were able to talk about it with folks who were teaching and folks who were researching. For folks who were researching, I think it would have felt more difficult to present the possibility of the strike to last, say, months. People would have been like, "Whoa, whoa, whoa!" There would have been a lot of tension and anxiety around that. That type of conversation would have required a level of one-on-one organizing that was beyond our capacity. If someone had come up to me early on and say that the strike could last for two months—which is what happened—it would have felt like a difficult calculus to figure out. I think it would have required a lot of more specific planning and conceptualization of *why* it's deeply crucial to win these things.

Having people think through this idea of lost time or lost progress would have been really challenging. As organizers, it was our responsibility to have people go further than workers thought they could, and that is only possible through this deep sense of collective empowerment that came through the strike.

We have one recent example in the US of how, through a strike, workers built a sense of empowerment that enabled them to stay out. A bunch of health care workers went on strike for, I think, twelve weeks. I talked to some friends who work there and they said that before going on strike, workers wouldn't have been comfortable with the idea of leaving their patients for a long time. It was the process of striking that changed their imaginaries and got them to persist.

Though I don't think it was ever an official rap, I think it was a mistake to try selling the strike as a one- to two-week thing, wherever this narrative came from, and it should not be a strategy moving forward. I think we could have mapped out a three- to four-week plan and asked ourselves, as organizers, "How can we make this plan possible? Who is facing retaliation and how do we set up an infrastructure to call out that professor?" There are ways by which we can make people feel like they can and need to be out on strike longer than they would have conceptualized for themselves.

Kien Le

Another outcome of the strike is learning about the flaws of how we spread information because there were a lot of factual inaccuracies posted on social media. And the lack of information really hurt the unity of our local. In the future, we may want to work on the flow of information, which is difficult because people can be overloaded with information they don't know how to navigate. I think the idea of a network of people spreading information is good and important.

Elsie Jacobson

I think our postdoc bargaining team did incredibly well. Remember I said that the postdoc numbers on strike dropped in the second week, and the university knew that, and we knew that. It was 15 percent of postdocs who signed up for at least one picket shift during the second week. And there, for sure, were postdocs who didn't sign up and went, and postdocs who signed up and didn't go. But still, we had maybe 20 percent of the biological sciences and chemistry postdocs at our picket line and that's not the strongest position to be bargaining from! If we'd had 90 percent out, then I'm sure things might have been different. But for the power that we had, the bargaining team did incredibly well. They did! Our contract is amazing.

Throughout the strike, I was not involved in bargaining one bit because I was 100 percent focused on our picket. I'm probably a little biased because my partner, who started as a Student Researchers United organizer, was on the bargaining team—and by the way, I didn't see him at all during the strike! We were basically long distance again for a couple of weeks during the in-person bargaining. Basically, at the end of the day, I know the bargaining team members and I trust them. They are postdocs who sacrificed a huge amount of time and energy to do this horrible job. I felt so sorry for them. We were out on the picket line, and, honestly, we were having a fun time, doing crafts, and making banners, and talking to our colleagues. Meanwhile, the bargaining team members were sitting in a windowless room with UC's labor relations negotiators and they weren't even allowed to talk to each other because everything was on record! I remember clearly one of the last bargaining sessions—they were streaming them on Zoom when they could—and they were in a windowless room with a row of postdocs on one side typing very quickly, having all these fast-paced conversations, and labor relations was on the other side being horrible. It seemed like awfully hard work.

And then, some people were saying that the bargaining team was negotiating under the table with the university, which is absurd! The bargaining team didn't get anything extra for all the hard work that they did. Everyone in the bargaining team is getting the same contract that everyone gets. Of course they were trying their best! And I think that without that trust—I'm missing the words because I'm reliving the frustration I felt back then. Without that trust, how are we going to get anything? I don't understand why there was mistrust toward them. I really don't.

Some postdocs were frustrated, feeling like we were almost done with our contract before the strike even started, and that things weren't moving fast enough. But I tried to stress that staying strong with the other units was key—if postdocs went alone, we wouldn't have won what we did. The university was stalling to weaken us, and the bargaining team was doing everything they could to keep things moving and keep us updated. The real concern wasn't "Why aren't we taking a good deal?" but "Why isn't this happening faster?" Some thought the delay was on us or part of the joint strategy, but it was UC slowing things down.

For postdocs, the final contract was announced just after Thanksgiving—if I recall correctly. I remember that on the Wednesday before Thanksgiving significant progress on the contract was announced. And the strategy was, "Let's try and see if we can get a little bit more." The UC proposed eight weeks of parental leave for everyone except for first-year postdocs, but the bargaining team countered and won eight weeks of parental leave for *everyone*! And since many postdocs only stay a couple of years, this was a big deal! I remember this clearly because we had a Thanksgiving picnic on the picket line and we had a bargaining team member on Zoom giving updates [*laughs*]. I remember there was still a microphone setup, and we announced it, "We got a win! Parental leave for everyone!" I was so happy. It had been frustrating waiting on the progress, but I think some people misplaced the frustration on the bargaining team instead of the UC.

Do I have any regrets about the strike? What a peculiar question! I kind of wish I'd gone into the Luskin occupation the first time [*laughs*]. But in all seriousness, I think there's always the sense that we could have done more—and I don't mean just during the strike. However, I don't really have any regrets around what happened during the strike because I see the strike as the end result of everything we did for the last couple of years, so there was not a huge amount that I could have done to change any of the outcomes. Of course, prestrike there's always more organizing that can be done. And maybe if we'd done that, our strike would have been even better. But honestly, I'm so happy. And in terms of specifically the strike, I really can't emphasize how great our picket was. We had a real sense of community and support and mutual aid. It is something I've never experienced before. And I think it was such an *amazing* experience. The experience of the strike was life changing for me, but I think for other people as well. I just think it was something really special that we all did together.

To finalize, I'll say something about my perception of the democratic processes of the strike and our union in general. First of all, I want to bring to the table a previous example of how I've seen democratic participation go very poorly. During the pandemic, the university created the COVID committees to manage the impact of the pandemic. And I know a couple of people that were on these committees right at the start of the pandemic and they were completely ignored. On the contrary, in our union and during the strikes, the stakes were high because we were making the decisions. We were making the decisions together and with a lot of people. In other words, the decisions we made, or the choices people made, had a direct impact. The fact that your choice has a direct impact on your life contrasts with how this country usually works.

Remember, I'm from New Zealand, so what I'm going to say is from an outsider's perspective. To some extent, in New Zealand the way you vote is felt in how the country looks. That is not what happens in the US. Here, sometimes it is really hard to see the impact of your choices. And I think that in our union and in the strike, there really were very direct impacts of the choices we made. And part of that actually is that it really forced serious, hard conversations and forced people to reckon with some things. And ultimately, people feeling empowered and people making choices that have impact is so important because when you feel like you're constantly making choices and then none of those choices *do* anything, you end up asking yourself what's the point. And so, I think it's so important experiencing these extremely direct outcomes. That is democracy that really matters. So, yeah, when you get that feeling that the choices you make can have an impact, you feel empowered. Before the strike, I don't think I would have ever thought about organizing a tenants' union, but now it feels really possible. Empowerment has ripple effects.

Emily Weintraut

Strikes are very emotional, and they hit very close to home. I genuinely believe that most people in our union—other than maybe the people who think we get paid too much, which is a teeny tiny, itty-bitty minority—have the same moral standing. The divisions come from just a strategic place, but because it's so emotional and we're going through a mentally difficult time, the differences get emphasized. I get that when someone says, "Let's do this," and no one wants to do it, they may feel isolated.

Thinking back on it, I would say that one of the issues we had to deal with during the strike is that once the demands were listed, we didn't have a structured way to decide priorities. We didn't ask ourselves what was the most important bargaining item. I don't think I would change the rhetoric from "$54K or we won't go away" to "We're asking for $54K, expect less," but I think that we should have explained bargaining to people so they fully understood that the bargaining team is going to try to get everything, but there should be space for movement. We needed to manage expectations and prioritize and maybe we should have started bargaining on wages earlier. It would have been different if we had been bargaining on wages for eight or nine months and getting horrible wages proposals from the UC for those eight months.

The thing that was more upsetting for me than not getting everything we dreamed on wages was not getting nonresident supplemental tuition remitted. It was hard when we dropped from $54,000, but I understood and I trusted the bargaining team. And with nonresident supplemental tuition, once I realized that there were legislative and legal issues that obstructed us from making more progress, I understood we needed to get rid of those barriers outside the bargaining process.

The bargaining team members went through a lot of vitriol during the strike. People screamed at them when they were trying to explain strategies or the reasoning behind some decisions. And still . . . I worked customer service for six years during Black Friday, where you get *a lot of vitriol* from customers to get, like, the twenty-five-dollar jean sales. But *I got far worse vitriol* and mistreatment from my own coworkers because they don't consider me an equal just because we disagreed. And still we continue to have campus organizing committee meetings, and none of the people who spread vitriol are coming. None of them are trying to help with membership. None of them are helping with grievances, even though we are constantly asking people to join that process. To me, it is so hypocritical to just bitch and moan and say how "the union" is the worst and how "the union" is corrupt. It's your union, you are a part of it, what are you doing to make it better? What are you doing to make it more representative? Those are the real questions. I don't know if they've had a lot of tough conversations with their coworkers.

And the thing is that there's tons of dissent in our union. We are a union of thirty-six thousand graduate workers. There's going to be tons of different opinions! But the vast majority of them are nice about it. I'll say some people believe in the Democratic Party more than I do, and whatever, I won't stop organizing with them for that reason. There are anarcho-leftists, there's communists in our union; and for me, just because you call yourself a communist or an anarchist, that doesn't make you the sole representative of that political ideology in our union.

I'm continuing to be here because if you care about something, you should stay. If you stopped, you clearly don't care enough. Don't just spew hate speech to degrade us online, don't put out false information about the proposal we got. Posting vitriol against your coworkers does nothing but hurt us! Getting involved is what helps.

Some people who opposed the contract talk about "union leadership" as if it was a third party. Union leadership is people who do stuff for our union on a regular basis. For me, if you come to our organizing committee meetings—which are open to whoever wants to come—then you can lead because you are helping strategize! It's called the organizing committee because we organize there! I've asked people who complain about leadership to come, and they don't come. It's almost like people want to third party us, so that they can complain about it, and say they are marginalized. For example, during the strike there was the Davis strike captains group chat, and every time anyone would complain about union leadership I'd say, "You are union leadership! You are a strike captain. You have taken on a leadership role for X amount of people. You are union leadership!" And they would get so frustrated because they wanted the union to be separate.

Most of union leadership is just people who are nice and who have social connections. I've talked a lot about Aarthi. Aarthi was elected unit chair for Local 2865 Academic Student Employees *because Aarthi talks to people and connects with people* and really understands them! And people like her and trust her. People have asked me to run for a steward position. I don't need that, but people say I've been helpful in our union. So, I'm like, "I guess this is another thing I need to do" [*laughs*]. Not super looking forward to it. But people have asked me to do it, and that's how a lot of our leadership functions. We ask people to help and then they step up and that's what union leadership is.

There are also complaints about the role of the staff from UAW International that I don't get. I see staff as support. The staff makes a point to make sure the choices are made by members. If we were saying something, the staff from UAW International would have been asking questions, not making decisions. They weren't saying what raise we should ask for. Our members were deciding what to bargain for. Our members were putting people in positions of power. If anything, I think that we would not need so much help from staff if more members got more involved in organizing. I think having staff is amazing! I love having staff. I love having people who understand unions, who work so hard.

Comm(unity)

Aarthi Sekar

We had an incredible group who, out of necessity, emerged in leading the picket line. The group was called the Cunties. These were—they still are—leaders that realized that the strike is what each of us makes it; the strike is nothing without each of us contributing and owning it. Over the first couple of weeks, the people who later became Cunties were full-time organizing the marches and the picket lines.

In the forefront of their mind, Cunties were thinking about how to get more of our coworkers out to the picket line and how to ensure an active collaboration with one another. And so, people found solidarity within the Cunties to be out in the cold morning unloading tables with frozen fingers and frozen shoes in the grass that was dew covered. It was a group to find friendships with each other, standing out there in the wind, enrolling and checking people in for strike pay, doing all of the coordination, and the traffic control. These workers' leadership *made the strike possible.*

Cunties was born out of the necessity of staying strong and united, and the realization that we can't be casting suspicion on each other during this fight, that our suspicion should only be for the UC because it's us against them. They were also very conscious about what it meant to be in a contract fight against UC. They understood too that our power came from workers being united as one front; and finally, they understood that division among us was detrimental to our fight.

Cunties, the name, came out of one of our leaders who is an undergraduate tutor, Willa Gibson, for whom the word *cunt* is used in a positive way in her family. You could say the name was born out of this very positive, strong association; and we all just fell in love with it. And who was part of Cunties? The group of folks who made up Cunties were not male, they were women and nonbinary folks for the most part. They were workers across many different departments, from plant pathology to neuroscience to genetics to biochemistry, from molecular biology to linguistics, from animal science to entomology to chemistry to undergraduates who work as tutors. They included workers who were in different points in their degree, anywhere from seventh year—like myself—to first year. We had many leaders who were in their first year, which is incredibly exciting because this contract is going to affect first years and second years more than anybody, not me who is about to leave. So I think they really own the campaign because of this recognition that *this is their contract.*

Joyce Chan

I was actively listening to the workers who advocated for not ratifying the contract. I mean, absolutely! As we were hearing more no voters speak, I became more active on trying to build bridges and trying to understand where each side was coming from. In fact, I changed my mind about them because my first impression of them was, "They are angry people," and it was hard for me to see where they were coming from because they were mistreating our bargaining team. But then

Vidya, a postdoc in the Health Sciences Department and a member of the bargaining team, was able to see past that and she made time to visit them at their respective picket lines and have actual conversations with them. I think they felt safe around Vidya because she was trying to get to the heart of the problem, and she said, "We need to change the way that we approach them." And at first, hearing that, I was skeptical because of my own feelings and my concern for my friends. But actually, sitting down, listening to their stories, especially at the Accessibility Teaching Rally, I was able to reflect and realized, "These are some of the most vulnerable people that we were trying to help with the new union contracts." And that changed my attitude—I was able to regard them with more respect.

In terms of lessons, the strike certainly taught me to be—this is going to come out as corny—more empathetic. Rather than being turned off when I see people using or spreading misinformation out of a kind of reflexive mistrust or expectation of harm, I'm now a bit more inclined to ask, "Why are they spreading misinformation?" I think there was one phrase that I learned from when I was doing the organizing with the Asian American groups, and that phrase was to "speak from the scar and not from the wound." This means you should not decide which lessons you have learned before the wound has healed, because you'd be speaking from a place of hurt. You'd be speaking from a place of anger and that can make you blind to the bigger picture, and prevent you from focusing on the people around you who might be able to help you through that wound. I was seeing people speaking from the wound, especially people who have been mistreated for being disabled academic workers, people who were unable to get the accommodations they needed or who were being pushed out. And the leaky pipeline in academia for new parents, women, and especially disabled workers was playing a role too. And so although I think experience is a very powerful informant, you have to take time to heal.

I'm also part of a group within our union actively working to change the processes and just make it less hellish for people here at UCSD to help fix that leaky pipeline for disabled workers, parents, and women. We even have a caretaker and new parent organization, which is run by people who are parents themselves or who have an aging or ill parent, which adds a lot of emotional burden. We are having consideration for different aspects of our lives that people can really connect over because it's important that workers *don't see our union as a service*. We are a community and we should be conducting ourselves more in such a way.

Kien Le

A personal win from the strike, for me, are the friends I made. Because before the strike, I was thinking, "I just want to get my degree and get out of grad school." I was a hater. I hated everyone. I was constantly asking myself, "Why are people so annoying?" It can be on the record, it's fine. People are so annoying; I hate everyone here. I feel that speaks to the culture of people in humanities. They are so isolated and they feel they have some intellectual superiority, which is funny. But when we went on strike, I was like, "Oh, not everyone is that crazy! These people involved in the strike; they know what they are talking about. They really understand the struggle. They really know what reality looks like. These are the people who I want to work with."

A few weeks ago, I had to go to the emergency room because I needed an emergency procedure. And people from our union showed up to the ER to visit me. And I never expected people to do that, to be honest. When I was in the emergency room, I was thinking, "I want to get out of here. I just want to get this over with." And then, before I went under the knife, people showed up because they wanted to, and that really make a difference. That is true solidarity.

I feel the strike helped us to build a stronger community because now, as we are talking, people show up to the actions against the university's retaliatory measures. In 2014 our membership rate was at 32 percent, which was low. And the strike was possible because we doubled the membership. Right now, we are at 62 percent. There is a structure of workers, department workers, head stewards, bargaining team, and unit chair, and it's a grassroots structure because all of them are our coworkers. And some people don't understand that; they don't understand our union is not a service. If you want something done, you have to organize it because it is your union.

In the 2014 contract vote, we did not even have two thousand people vote, statewide! And in 2022, at Irvine alone we had like two thousand people vote, which is such a difference. That never happened before. And now people are getting more involved! Before the strike, how many people showed up to our monthly membership meeting? Less than thirty people. At the last monthly membership meeting, in February 2023, we had seventy people. We disagree, but we realized we need to work together in order to win more.

This is the great outcome of the strike: we have more participation. This is something more people need to understand. Whatever radical move you want to make, you need to make sure everyone will come out for that. It doesn't work if you just expect people to follow because it is morally righteous. You need to go through a process of building majority support. We need power and we need numbers.

Emily Weintraut

One of the great outcomes of the strike is what I call my "picket friends." Prestrike, people were talking to their coworkers in their immediate area, but that changed thanks to the strike. I can name all the people with whom I had great times on the picket line. I had never seen them before in my life, but they became my *community*. My worker experience is more interdisciplinary now.

The strike also brought together a community of organizers called the Cunties. This is my version of the story of why we are called the Cunties and how we came to be together. In the lead-up to the strike, we made a group chat for strike captains as an organizing tool. We chose to do it on WhatsApp because it seemed like the most universal and user-friendly platform because everyone had used it before. The strike captains are leaders who signed up to talk to other people in their labs and departments to bring them information—even if some of them don't want to think of themselves as such. So, the point of that group chat was to help disseminate information and organize the picket line; it was also supposed to help to have more of a back and forth with bargaining. In short, the goal of the group chat was to connect with every worker—via the strike captains—so the bargaining team didn't need to talk to every single worker on campus. We were hoping it would be the workers on the picket talking to their strike captains and the strike captains talking to the bargaining team, and vice versa. However, the group of people who opposed the Davis bargaining team blew up our system and we could no longer use that chat to organize—especially logistical stuff—because there were political discussions going on. And then some of the strike captains were not always checking in, so we couldn't count on them to pass the information.

As a result, we created another chat to organize logistics because we needed that space. We couldn't have done many actions, like the occupation of the Mrak Building, without a chat like that. Cunties is that group chat. The Cunties chat was just tens of people—a lot of them I hadn't personally met until week three of the strike—who were trying to be productive. We are tens of people with different political beliefs and different niches. I'm way closer with certain people than with others. I wouldn't invite all the Cunties to my wedding [*laughs*]; it's not like that. Its original name was not Cunties, it was "Davis organizing" or something, but then the chat was named "Cunties" because Willa—an undergrad who works as a tutor—and I were screwing around and we came up with that name. There was a poll in the chat to name it, there were many names, all vaguely inappropriate and related to the fight against the UC. Cunties was the most voted name.

As with many organizing spaces, the Cunties chat became very social very quickly because people—the bargaining team, for example—needed emotional support to outlive the vitriol. This was not unusual; I remember I was part of a group chat once during a statewide caucus just for people to share their anxieties while in the meeting. We were organizing through Cunties, but it was also a very effective emotional support tool. Cunties is where I saw a lot of people cry and I cried myself just talking with people and de-stressing. I mean, some of our coworkers were being so loud with the vitriol, they were saying horrible, racist, misogynistic things, especially against the bargaining team members. They were fully displaying their biases, but then they acted as if they're the vanguards of the revolution. That's why the emotional support we got in Cunties made some of us very close.

Some people say that Cunties is a secret union clique. It's not. We asked everyone to join meetings in person and over Zoom, and the people who were against us never joined. They can't say we are secret if we invited them. What we do is hang out a lot because we work together so much that now some of us are friends.

Besides, now that the emotional part of the strike is over, we use the Cunties chat just as an easy method of communication. And we're now creating a Slack to help with organizing: to expand the organizing network, develop leaders, and empower people to take on more leadership roles. Cunties is dying, but it was an interesting way to bring people from different backgrounds together, different beliefs, different everything. Cunties was like an extension of your picket friends, essentially.

There is an important note I want to add about Cunties: we are pretty diverse. Everyone is at least left of center, but we do not agree on everything. There is a person who I always make fun of because they read communist theory, and I make jokes, "Theory is just fan fiction. I'm not going to read that." And they also tease me, "What do you believe then?" I don't have a political term to call myself because I don't think they're encompassing enough to represent every part of my political ideology—communism doesn't necessarily talk about abortion rights, and so on. The point is, I organize with people who have different beliefs. It would be bad if we all agreed on everything, having different opinions helps us to strategize better, and it empowers us. I'm a scaredy cat when it comes to escalation, but then I know many others who are always ready to escalate. And I even had some hard conversations because I was very scared to escalate.

How is it possible to build unity with the people who actively voted no on ratification and were against the majority of the bargaining team? I think they need to physically be present. It's been frustrating how just a handful of people came to our biweekly organizing committee meetings in January and February 2023. My perspective is, "I will unite with you, but you need to show up to something at some point; you need to actually organize. You can't just complain all the time about how it's undemocratic. It doesn't mean it's undemocratic just because you weren't there." I'm united with lots of people I disagree with because they continue to organize. For example, one person reached out to me, they went to one organizing committee meeting I facilitated, and they were expecting to facilitate the next meeting, but *for once* there were people already scheduled to facilitate the following meetings. So I told them they could reach out to the person who was going to facilitate next and see if they were willing to change dates. And I didn't get a response to that, and they didn't show up again. That makes me think they were just trying to get an excuse to say, "I'm actively trying to participate and they didn't let me coordinate a meeting." We're so open to unity, but it's like these people are trying to get you in "Gotcha!" moments.

Reshaping Academia

Aarthi Sekar

We, academic workers, won *so much* through the strike. I don't even know where to start. The UC strike won the best academic workers' contracts in the country up to this point. Also, after going on strike, we now *know* that we have the power to make fundamental changes to our working conditions and how academia is going to be moving forward. The UC strike has inspired other academic workers across the country to unionize; it has pressured other institutions to acknowledge that they are not paying living wages to academic workers. The UC strike has generated hundreds of incredibly motivated workers within UC and new leaders who understand how important collective action is. They are going to keep on changing our workplace, and we're only going to keep growing. The UC strike has generated the knowledge that as we move into new sectors, we can unionize all of those sectors. It's going to be us branching out into different sectors that need unions, like the biotech and engineering industries, and making strong those professions that already have unions, like teaching. The impacts of the strike are immediate and apparent, but they are also going to be lasting well into the future.

Yes, the strike was tough and it was long, but now that we are filing grievances based on the new contract language, we are moving on from the infighting. There is a group of workers in a lab who don't get paid on a monthly basis; they get paid a lump sum in the summer and they don't fully get that. And as soon as the student researchers' contract was ratified, they read it, reached out, and said, "Hey, we are having our rights violated and we would like to file a grievance," because they can now! There are so many people that would have been terrified to take any action, but after having been on the picket line, they—and we all—realize our worth and our power, and they are taking their situation into their own hands.

Our fight was not just about the over thirty-six thousand graduate workers or the forty-eight thousand academic workers in the system who are going to be affected for the next five years. This was a fight for our futures. All across the world, people are challenging the way academic institutions treat academic workers who provide instructional labor and research labor. This is a fight to challenge these institutions that are running as corporations and are making profits and have administrations amassing large fortunes and living luxurious lives.

Dez Manuel Fonseca

When I'd talk to academic workers outside of UC, I tried to not lead with my opinions on ratification or on the contract, which became the big story online, even if organizing should be the big story because it was only through organizing that we got or didn't get whatever contract. And because I did this, I'd get different perspectives on the strike, most of them based on what people saw online. There would be people who came to me and said, "I heard you got a shit contract." And other people would tell me, "I heard you got an amazing contract." Both sides because of what they saw on Twitter. A lot of people I talked to thought I would be against ratification. But also, the majority of people outside of UC knew that my perspective would be more informed than Twitter. So, I had good conversations with people, and they ended up understanding that a contract with 55 to 80 percent increases over two and a half years is not a shit contract!

The outcome of our strike, and the conversations that came from it, gave people a lot of hope to organize; friends at UT Austin and friends at Johns Hopkins have their own union campaigns or preliminary union campaigns—our struggle gave them a lot of hope. They talk about how much they need a contract like this to be able to live and work where they do.

One of the challenges we face in organizing because we are academic workers is that we can think a lot about theory. Our job is often abstract theorizing and thinking. Our job is not practice unless it comes to teaching. But it's important not to let that theorizing part substitute for the actual hard work of organizing and of practice. The theory only comes out of practice and not vice versa, and this argument has its own theoretical roots. Maybe that's specific to me and the social sciences. I had a lot of misconceptions, and ideas about the world, ideas about organizing, ideas about politics, ideas about labor, ideas about being a militant or being a radical whatever. And it was very different when I actually tried to put these ideas into practice. My notions of what it's like to actually talk to a coworker changed because we were not talking about theoretical things but about our workplace. We were not just thinking of ourselves as workers, but realizing that we are workers, realizing that we work for a wage, and that we're no better off materially in our jobs than the service workers who run this economy, who run this country, but that are ultimately exploited by this economy and by this country.

Academia is so competitive for the same reasons why academia is such a precarious workplace to be in. There's no jobs, there's no funding! You have to compete for jobs, you have to compete for funding, and that's a direct result of the defunding and deregulation of higher education in this country. For example, during my undergrad years there were three positions open and *a thousand people* applied. What that means is that the university is never going to run out of applicants; in consequence, the pay doesn't even have to be that much because people can't get another job.

Our movement as academic workers fights against that negative and unhealthy competition where we're workers in the precariat. Basically, we're just—as adjunct professors and grad students—gig workers begging for a teaching assistantship, begging for a class to teach. And there's no real reason aside from the profit motive that higher education should be organized in that way. So fighting to eliminate that gives me a reason to stay in academia. I don't just have to sit idly by and be in this industry that has become soul crushing. If it wasn't for the workers' movement, academia would keep crushing souls.

Curtis Rumrill

The university agreed to a contract that they never imagined they would agree to. They agreed to money and changes they never thought they would be agreeing to. Somehow the administration was not paying attention to the organizing that was happening and missed the kind of power that we were building going into the strike. And they have deep buyer's remorse on the contract that they have signed. You can see it down to the faculty level. You can see the faculty saying, "We don't know what our departments are going to look like anymore as a result of this contract, because we are obligated to spend money we don't have." Because they've been underpaying us for so long that now they're required to rectify that and they can't figure out how because they're used to running on nothing; they're used to using us as deeply cheap labor. I think the administration is weeping about how bad the contract is for them. They have no idea how to make what they have promised happen. And that is just a *huge* banner of success for us. We finally used our power and we forced them to change things that they never even imagined they could change. And so, from that perspective, I think that the strike needs to be deeply celebrated. And I think the narratives that are coming out that we somehow squandered our power or that the UAW squashed our strike are just absurd and dishonest. Maybe naive is the best reading of them. But I think a lot of them are deeply dishonest.

Kenzo Esquivel

Realistically speaking, we're the only group that has the power to fundamentally shift how universities work. And this is why I'm engaged in our grad union: it feels like it is the only realistic and meaningful way to really reshape institutions of higher education and academia as a workplace, and all that encompasses. One of the things coming out of the strike that's been really interesting to talk to people about is the way in which faculty feel a lot of tension around this idea that we're just workers and not students or trainees, and really reckoning with the issues of the model as it has existed. This trainer-trainee model no longer works in the world that we live in. And getting them to reckon with that has been a really interesting outcome of the strike. But fundamentally, if we want to see institutions of higher education that really embody the values that we were fighting for in this contract fight, I don't know of any other group that has the power to be able to do that. And I mean, more and more as I engage with universities, I'm like, "There's little to save here. We need to completely dismantle everything about it and start anew." But to the extent that that's maybe a far cry from where we're at, in the world as it is now, our grad worker unions are our best hope for reshaping the institutions in a way that hopefully can be geared toward better inclusivity and better actual quality of education, actually holding our institutions to the values that they purport. I just don't think that there's any other realistic accountability mechanism that exists beyond us. I maintain hope, though I will hopefully graduate before the next year, that we can take this up.

Part of what a union can do is build a long-term vision of what the university *should* look like. And the process of articulating that vision is bringing people to understand and cocreate that vision. Especially in the academic space, people haven't historically conceptualized themselves as workers, so there is an explicit process of conscientization that needs to take place about what it means to do labor in the academic space. The key first step that we play as a union is to get people to understand what their relationship is to the university. And then ultimately to give folks a sense that they can also control or have some say in our workplace.

Something that I remain hopeful about is that our movement can be the start of a new phase in how our union interacts with the university and how the academic spaces across the country think about our types of work and its importance in the functioning of a university system. And I think that our strike did serve the purpose of starting that conversation and energizing people at different universities to reckon with these questions. And we have a two-and-a-half-year contract, so I'm hopeful that the strike was the trial run.

It was historic, something we'd never done before. We should give ourselves, including the leadership, some grace—they didn't know how to run the biggest academic strike in US history, and neither did we! My frustration came from feeling like this needed to be a collective effort. But the bargaining team seemed to feel they had to act as the experts, making strategic decisions instead of making it a communal process where we all understood the stakes and fought for the best contract together.

Maddy Duong

The new contracts are having an impact in people's lives. I think the new conditions are going to make the experience of working in UC so much better. I mentioned that I know a lot of parent workers, so the paid parental leave is really important to them. Also the ability to file a grievance against abusive conduct is really important because there are so many people, especially international workers, who face a lot of abusive conduct from their principal investigator, and having that in the contract and educating people about what's in the contract will hopefully make people feel like they can do something about that.

If I were to give advice to workers organizing in other universities or colleges, I would say that you need to have a lot of one-on-one conversations! Don't send emails, don't send forms. Academic workers do not read their emails [*laughs*]! They do not pick up their phones. You literally have to go find them. But I think that's one reason why this works so well is because the union is literally the workers who talk to their coworkers. So, I feel like mobilizing the workers in each department is really important because they do isolate us. It's crazy! So, you have to get people from each department to organize their space. And I think it really works like that because then people know that person and *they're* able to have those one-on-one conversations with coworkers they know.

And if you come to the point of considering going on strike, I would say it's important to make people see that they have a personal investment in it. It's important to make them see that the union is them. And how else are we going to build power but to do this? Having an *engaged membership* is how you have a strong, sustained strike. It's important that the organizing committee is made up of the right group of workers—workers that other workers can identify with. By "right group of workers" I mean . . . if it was all men, then I wouldn't feel compelled to be part of this group. But I saw international students like Vietnamese international students. That made me feel, "I'm Vietnamese, I can identify with this person." I saw other women leading chants, like Tia, so I was like, "Okay I can identify with this person." People that other workers can identify with, so they don't feel like it's an exclusive space.

Elsie Jacobson

When it comes to what we won with the strike, and with the bargaining process that began months before, I would say that we made genuine, meaningful progress on everything—and I mean *everything*—that we wanted to make progress on. For example, in our previous contract we had four weeks of parental leave, but now we have eight weeks. And now it is called family leave, so it can be used for a variety of family emergencies. Also, in the previous contract there was no support for childcare, and now we have $2,500 a year, and it goes up $100 every year. Obviously, we want more, but given that we had nothing, it is pretty good. But more importantly, these wins are a strong base to build on in the future.

There is a postdoc in my area who, literally, his wife gave birth the week after ratification, and they got those benefits straight away! And that's going to make a massive impact in their lives. I really felt good seeing him so happy about the contract. I always get emotional talking about this case [*crying*]. Seeing an immediate direct benefit was amazing.

Another win I would emphasize is, obviously, the disability article. The progress we made is really exciting. Previously the reasonable accommodations article said, "Reasonable accommodations must be provided." But there wasn't much around the time frame, and the "reasonable" could be interpreted almost at the will of the university and the principal investigators. I have a friend who was part of the Gonda picket, and their story with the old disability article was so upsetting. They needed accommodations for their disability and it took months, *actual months*, to set up. And it was expected for them to carry on with business as usual—as if they didn't have a disability—in the meantime. What we have now are "interim measures," which means that even if setting up the accommodation takes a while—because some physical accessibility things do just take time—there have to be interim measures so that no one is having to work in unsafe conditions while also having to manage their disability. So, the "interim measures" thing is a really important thing—I just can't stress what a *huge* deal it is.

Another important thing incorporated into the disability article is the Joint Labor Management Committee. This committee has potential to make a big impact, but it also requires our serious engagement for it to work; it is not guaranteed. The purpose of this joint committee is to intervene whenever the accommodation processes aren't working for people or when the accommodations need to be secured in a more systematic way. For example, if you need an accommodation like an expensive electronic pipette for lab work, maybe you are worried about asking for that because it's going to cost a lot of money and typically your principal investigator would pay for it, and if your principal investigator pays for your accommodation there is always a worry that it is going to affect the funding for your lab work; or maybe you require the accommodation but your principal investigator or the university does not want to comply because they consider it too expensive. In these cases, the workers could file a grievance so the Joint Labor Management Committee—where there are representatives from the university and the union—has a discussion about the resources and strategies regarding accommodations so the solution is better and systematic.

And then, regarding the salaries, well, the salary was one of the earliest discussions we had in the disability working group because one thing that disabled people need is a better salary because it's expensive to have a disability, between medical bills and paying more for conveniences that are necessary. This is the case for parents too, for whom having more money makes a huge difference. So, the wages we got in the new contract are amazing. It felt amazing seeing people thrilled looking at the wage calculator. Our new contract is going to change people's lives; it already is changing them, I'm sure.

For international workers' rights, what's really awesome is that we now have visa leave, which is new for the first time, meaning postdocs have paid time off to deal with issues and appointments related to our visas. We also have some protections against changes in the visa laws, which were especially important because of the changes that happened during the pandemic and the Trump presidency. Travel and visa renewal became more difficult with the pandemic and lockdowns, meanwhile Trump was attempting to limit student visas and ban immigrants from Muslim-majority countries. Now we have some protections around that. Also, the work appointment lengths changed, which is especially important for international workers because the system we had was that the appointment length for new postdocs was one year at the start, then two years, and then one year again. But often the two-year appointment wasn't actually given—who knows why, they have all sorts of excuses, they always do! And now the first contract *has* to be for a minimum of two years. And that is really important because, again, the longer your visa is, the less frequently you have to renew it, and renewing your visa requires going to your home country for an indefinite period of time, every time. Not having to renew their visa every year makes a huge difference for international workers.

Another thing I would say is that I think at the most simple, basic level, better working conditions are good for everyone, and I think poor working conditions do disproportionately affect different groups of people. For instance, because of my disability, I'm much less resilient to poor working conditions. For example, if I can't take sick days and work from home when necessary, I would be pushed out of the system. Higher wages mean that, for example, people who have to support families can actually be in the system and work here without having to sacrifice things that are impossible to sacrifice. I think that in itself is really important to start with. For all UC talks about equity, our contract provides practical support to diverse scholars.

On top of that, our movement has an impact on social equity too. I mean, climate change is inextricably linked with everything! I think the poorer working conditions we have, and the more personal problems we're struggling with to get through the day, the harder it is to focus on the bigger systemic issues. That's part of how capitalism works; it makes people constantly fight for their own survival, so that it's hard to have any energy left over to fight for the long-term survival of everyone.

Emily Weintraut

The institution of academia is going to change so long as our union is empowering people and these people continue to work in academia. Just with the antiharassment protections that we have, things are changing. There was a time when, if you were a man, you couldn't report your advisor if they were screaming or saying horrible things to you. It was hard to fight against that. The protections we won with our strike break that down. Now you don't have to be a protected class—like a woman working with a male principal investigator—in order to prove that you have been harassed and abused. That's going to be a big thing for women in female-dominated fields in STEM where you have women who are in positions of power. Because, you know, women can be abusive to other women, but before our contract, if it wasn't a man abusing a woman, it was hardly considered abuse.

Also, childcare, transportation benefits, and wage increases will help to break down the barriers in academia. My mom went to college when I was growing up. I think that if she had childcare benefits like the ones we won, she would have gone to grad school right after undergrad. We wouldn't have been extreme couponing to stay afloat and out of debt. I think a contract like ours is going to incentivize some people to stay in grad school; it's also going to push departments to make good on their DEI commitments. And I say this as someone who doesn't want to stay in academia because I know how toxic a lot of the culture is, but I genuinely do think it's going to get better.

We are seeing other universities organizing to be unionized, or to strengthen their contracts, like Temple University or Rutgers, where workers took a strike authorization vote recently, in March 2023. We are communicating with people in Rutgers through the TikTok account and in other ways too.

And if you are reading this, thinking of organizing with your coworkers at your university, I would tell you that the way that you start is by talking to your coworkers. That's how it all starts: you talk to your coworkers. A union is not effective if it's just some political agenda executed by a couple of people and you aren't talking to their coworkers about it. Your coworkers are not going to support that if they don't feel heard. They're going to feel disenfranchised by it. The way that you have an effective union and one that can make such transformative change is you talk to your coworkers.

The Future

Aarthi Sekar

I've thought about the fact that I'm not going to benefit as much from this contract because I'm in my seventh year. I thought about it in the middle of the conflicts among workers, but I didn't struggle with it. I'm really happy that I fought for one of the best academic workers' contracts in the US. I am really proud of what I contributed and it doesn't bother me that I won't see it affect my working conditions for long because this contract is going to provide basic protections and rights for the generation after me. I got into this fight because I don't want people to go through what I did. And now I'm really proud because, yes, this is going to change the trajectory of academia.

Dez Manuel Fonseca

The strike was the craziest thing I've done in my life, probably. The most intense experience of my life. And here I talked a lot about regrets and wishful thinking, but it was really positive! At the same time ... I'm glad it's over! I don't know if that's the right expression, but it was really intense and with intensity comes positives, comes negatives. There was a lot of bad blood at some points between workers, and I tried to play peacemaker a lot. I wasn't sleeping. I was running myself into the ground. I was barely eating—I lost fifteen, twenty pounds during the strike. If you had asked me about the strike on December 24, oh man! I wouldn't even take your call! I was relieved it was over. Ratification felt like the most intense battle! Even though the big battle was against the university. I think in that period of internal debate we cared about our coworkers deeply in a way we don't care about the university, the admin, the bosses, the capitalists. It was no problem beefing with them, no problem beefing with the university but having those internal, political discussions and debates was very difficult.

Now that the strike is over, organizing and trying to maintain academic progress is harder. But I'm trying to capture the momentum of the strike and turn it into long-term organizing, which is difficult because it's hard to get people to keep making the sacrifices they made during the strike for the strength of our union and organized labor. And some people who have committed years to our union, and who have put off their dissertation for years, are now stepping back, understandably. And some people who got involved during the strike, are staying involved and will stay involved for years. And some people who were really involved in the strike have taken a step back and maybe they'll join later. But I know I'm super involved. I'm having several meetings a week regarding different campaigns. We didn't come close to winning everything we wanted to win. Nobody should think otherwise. We deserve a lot more, and we have to organize if we want to actually win those things. It's not enough to lament the fact that we didn't get it; we have to do something about it.

We are doing a lot right now. We are underway with organizing politically to expand the right to strike and to sympathy strike.[1] We're also really fighting back against those poison pills in the Taft-Hartley Act of 1947, fighting back against the assault on labor that began then and intensified in the seventies and eighties. Making sure the contract is enforced, filing grievances because the university is not going to magically decide to respect all terms of the contract. We are also building membership participation and doing so in a way that facilitates democratic participation and educated participation. We are doing political education. We are working with other unions to think about cross-union solidarity. I have a lot of work. But I also feel like organizing has made my life more efficient. I know how to spend my time wisely now.

Joyce Chan

This strike made me grow in different ways. It definitely helped with my confidence. I don't think I've ever really had a space to really be vocal about my needs, be vocal about standing up and advocating for others because working within the system—as I did in my PhD—was very, very different from what union and labor organizing does. I think I was able to surprise myself by speaking in front of a huge crowd because

---

1 A sympathy strike is a type of strike in which workers stop working to show solidarity with another group of workers who are already on strike. In addition to demonstrating solidarity, the purpose of these strikes is to increase pressure on the boss targeted by the original strike.

I felt safe at that time! I felt safe. I felt *belonging*! And I felt that even if I stumbled or messed up, everyone would be understanding of that.

I never told my parents I was on strike. They found out in a Chinese-language newspaper because during the strike we had reporters from India, from Europe, from China, come and interview our striking members. And it just so happened that it made it all the way back to New York in a Chinese-language newspaper. And then my mom remembered I had told her about my elected position in the union, and she phoned me and asked, "Did you get your raise? How much was it?" [*laughs*]. And I don't think she even knew that we were striking, she just knew that *something* was happening. She probably felt I was too good a daughter to not work, so she was not worried about me getting in trouble or withholding labor. She just wanted to know the raise amount [*laughs*].

Curtis Rumrill

Optimistic me says this is the birth of a functional organization because we're going from a situation in which we had extremely low participation in our union to being a mass participation organization. And I think the long-term organizing that has to happen is in building coalition and alliances and relationships with people that disagree with each other, to bring people together who have disagreed vitriolically, as long as they are capable of acting in good faith and can participate in the actual decision-making processes of the union. I think that if we can do that work, then we are in a position to be a really good, functional organization.

Kenzo Esquivel

I feel okay about the strike now. When I was thinking about doing this interview this morning, I was like, there's a 70 percent chance I will cry. I was feeling nervous about processing it because, well, so much time and energy went into it, and there was, in the end, so much tension and strife and challenging dynamics at play. So part of the reason why I did agree on doing this project is because I do want to process, I do want to think through this. But the spaces—a joint council meeting at the end of January—that were created to do this type of reflection, at least within our union structure, had a very specific timeline and space and bent that wasn't the best for me because, one, I wasn't able to go in person and Zooming in felt very removed; and two, there was a sense that we needed to celebrate what happened, which makes it hard to reckon with a lot of what happened that wasn't as positive.

Today, in March 2023, as we speak, we have a number of late pay issues in my department. So we're trying to resolve those. The biggest issue right now for us is resolving and getting clarity around what the actual implementation of our new wages will be for next year. But this feels like a mess and is another place where I personally was pushing for us to get a lot more concrete language within our contract because right now, it is a case-by-case, department-by-department issue. And hopefully we'll have some more clarity around a statewide way of dealing with this.

Maddy Duong

On a more personal basis, I'm a different person after the strike. For example, I think it definitely would have taken a little bit more convincing for prestrike Maddy to do a disruptive action or participate in civil disobedience. I think the strike made me more comfortable around that idea, because previously I haven't thought about protesting in terms of my workplace. I had participated in protests around social issues, social justice or environmental justice, such as the Black Live Matter protests and Iran. But I hadn't thought I would be part of a rally or anything like that to change something in my workplace.

When the strike ended, a part of me actually missed seeing my strike friends every day, although I'm working on something important with them. I think everybody experienced that poststrike, like, "Oh, I miss my strike friends" [*laughs*]. But I definitely didn't miss the strike pizza and the strike donuts. So, it was good to get back into regular life. And I've been actively participating in organizing, which feels good. This experience, the strike, made me better in every way. It really empowered me as an individual! It was like a speed-trial leadership thing that enhanced my leadership skills.

What's next for me, as an organizer, is telling people about their rights and educating everyone about what's in their new contracts, how they can enforce their new contract, catching those grievances, and engaging more members for the next time we go into bargaining so we can build up power and resources.

And in life, I'm going to grad school. I don't know yet if I'm going to go to UC. I'll be really sad to leave the UAW if it does come to that. But

I've already reached out to the unions at the other school to see what's going on. At first, when I was looking for where to go to grad school, it felt important to be in a unionized school. But then I realized it would be cool to unionize a school. So, whatever happens, I'm going to keep being an organizer.

Kien Le

Right now I'm a part of the organizing committee. We organize orientations for new workers. We want to have as many members as we can, and grow in numbers. We are also organizing actions against UC cutbacks. Even though the strike is over, organizing is not; we need to keep pushing. We need people to get more involved. It's not the time for people to turn away. We need to build more power. That's what I have been doing; that's what I'm trying to achieve. I'm trying to encourage other people to step up: if you are a member, you can sign up to be a department steward now. If you're a department steward and you want other people to get involved, you can recruit more people to share that responsibility, or you can run for head steward. I just want people to know they need to keep organizing rather than waiting for something to happen.

Elsie Jacobson

I know I'm not the same person I was before the strike. But it's kind of hard to say for sure how I'm different. It is an experience that is going to be with me forever, even if I have a lot of specific events I don't remember as well as I would like.

I feel I learned a lot about how power works, and how the university works, and how academia works. In some ways it really opened my eyes because when we are in the lab on a day-to-day basis, we can feel very disconnected from everything else. In a lot of ways, doing lab research feels a little bit like you're working in your tiny little setup by yourself. And the strike was like stepping back and seeing the whole thing as one entity that we're part of. That was really a kind of eye-opening thing for me.

And knowing for a fact what we can achieve when we work together was also eye-opening. Right now, I'm organizing along with people who, like myself, live in UCLA housing, and I know the strike is the foundation of this new organizing. We have a lot of problems in our building and the UCLA management doesn't do enough maintenance and when something goes wrong, they will sometimes quite literally stick a band-aid over it. A friend had a ceiling leak and, instead of seriously attempting to fix the leak, they literally put a piece of paper over it and they said, "We'll come back," which didn't happen. So, right now, one particular problem that we are having is that the sewage comes out of the toilets, in some cases out of the kitchen sinks, and it floods the apartments on the first floor. So far, UC has had to rip out part of the walls and part of the floor because it's all contaminated with sewage—my partner and I have bags of contaminated stuff. But UC knows they have us trapped because we pay below-market-rate rent, so they just absolutely skimp on everything they possibly can, and if you want them to fix something you have to make a job out of complaining. Right now we are demanding a housing complex where if something bad happens, there is a standardized protocol for compensation and reimbursement, and—for example—free rent for the period that you've got literal sewage flooding your house. I'm doing my best to take what I learn from the strike and use it to make housing at UCLA better.

Emily Weintraut

Personally, I'm more and more frustrated with UC now that the strike has ended and I've continued to organize. For example, just in February 2023—two months after the strike ended—I got an email from UC's labor relations office in response to an abuse grievance we filed in my department and I felt *literally* nauseous about how the university continues to deny that abuse and harassment happen. We won these transformative protections, but so far, instead of becoming a better workplace, the university is stalling on enforcing the contract and we've been having to use direct action to force them to do their job. And we're going to keep fighting and forcing them to respect and enforce the contract—they signed it, they must uphold it.

People don't come into my lab as much because of this abuse grievance currently happening with a staff member who has access to my lab. He has a new victim every single time, and it gets worse the more that you interact with him. One of my coworkers only works on weekends, and another has completely relocated because the university has refused to implement interim measures or do anything.

What does the future look like for me in our union? I would love for other people to step up to replace some of the work I'm doing. That's the dream. But right now, I'm running for head steward of Local 2865 in UC Davis just because people have asked me. If I get elected, I have two goals: to vocalize people's concerns and to find someone to replace me. If I don't get elected, I'm not going to be that upset about it.

Right now, our biggest concern is getting more members involved, because once you get that involvement, it's like a snowball. If people were to get involved, it would be much easier for everyone. That's what happened with me. I kind of just fell into union organizing. I never saw myself being as involved with a union. I never saw myself doing any of this ever. I also didn't want to go into academia because of all the issues that we are fighting against. But our union really has transformed my life. I so strongly believe in what we're doing.

Bibliography

Brown University. "Brown Succeeds on Appeal." Brown University. July 16, 2004. https://www.brown.edu/Administration/News_Bureau/2004-05/04-004.html.

Graduate Assistants United. "Our History Timeline." Graduate Assistants United. Accessed May 4, 2024. https://www.ufgau.org/history.html.

Graduate Employee Organization. "GEO History." Graduate Employee Organization. Accessed May 4, 2024. https://www.geo3550.org/about/history.

Graduate Teaching Fellows Federation. "Our History." Graduate Teaching Fellows Federation. Accessed May 4, 2024. https://gtff3544.net/about/history.

Herbert, William, Jacob Apkarian, and Joseph van der Naald. "2024 Directory of Bargaining Agents and Contracts in Institutions of Higher Education." National Center for the Study of Collective Bargaining in Higher Education and the Professions. September, 2024. https://research-data.hunter.cuny.edu/ncscbhep/2024DirectoryofBargainingAgentsandContractsinInstitutionsofHigherEducation.

Kelly, Kim. *Fight Like Hell: The Untold History of American Labor*. Atria/One Signal Publishers, 2022.

Langin, Katie. "Fewer U.S. Scientists Are Pursuing Postdoc Positions, New Data Show." *Science*, March 25, 2024. https://www.science.org/content/article/fewer-u-s-scientists-are-pursuing-postdoc-positions-new-data-show.

Lynd, Staughton. "Part 2: Rebuilding the Labor Movement from Below." In *Doing History from the Bottom Up: On E. P. Thompson, Howard Zinn, and Rebuilding the Labor Movement from Below*, Haymarket Books, 2014.

McAlevey, Jane. *A Collective Bargain: Unions, Organizing, and the Fight for Democracy*. Ecco, 2020.

McAlevey, Jane. *Raising Expectations (and Raising Hell): My Decade Fighting for the Labor Movement*. Verso, 2012.

Mohan-Ram, Vid. "NYU Graduates Win Right to Form Union." *Science*, November 3, 2000. https://www.science.org/content/article/nyu-graduates-win-right-form-union.

Ochoa, Ricardo. "Barbarians at the Gate." *California Public Employee Relations* no. 143 (2000).

Price, Michael. "Nontenure-Track Researchers Ratify First Contract with the University of California." *Science*, November 14, 2019. https://www.science.org/content/article/nontenure-track-researchers-ratify-first-contract-university-california.

Teaching Assistant Association. "History." Accessed May 4, 2024. https://taa-madison.org/history.

Thompson, E.P. *The Making of the English Working Class*. Victor Gollancz Ltd., 1963.

Thompson, E.P. *The Poverty of Theory and Other Essays*. Monthly Review Press, 1978.

UAW 2865. "SRU Contract Ratification Results." UAW 2865 Mailchimp, December 23, 2022. https://mailchi.mp/6f8d2bd383ea/2865-sru-contract-ratification-results.

UAW 2865. "UAW 2865 Membership #s, 2008-22." Unpublished internal document. Accessed May 4, 2024.

University of California. "Budget for Current Operations. Context for the Budget Request. 2023-2024." University of California Office of the President. Accessed May 4, 2024. https://www.ucop.edu/operating-budget/_files/rbudget/2023-24-budget-detail.pdf.

University of California. "Fall Enrollment at a Glance." University of California Information Center. Last updated January 19, 2024. https://www.universityofcalifornia.edu/about-us/information-center/fall-enrollment-glance.

University of California. "UC Hispanic-Serving Institutions Initiative." University of California Office of the President. Accessed May 4, 2024. https://www.ucop.edu/hsi-initiative/index.html.

University of California. "Undergraduate Students: Admissions and Enrollment." *University of California Accountability Report*. July 16, 2021. https://accountability.universityofcalifornia.edu/2021/chapters/chapter-1.html.

University of California. "The University of California Leads in US Patents." UC Newsroom. June 12, 2018. https://www.universityofcalifornia.edu/news/university-california-leads-us-patents.

About the Editors

Aleida García Aguirre is an independent history researcher specializing in the study of processes of subjectivation of young revolutionaries in Mexico and Latin America during the seventies, and the social history of student movements and armed organizations in provincial Mexico during the Cold War. Her methodologies and theory are rooted in history from below, social history, oral history, and memory studies and the narratives of the self. She has been awarded a Doctoral Scholarship by the Ministry of Education of Argentina and a Fulbright Scholarship, and has worked as a professor in various institutions in Mexico, and in Human Rights Research for the Mexican Secretaría de Gobernación (Secretariat of the Interior). She is the author of *Memorias inquietas: De estudiantes rurales a guerrilleros urbanos* (Restless Memories: From Rural Students to Urban Guerrillas) and "The Subject Is Still There: Judicial Statements and Mexican Political-Military Organizations in the Seventies." She lives in Oakland, California.

Molly Vine became a UAW member while earning an MFA in documentary film at San Francisco State University. Following grad school, she directed and produced documentaries related to labor and social movements. She then went on to become one of the lead organizers in the 2022 UAW strike at UC. Molly lives in Oakland and works as a UAW organizer focused on helping workers form new unions.

Patrick Dexter became a member of UAW 2865 while earning a Master of Urban and Regional Planning degree at UCLA. In 2020 he joined the campaign to form Student Researchers United–UAW and then became a lead organizer with UC-UAW during the 2022 strike. He now works as an organizer for UAW Region 6 and lives in Los Angeles.

ABOUT PM PRESS

PM Press is an independent, radical publisher of critically necessary books for our tumultuous times. Our aim is to deliver bold political ideas and vital stories to all walks of life and arm the dreamers to demand the impossible. Founded in 2007 by a small group of people with decades of publishing, media, and organizing experience, we have sold millions of copies of our books, most often one at a time, face to face. We're old enough to know what we're doing and young enough to know what's at stake. Join us to create a better world.

PM Press
PO Box 23912
Oakland, CA 94623
www.pmpress.org

PM Press in Europe
europe@pmpress.org
www.pmpress.org.uk

FRIENDS OF PM PRESS

These are indisputably momentous times—the financial system is melting down globally and the Empire is stumbling. Now more than ever there is a vital need for radical ideas.

In the many years since its founding—and on a mere shoestring—PM Press has risen to the formidable challenge of publishing and distributing knowledge and entertainment for the struggles ahead. With hundreds of releases to date, we have published an impressive and stimulating array of literature, art, music, politics, and culture. Using every available medium, we've succeeded in connecting those hungry for ideas and information to those putting them into practice.

Friends of PM allows you to directly help impact, amplify, and revitalize the discourse and actions of radical writers, filmmakers, and artists. It provides us with a stable foundation from which we can build upon our early successes and provides a much-needed subsidy for the materials that can't necessarily pay their own way. You can help make that happen—and receive every new title automatically delivered to your door once a month—by joining as a Friend of PM Press. And, we'll throw in a free T-shirt when you sign up.

Here are your options:

- **$30 a month** Get all books and pamphlets plus a 50% discount on all webstore purchases
- **$40 a month** Get all PM Press releases (including CDs and DVDs) plus a 50% discount on all webstore purchases
- **$100 a month** Superstar—Everything plus PM merchandise, free downloads, and a 50% discount on all webstore purchases

For those who can't afford $30 or more a month, we have **Sustainer Rates** at $15, $10, and $5. Sustainers get a free PM Press T-shirt and a 50% discount on all purchases from our website.

Your Visa or Mastercard will be billed once a month, until you tell us to stop. Or until our efforts succeed in bringing the revolution around. Or the financial meltdown of Capital makes plastic redundant. Whichever comes first.

Mutiny in the Mountains: West Virginia Public Workers 1969–2019

Gordon Simmons

ISBN: 979-8-88744-153-5
$19.95 192 pages

Mutiny in the Mountains uses labor history to show the way forward for millions of workers struggling in an age of uncertainty.

In 1969, thousands of West Virginia state highway workers went on strike in fear that they faced impending loss of their jobs as they were excluded from civil service protection. Although the walkout coincided with one of the most severe winters to affect road conditions, the newly elected governor fired the strikers. The 1969 State Road Strike inaugurated a half decade of public sector organizing and protest that culminated in the historic public-school strikes of 2018–19 that shut down all schools across the Mountain State and inspired a wave of public education strikes in Arizona, Oklahoma, Kentucky, and beyond.

Beginning with the nation's first general strike in 1877, that started with railroad workers in Martinsburg, West Virginia, and including the early coal strikes in 1912–13 and an armed insurrection in 1921, most treatments of the state's labor history have focused on the private sector. This is the first comprehensive history of the struggles waged by state and local government workers in West Virginia. The involvement of numerous unions and interventions of the state legislative and executive branches is traced in order to provide context for those struggles. Relying on journalistic sources, legislative enactments, court decisions, and participant interviews, *Mutiny in the Mountains* accounts the fifty-year struggle of West Virginia's public sector workers to assert power without the benefit of significant collective bargaining rights or political leverage.

Labor Power and Strategy

John Womack Jr.
Edited by Peter Olney and Glenn Perusek

ISBN: 978-1-62963-974-1
$16.95 192 pages

What would it take to topple Amazon? To change how health care works in America? To break up the media monopolies that have taken hold of our information and imaginations? How is it possible to organize those without hope working on the margins? In *Labor Power and Strategy*, legendary strategist, historian and labor organizer John Womack speaks directly to a new generation, providing rational, radical, experience-based perspectives that help target and run smart, strategic, effective campaigns in the working class.

In this sleek, practical, pocket inspiration, Womack lays out a timely plan for identifying chokepoints and taking advantage of supply chain issues in order to seize and build labor power and solidarity. Interviewed by Peter Olney of the International Longshore and Warehouse Union, Womack's lively, illuminating thoughts are built upon by ten young labor organizers and educators, whose responses create a rich dialogue and open a space for joyful, achievable change. With stories of triumph that will bring readers to tears this back-pocket primer is an instant classic.

"In Our Revolution we shout, 'When we Organize, We Win,' but organize who and win what? Labor Power and Strategy *is a great collection of Womack and 10 organizers debating strategic workplace organizing vs associational or more general organizing at workplaces or in communities. Womack, in a long initial interview and in the conclusion, argues that without organizing workplace chokepoints, we are left with the spontaneous movements that come and go. Several of the 10 organizers essentially argue that the spontaneous can become conscious and long lasting. Grab the book and take up the debate."*
—Larry Cohen, board chair of Our Revolution, past president of Communications Workers of America

"In this fascinating and insightful dialogue, the distinguished historian John Womack and a set of veteran labor activists probe the most fundamental of questions: How do we organize the 21 century working-class and give it the power to transform world capitalism? Are workers with vital skills and strategic leverage the key to a labor resurgence, or should organizers wager upon a mobilization of working people whose relationship to the economy's commanding heights is more diffuse? Or can we arrive at some dialectical symbiosis? Whatever the answer, this is the kind of constructively radical conversation essential to the rebirth of working-class power in our time."
—Nelson Lichtenstein, historian and author of *Capitalism Contested: The New Deal and Its Legacies*

Insurgent Labor: The Vermont AFL-CIO 2017-2023

David Van Deusen with a Foreword by Kim Kelly and an Introduction by Steve Early

ISBN: 979-8-88744-036-1
$19.95 288 pages

Insurgent Labor tracks the trials and tribulations of bringing a formerly stagnant labor council into national relevance with an unapologetically left-wing agenda.

David Van Deusen charts the rise of the UNITED! slate to create a progressive and militant labor organization. He chronicles the many victories throughout his tenure including expanding union democracy into the rank and file, moving power away from single individuals and into democratic structures, supporting farm workers, supporting Black self-determination, and providing solidarity with the Revolution in Rojava.

The boldest step undertaken by the Vermont AFL-CIO—and marker of years of steady progress in labor organizing and raising of political consciousness in Vermont—was authorizing a call for a general strike throughout Vermont as a possible response to the November 2020 coup threat by then US President Donald Trump.

This book should be of interest to anyone, whether they have merely thought of joining a union or are an old union hand. Most importantly, Insurgent Labor offers a blueprint for militant labor's advances in an era of capitalist polycrisis and offers hope for a brighter future based around equality, justice, and true democracy.

"Employing historically effective left strategies Van Duesen shows how a Central Labor Body organized to fight for both the economic and political interests of workers can unite with other social movements to blunt right-wing attacks on workers at the workplace and globally. Essential reading for those who believe in democracy."
—Fernando E. Gapasin, principal researcher for AFL-CIO 1996 "Union Cities" project and coauthor with Bill Fletcher, Jr. of *Solidarity Divided*

"Labor Councils focused on member involvement and action are needed now more than ever. Vermont is a model for cross union solidarity and David Van Deusen's account should inspire others."
—Larry Cohen, former national president of Communications Workers of America and AFL-CIO Executive Council member; current chair of Our Revolution

Working Class History: Everyday Acts of Resistance & Rebellion

With a Foreword by Noam Chomsky

ISBN: 978-1-62963-823-2 (paperback)
978-1-62963-887-4 (hardcover)
$20.00/$59.95 352 pages

History is not made by kings, politicians, or a few rich individuals—it is made by all of us. From the temples of ancient Egypt to spacecraft orbiting Earth, workers and ordinary

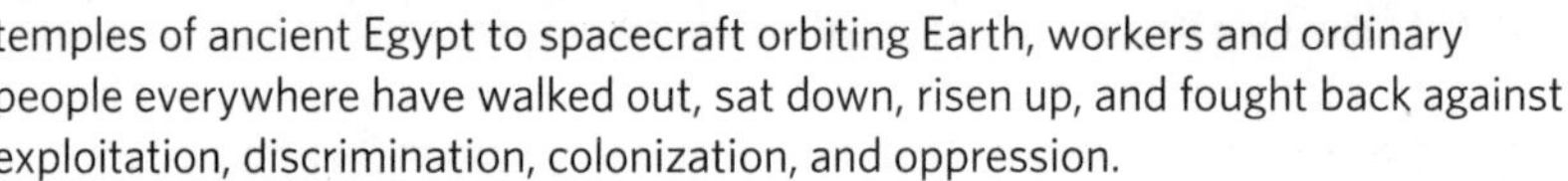

people everywhere have walked out, sat down, risen up, and fought back against exploitation, discrimination, colonization, and oppression.

Working Class History presents a distinct selection of people's history through hundreds of "on this day in history" anniversaries that are as diverse and international as the working class itself. Women, young people, people of color, workers, migrants, Indigenous people, LGBT+ people, disabled people, older people, the unemployed, home workers, and every other part of the working class have organized and taken action that has shaped our world, and improvements in living and working conditions have been won only by years of violent conflict and sacrifice. These everyday acts of resistance and rebellion highlight just some of those who have struggled for a better world and provide lessons and inspiration for those of us fighting in the present. Going day by day, this book paints a picture of how and why the world came to be as it is, how some have tried to change it, and the lengths to which the rich and powerful have gone to maintain and increase their wealth and influence.

This handbook of grassroots movements, curated by the popular Working Class History project, features many hidden histories and untold stories, reinforced with inspiring images, further reading, and a foreword from legendary author and dissident Noam Chomsky.

"This ingenious archive of working class history, organized as an extended calendar, is filled with little and better known events. Reading through the text, the power, fury, and persistence of the working-class struggles shine. 'Working class' is broader than unions and job struggles, and rather includes all emancipatory acts of working-class people, be they Indigenous peoples fighting for land rights, African Americans massively protesting police killings, anticolonial liberation movements, women rising up angry, or mass mobilizations worldwide against imperialist wars. It is international in scope as is the working class. This is a book the reader will open every day to recall and be inspired by what occurred on that date. I love the book and will look forward to the daily readings."
—Roxanne Dunbar-Ortiz, author of *An Indigenous Peoples' History of the United States*

Free City! The Fight for San Francisco's City College and Education for All

Marcy Rein, Mickey Ellinger, and Vicki Legion with a Foreword by Pauline Lipman

ISBN: 978-1-62963-829-4
$20.00 288 pages

Free City! The Fight for San Francisco's City College and Education for All tells the story of the five years of organizing that turned a seemingly hopeless defensive fight into a victory for the most progressive free college measure in the US. In 2012, the accreditor sanctioned City College of San Francisco, one of the biggest and best community colleges in the country, and a year later proposed terminating its accreditation, leading to a state takeover. *Free City!* follows the multipronged strategies of the campaign and the diverse characters that carried them out. Teachers, students, labor unions, community groups, public officials, and concerned individuals saved a treasured public institution as San Francisco's working-class communities of color battled the gentrification that was forcing them out of the city. And they pushed back against the national "reform" agenda of corporate workforce training that drives students towards debt and sidelines lifelong learning and community service programs. Combining analysis with narrative, *Free City!* offers a case study in the power of positive vision and solution-oriented organizing and a reflection on what education can and should be.

"Free City! *is a timely and urgently needed saga of successful resistance to the corporate forces threatening the very existence of public higher education in California. It is a meticulously documented history, a breathless narrative, and a comprehensive guide to action all in one. The lessons learned in the fight to save City College of San Francisco need to be widely understood and applied by all educators, students, and community members committed to the struggle for education for all."*
—Justin Akers Chacón, professor of Chicano/Chicana Studies, San Diego City College, coauthor of *No One is Illegal: Fighting Racism and State Violence on the US-Mexico Border* and author of *Radicals in the Barrio: Magonistas, Socialists, Wobblies, and Communists in the Mexican-American Working Class*

"The struggle and success of Free City! *proves that when people organize, persist, and resist injustice, they win!"*
—Diane Ravitch, founder and president, Network for Public Education, author of *The Reign of Error: The Hoax of the Privatization Movement and the Danger to America's Public Schools*

Strike! 50th Anniversary Edition

Jeremy Brecher with a Preface by Sara Nelson and a Foreword by Kim Kelly

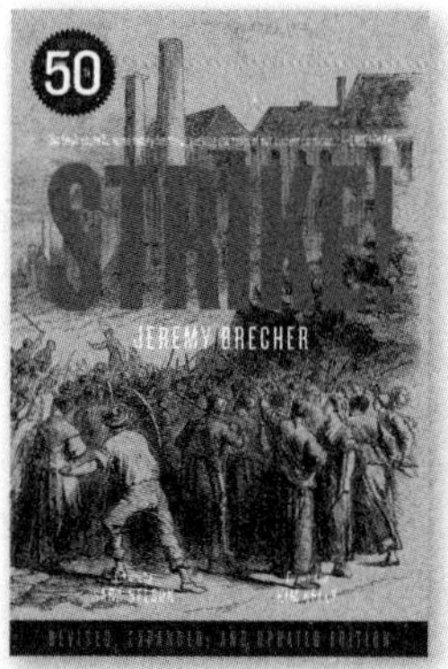

ISBN: 978-1-62963-800-3 (paperback)
978-1-62963-856-0 (hardcover)
$28.95/$60.00 640 pages

Jeremy Brecher's *Strike!* narrates the dramatic story of repeated, massive, and sometimes violent revolts by ordinary working people in America. Involving nationwide general strikes, the seizure of vast industrial establishments, nonviolent direct action on a massive scale, and armed battles with artillery and tanks, this exciting hidden history is told from the point of view of the rank-and-file workers who lived it. Encompassing the repeated repression of workers' rebellions by company-sponsored violence, local police, state militias, and the US Army and National Guard, it reveals a dimension of American history rarely found in the usual high school or college history course.

Since its original publication in 1972, no book has done as much as *Strike!* to bring US labor history to a wide audience. Now this fiftieth anniversary edition brings the story up to date with chapters covering the "mini-revolts of the 21st century," including Occupy Wall Street and the Fight for Fifteen. The new edition contains over a hundred pages of new materials and concludes by examining a wide range of current struggles, ranging from #BlackLivesMatter, to the great wave of teachers strikes "for the soul of public education," to the global "Student Strike for Climate," that may be harbingers of mass strikes to come.

"Jeremy Brecher's Strike! *is a classic of American historical writing. This new edition, bringing his account up to the present, comes amid rampant inequality and growing popular resistance. No book could be more timely for those seeking the roots of our current condition."*
—Eric Foner, Pulitzer Prize winner and DeWitt Clinton Professor of History at Columbia University

"Magnificent—a vivid, muscular labor history, just updated and rereleased by PM Press, which should be at the side of anyone who wants to understand the deep structure of force and counterforce in America."
—JoAnn Wypijewski, author of *Killing Trayvons: An Anthology of American Violence*

"An exciting history of American labor. Brings to life the flashpoints of labor history. Scholarly, genuinely stirring."
—*New York Times*